INTRODUCTION TO SOCIOLOGY

A PUBLIC SOCIOLOGY FRAMEWORK

FIRST EDITION

Edited By Amy Alsup, M.A.

San Diego Miramar College

Bassim Hamadeh, CEO and Publisher
Mieka Portier, Senior Acquisitions Editor
Tony Paese, Project Editor
Susana Christie, Senior Developmental Editor
Celeste Paed, Associate Production Editor
Asfa Arshi, Graphic Design Assistant
Trey Soto, Licensing Specialist
Natalie Piccotti, Director of Marketing
Kassie Graves, Senior Vice President of Editorial
Jamie Giganti, Director of Academic Publishing

Cover image copyright © 2019 iStockphoto LP/Orbon Alija.

Printed in the United States of America.

3970 Sorrento Valley Blvd., Ste. 500. San Diego, CA 92121

CONTENTS

Unit VIII   Social Change, Social Justice, and Social Movements 245

PREFACE

This book is designed to introduce students to sociology from a civic-minded framework. The readings in this anthology echo the academic call to public sociology. Although not all the works in this volume are written by sociologists, each reading aligns with the mission of public sociology in some way. Like Frances Fox Piven (2007), I define public sociology broadly. I see it as using sociological insight to inform public dialogue and political action. When Michael Burawoy introduced this framework to sociologists in 2004, he emphasized the need to bring sociology to audiences outside academia. Students participate in this mission all the time, discussing what they learn in the sociology classroom with friends, family, and their broader communities. This anthology is meant to encourage an active level of engagement and bring students in conversation with their communities.

Sociologists have debated the meaning of public sociology over the last fifteen years. Some have wondered whether or not naming this movement is productive. I hear these concerns and acknowledge them. Importantly, scholars like Patricia Hill Collins point out that people of color have been doing the work of public sociology for years, but without the label or the recognition (Collins, 2007). I believe that we should take this knowledge seriously and make sure that we recognize that women, people of color, LGBTQ+ individuals, and working-class people have been performing the work of public sociology, both in academia and their communities, without acknowledgment for years. In this anthology, I have attempted to center these voices. I believe that students will benefit from hearing these sociological insights directly from people situated in marginalized communities. I think the most empowering way to teach sociology is to introduce students to social inequalities and then challenge them to address these inequalities by spreading knowledge and making a difference in their communities.

The reason many students become interested in sociology is because of its social justice orientation and potential to revolutionize the world. The readings in this anthology are designed to encourage students to think critically about society.

By orienting the student toward public sociology, the hope is to encourage direct engagement with society.

In the first series of readings, students are introduced to important sociological frameworks and theories. In subsequent units, students learn about specific topics such as gender, sexuality, race, ethnicity, the family, education, the environment, and social movements. These readings can easily stand on their own, or they can accompany readings in an introductory sociology textbook. The post-reading questions in each unit encourage students to think about social injustice, social policy, and social change. This book differs from other introductory sociological texts by its specific focus on public sociology and its social-justice orientation. It can be a great resource for students who want to become more involved in social causes and carry sociological knowledge outside the classroom.

References

Collins, P. H. *"Going Public: Doing the Sociology That Had No Name."* In Public *Sociology: Fifteen Eminent Sociologists Debate Politics and the Profession in the Twenty-First Century, edited by D. Clawson et al.* University of California Press, 2007.

Piven, F. F. *"From Public Sociology to Politicized Sociology."* In *Public Sociology: Fifteen Eminent Sociologists Debate Politics and the Profession in the Twenty-First Century, edited by D. Clawson et al.* University of California Press, 2007.

INTRODUCTION

Sociology delivers a unique perspective on the world. It not only provides a window into human behavior but also offers us theories and practices that we can adopt to make the world a better place. When we look around, we see that our society is unequal. There is a growing divide between the rich and the poor. Women and LGBTQ+ individuals have long faced social injustices. People of color have endured widescale systemic racism for centuries. Karl Marx, who greatly influenced the discipline of sociology, famously wrote in 1845 that "philosophers have hitherto only interpreted the world in various ways; the point is to change it" (Marx 1978, 145). This book is aligned with that mission. The readings included in this volume are not only meant to inform you of important social patterns of inequality but also to encourage you to use this knowledge to actively make society are more equitable place.

The readings in this anthology are designed to introduce you to a movement called public sociology. Public sociology is the mission to bring sociology to the public and to use sociological knowledge and research findings when solving social dilemmas. Even in its infancy in the mid-nineteenth century, the discipline of sociology tackled complex public issues with the goal of social change.

In unit 1 of this anthology, you will uncover the history of sociology. You will gain insight into early sociological thinking and practice. Furthermore, you will learn how to think about the world sociologically. In unit 2, you will learn early sociological theories that continue to shape the discipline today. In unit 3, you will see patterns of gender and sexuality in society. Some of the topics you will explore here include gender inequality, feminism, LGBTQ+ identities, and social issues. In unit 4, the focus shifts to race and ethnicity. Here, you will view how race and ethnicity shape people's identities and experiences. You will also unearth trends in immigration. In unit 5, you will gain knowledge about families. You will examine social debates about families headed by same-sex couples and learn about some common struggles that single mothers face. In unit 6, you will encounter readings about education and schooling. The authors in this section illustrate that schools in the United States face massive inequalities. The unit 7 readings focus on the environment, social debates about climate change, and social problems caused by environmental damage. Finally, in unit 8, the authors explore social movements. You will learn about how activists use new information technology, including the internet, to make social change. You will also gain insight into some of the contemporary social movements happening in society today.

Many of the readings in this anthology focus on social inequalities. As you read, I encourage you to consider how sociology can be used as a tool to combat these injustices. How can you use sociological knowledge to understand inequality better? What can you do specifically to fight for social change? What are some practical ways that you can publicize sociology, sharing the insights it has to offer with your friends, family, and community? As you embark on this journey, I hope you find a sense of freedom in the insight offered here. Sociology can be a powerful tool to change the world for the better.

References

Marx, K. 1978. (1845). "*Theses on Feuerbach.*" In R. C. Tucker, (Ed.), In *The Marx–Engels Reader, 2nd ed.*, edited by R. C. Tucker. W. W. Norton & Company.

UNIT I

SOCIOLOGICAL
FRAMEWORKS AND PUBLIC
SOCIOLOGY

Key Terms and Definitions

Review the key terms and definitions below to strengthen your understanding of the readings in this unit.

The Chicago School: The Sociology Department at the University of Chicago that rose to prominence during the 1920s for its contributions to urban sociology (the study of social interactions in metropolitan cities).

The Enlightenment: An intellectual movement that emerged in Europe in the late seventeenth century that challenged traditional authority and religious frameworks and prioritized science and rationality.

Issues: Social patterns that impact groups of people.

Public Sociology: The mission to use sociology to solve public and political issues in society. The purpose of public sociology is often to enhance society by making it more equitable for all people.

The Scientific Method: A systematic approach to research that often begins with the formation of a hypothesis followed by a test or experiment. Research results are then evaluated, and the researcher draws a conclusion.

Social Construction: The process by which social meanings are created through human interaction.

Sociological Imagination: A term coined by the sociologist C. Wright Mills that describes a framework for understanding society. This approach asks individuals to connect their own personal experiences (troubles) to broader social patterns in society (issues).

Sociology: The methodical study of society and the forces that drive human interaction.
Troubles: Personal matters that are exclusive to the individual.

Introduction

Since the beginning of human history, people have thought about how society shapes our beliefs, values, social norms, and interactions. During the seventeenth and early eighteenth century, an intellectual movement known as **the Enlightenment** emerged in Europe. Enlightenment thinkers questioned many of the "common sense" assumptions about society. Up until this time, most Europeans viewed the world almost exclusively through religious frameworks. As technology advanced, people began to question supernatural explanations about the world. Scientific developments steered people instead toward rational, calculated, scientific modes of thinking. This led to new research approaches such as **the scientific method**, in which researchers explore hypotheses by conducting experiments and other types of research studies.

The Enlightenment gave rise to new academic disciplines like **sociology**. Sociology emerged during roughly the same time as the Industrial Revolution in Europe. Industrialization profoundly altered human experiences and interactions. People flocked to cities from agricultural regions and began working in factories and specializing in trades. This created a population boost and exposed people to new ideas and diverse groups of people. These massive changes provoked an intellectual curiosity among scholars. Sociologists began to ask questions such as, "How do technology and science alter our relationship to society?" and, "How does city life transform our social relationships?" In this historical moment, sociology was born.

The readings in this section are meant to introduce you to sociology as an academic discipline and provide models of how to think about the world in a sociological fashion. In the first selection, "How to Think Sociologically," Steven M. Buechler explains how Enlightenment thinking gave rise to sociology as a discipline. Adopting the terminology of C. Wright Mills, a scholar who was active in academia from the late 1940s through the early 1960s, Buechler proposes that ordinary people can adopt a **sociological imagination**. They can do this by connecting their own personal experiences, or **troubles**, to broader social patterns, or **issues**. This intellectual exercise reveals that the circumstances which we often perceive to be *personal* and *individual* many times instead reflect wider social trends. Buechler challenges his readers to think critically about the world and to question taken-for-granted assumptions about reality. Instead of accepting the status quo as the natural order, through sociology, we can envision how reality is a **social construction**. Society is not set up the way it is because of fate or destiny, but instead is the product of countless, unique social interactions and developments. Put another way, our immediate environment might look radically different if events had unfolded in a different fashion.

In the next reading segment, Devereaux Kennedy elaborates upon the meaning of the **sociological imagination**. In this excerpt, the author highlights how ordinary people can advance the cause of **public sociology** through imagining how personal problems may connect to broader public issues. Using the sociological imagination allows us to develop theories about the social world to understand society better. Furthermore, adopting this tool allows us to create solutions for social problems, advancing the causes of social justice and equity.

In the third reading, "Race and the Birth of American Sociology," Aldon Morris challenges the common assumption that the **Chicago School**, which rose to prominence in the 1920s, was the first American school of sociology. Instead, he asserts that the first American school of sociology was founded in Atlanta right before the turn of the twentieth century by the African American sociologist W. E. B. Du Bois. In some circles, W. E. B. Du Bois is appreciated for his contributions to the discipline of sociology. However, he is rarely acknowledged as a founder of sociology's first school of sociology. As a predecessor of C. Wright Mills, W. E. B. Du Bois established similar connections to **public sociology** and should be regarded as a pioneer of this approach. In particular, he studied the impact of race in US society, showing that it is a **social construction** without a biological basis. In other words, Du Bois emphasized that even though we define race by physical markers, it is society that gives racial categories meaning and power. Ultimately, Du Bois's scholarship, and the Atlanta school of sociology desires recognition. Du Bois's community-based research and contributions to our contemporary understandings of race still profoundly shape the world of sociological research today.

In the final reading, "From Public Sociology to Politicized Sociologist," Frances Fox Piven embraces a broad definition of the term **public sociology**. In her view, public sociology happens when we use sociological ideas to solve public and political issues. She remarks that classical sociological figures like Karl Marx, Max Weber, and Emile Durkheim emphasized the political problems of their time in their work. Each of these figures wrote about the public impact of the Industrial Revolution (albeit from different perspectives). Piven notes that sociologists continued in this tradition in later years, focusing on social problems and potential policy interventions or public solutions. Ultimately, she concludes that sociology should focus on the needs of the poor and working class, marginalized racial groups, women, undocumented immigrants, and other groups of people who face injustice in society. To her, this is the mission of public sociology.

Each reading in this section contains an underlying assumption that sociology can and should be made "public." The first two readings show the reader how to understand the world from the perspective of a public sociologist. The third reading shows that American sociology has roots in community-based approaches in line with public sociology. Although the Atlanta School and W. E. B. Du Bois often fall under the radar, the world would greatly benefit by recognizing their contributions. The final reading emphasizes how sociology can be used to solve public and political issues in society. Ultimately, sociology is more than an academic discipline. It is a systematic template for critical thinking and a platform for questioning long-held assumptions about society. Adopting a **sociological imagination** and embracing the pursuit of **public sociology** allows the discipline to have a lasting impact inside the classroom and beyond.

How to Think Sociologically

Steven M. Buechler

People have always tried to make sense of the world around them. Myths, fables, and religion provided traditional ways of making sense. More recently, science has provided additional ways of understanding the world. Sociology is part of the rise of science as a means of making sense of the world.

As we know in our own time, there can be tension between religious and scientific views. Contemporary disputes over evolution, sexuality, marriage, and even the age of our planet often pit religious values against scientific interpretations. More broadly speaking, both at home and abroad, religious fundamentalisms rest uneasily alongside modern, secular worldviews. These familiar tensions have a history that takes us back to the origins of sociology itself.

Sociology and Modernity

The rise of sociology is part of a much larger story about the emergence of the modern world itself. Modernity emerged in European societies through a long process of social change that unfolded from the sixteenth to the nineteenth centuries. During this time, virtually everything about organized social life in Europe was fundamentally transformed. In our day, we speak of globalization as a force that is changing the world in the most basic ways. But current patterns of globalization can be traced back to the rise of modernity itself; in many respects, they are a continuation of the changes that ushered in the modern world.

Economically, modernity transformed most people from peasants to workers in a complex division of labor. Politically, modernity created distinct nation-states with clear boundaries. Technologically, modernity applied scientific knowledge to producing everything from consumer goods to lethal weapons. Demographically, modernity triggered population growth and massive migration from small, familiar, rural communities to large, urban, anonymous cities.

When social worlds change like this, some people benefit while others are harmed. In addition, most people find rapid change and its inevitable conflict to be unsettling, and they seek to understand what is happening. It was this moment that gave rise to sociology. Explaining modernity became sociology's task at the same time that modernity was making sociology possible in the first place.

The link between modernity and sociology was the Enlightenment. This intellectual revolution accompanied other revolutionary changes occurring throughout Europe. In the broadest terms, the Enlightenment challenged religious belief, dogma, and authority. It sought to replace them with scientific reason, logic, and knowledge.

Four basic themes pervaded Enlightenment thought (Zeitlin 1987). First, human reason was the best guide to knowledge, even if it meant that scientific skepticism displaced religious certainty. Second, reason must be paired with careful, scientific observation. Third, Enlightenment thought insisted that social arrangements be rationally justified; if not, they must be changed until they could be rationally defended. Finally, Enlightenment thought assumed that with the systematic application of reason, the perfectibility of people and the progress of society were all but inevitable.

Enlightenment thought contained some potentially fatal flaws. It was a Eurocentric worldview, created by privileged white men, that made universal pronouncements about all people in all times and places. While applauding Europe's progress, it ignored the colonial domination of the rest of the world that provided the labor, goods, and wealth that underwrote that progress. Generalizations about "humanity" meant "males," to the exclusion of women, and pronouncements on the "human race" meant white Europeans, to the exclusion of darker people, who were viewed as subhuman.

The Enlightenment was much more than a justification of imperialism, sexism, and racism, but it could become that as well. More than two centuries later, the jury is still out on whether Enlightenment biases can be overcome and its promises be fulfilled. Some postmodernists see little hope for this to happen. Others, myself included, think that the critical spirit of the Enlightenment can help uproot its biases. The project is already under way as feminists, people of color, and postcolonial writers find their way into contemporary sociological discourses (Lemert 2013).

In its own day, the Enlightenment provoked a "romantic conservative reaction" (Zeitlin 1987) that rejected the elevation of reason and science over faith and tradition. It defended traditional customs, institutions, and ways of life from the new standard of critical reason. The debate between Enlightenment progress and conservative reaction set the agenda for sociology as the social science of modernity. Progress or order? Change or stability? Reason or tradition? Science or religion? Individual or group? Innovation or authority? Such dichotomies framed the subject matter of the new science of sociology.

The classical era of sociology refers to European thinkers whose ideas brought this new discipline to maturity from the late eighteenth to the early twentieth centuries. The very different sociologies of Auguste Comte, Herbert Spencer, Ferdinand Toennies, Karl Marx, Max Weber, Georg Simmel, Emile Durkheim, and others are variations on sociology's main theme: How do we understand modern society? Given these efforts, we might think of sociology as the ongoing effort of human beings to understand the worlds they are simultaneously inheriting from earlier generations and maintaining and transforming for future generations.

This approach has been described as the "sociological imagination." It arises when people realize that they can only know themselves by understanding their historical period and by examining others in the same situation as themselves. We think sociologically when we grasp how our historical moment differs from previous ones and how the situations of various groups of people differ from each other (Mills 1959).

The sociological imagination is guided by three related questions. The first concerns the social structure of society. How is it organized, what are its major institutions, and how are they linked together? The second concerns the historical location of society. How has it emerged from past social forms, what mechanisms promote change, and what futures are possible based on this historical path? The third concerns individual biography within society. What kinds of character traits are called forth by this society, and what kinds of people come to prevail? The sociological imagination is thus about grasping the relations between history and biography within society.

The sociological imagination sensitizes us to the difference between "personal troubles" and "public issues." A personal trouble is a difficulty in someone's life that is largely a result of individual circumstances. A public issue is a difficulty that is largely owing to social arrangements beyond the individual's control. The distinction is crucial because common sense often interprets events as personal troubles; we explain someone's difficulties as springing from individual shortcomings. The sociological imagination recognizes that such difficulties are rarely unique to one person; they rather happen to many people in similar situations. The underlying causes derive more from social structures and historical developments than the individual alone. If our goal is "diagnosis," the sociological imagination locates problems in a larger social context. If our goal is "treatment," it implies changing the structure of society rather than the behavior of individuals.

This applies to success as well. Common sense often attributes success to individual qualities. The sociological imagination asks what social and historical preconditions were necessary for an individual to become a success. Many successful people, in Jim Hightower's memorable phrase, "were born on third base but thought they hit a triple." The point is that whereas common sense sees the world in individual terms, sociological thinking sees it in structural terms. Only by seeing the connections between structure, history, and biography can we understand the world in a sociological way.

This discussion implies that professional sociologists and ordinary people see the world differently. This is often true, but the issue is more complicated. Modernity has also led ordinary people to develop a practical sociology in their everyday lives. Think about it this way. Sociology sees the world as a social construction that could follow various blueprints. Indeed, social worlds *are* constructed in very different ways in different times and places.

In our time, an awareness of the socially constructed nature of social worlds is no longer the privileged insight of scholars, but has become part of everyday understanding. Whether owing to rapid change, frequent travel, cultural diffusion, or media images, many people understand that we live in socially constructed worlds. Some people are distressed by this fact, and others rejoice in it, but few can escape it. Thus, an idea that was initially associated with professional sociology has become part of the everyday consciousness of ordinary people today.

The result is that many people without formal sociological training understand social processes quite well. Put differently, the objects of sociological analysis are people who are quite capable of becoming the subjects of the sociological knowledge created by that analysis. Although few people can explain how quantum mechanics governs the physical world, many can describe sociological processes that shape the social world.

Certain circumstances prompt people to think sociologically. Perhaps the key stimulant is when familiar ways of doing and thinking no longer work. It is when people are surprised, puzzled, challenged, or damaged that they are most likely to think sociologically (Lemert 2008). People then develop sociological competence as they try to make sense out of specific, individual circumstances by linking them to broader social patterns. In this way, sociological awareness begins to understand bigger things as a by-product of wrestling with the practical challenges of everyday life.

Circumstances do not inevitably provoke sociological consciousness. Some people redouble their faith or retreat into ritualism. So perhaps we can conclude this way. Societies confront people with problems. These problems have always had the potential to promote a sociological awareness. In our times, there is a greater awareness of the socially constructed nature of the world. This makes it even more likely that when people in this society are confronted with practical challenges, they will develop sociological competence as a practical life skill. In late modernity, everyone can become a practical sociologist.

Thinking Sociologically

The sociological perspective involves several themes. They overlap with one another, and some may be found in other social sciences as well as everyday consciousness. Taken together, they comprise a distinctive lens for viewing the social world. Here are some of those themes.

Society Is a Social Construction

People construct social order. Sociology does not see society as God-given, as biologically determined, or as following any predetermined plan beyond human intervention. At the same time, this does not mean that everyone plays an equal role in the process or that the final product looks like what people intended.

Social construction begins with intentions that motivate people to act in certain ways. When many people have similar goals and act in concert, larger social patterns or institutions are created. Goal-driven action is essential to the creation of institutions, and it remains equally important to their maintenance and transformation over time. Put succinctly, society is a human product (Berger and Luckmann 1966).

Basic human needs ensure some similarities in the goals that people pursue in all times and places. But these pursuits also unfold in specific historical circumstances and cultural contexts that have led to a dazzling variety of social worlds. This variety is itself the best evidence of the socially constructed nature of social worlds. If biology or genetics were the determining force behind social worlds, wouldn't they look a lot more similar than what we actually see around the globe?

Social constructionists thus insist that society arises from the goal-driven action of people. But they also recognize that the institutions created by such actions take on a life of their own. They appear to exist independently of the people who create and sustain them. They are experienced by people as a powerful external force that weighs down on them. When this external force becomes severe enough, people are likely to lose sight of the fact that society is a social product in the first place.

The value of the social constructionist premise is this dual recognition. On one hand, society is a subjective reality originating in the intentions of social actors. On the other hand, it becomes an objective reality that confronts subsequent generations as a social fact that inevitably shapes *their* intentional actions—and so it goes. Understood this way, the idea that society is a social construction is at the heart of the sociological perspective.

Society Is an Emergent Reality

Another premise of sociology is emergentism. This reveals sociology's distinctive level of analysis. For psychology, the level of analysis is the individual, even if it is acknowledged that individuals belong to groups. For sociology, the level of analysis is social ties rather than individual elements. Emergentism recognizes that certain realities only appear when individual elements are combined in particular ways. When they are, qualitatively new realities emerge through these combinations.

Take a simple example. Imagine a random pile of ten paper clips. Now imagine linking these paper clips together to form a chain. There are still ten paper clips, but a new emergent reality has appeared that is qualitatively different from the random pile because of how the elements are related to one another. Or consider human reproduction. Neither sperm nor egg is capable of producing human life on its own; in combination, qualitatively new life begins to emerge from a particular combination of elements.

Sociology specializes in the social level of analysis that emerges when elements are combined to create new, larger realities. Emergentism also implies that when we try to understand elements outside of their context, it is at best a simplification and at worst a distortion. The parts derive meaning from their relationship with other parts, and the sociological perspective is fundamentally attuned to such relationships.

Society Is a Historical Product

Thinking historically is a crucial part of the sociological imagination (Mills 1959). Classical sociologists thought historically because they lived in times of rapid social change and it was a major challenge to understand such change. Modern sociology tends to be more static, and modern people tend to be very present-oriented. Both professional and practical sociologists would benefit from a more historical perspective on the social world.

Seeing society as a historical product means recognizing that we cannot understand the present without understanding the past. Historical knowledge of past social conditions provides crucial comparisons. Without such benchmarks, it is impossible to understand what is genuinely new in the present day. Without a historical referent for comparison, sociology is clueless when it comes to understanding social change. Historical knowledge also provides the raw material for categories, comparisons, typologies, and analogies that are crucial to understanding both the present and possible future worlds.

The concept of emergentism applies here because the importance of seeing relationships between elements also works chronologically. If we look at society at only one point in time, we sever it from its past and its potential futures. Its very meaning arises from these relationships; to ignore them is to distort even the static understanding of society at one point in time. Consider the difference between a photograph and a film that presents a succession of images. We can learn something from the still photo, but its meaning often changes dramatically when we see it as one of a series of interrelated images.

Society Consists of Social Structures

Sociologists use the term *structure* to refer to the emergent products of individual elements. Structure implies that the social world has certain patterns or regularities that recur over time. Put differently, sociologists are keenly interested in social organization.

Structures are products of human purposes, but they acquire an objective reality and become a powerful influence on human action. Think about how physical structures like buildings shape action. We almost always enter buildings through doors; in rare cases we might do so through windows, but walking through walls is not an option. Social structures are less visible and more flexible than buildings, but they also channel people's actions, because they make some actions routine and expected, others possible but unlikely, and still others all but impossible.

Like buildings, social structures often have a vertical dimension. Social structures ensure that some people are better off than others and that some are not very well off at all. Some residential buildings have penthouses at the top, premium suites near the top, standard accommodations below them, and housekeeping staff in the basement. Social structures are also stratified, granting power, privilege, and opportunity to some while limiting or denying them to others. Sociologists are especially interested in the hierarchical dimension of social structures.

Sociologists traditionally thought of social structures as powerful forces weighing down upon the individual. In this image, structures constrain freedom of choice and behavior. But this is a one-sided view. Structures are constraining, but they are also enabling. These established patterns of social organization also make many actions possible in the first place or easier in the second place. Without preexisting social structures, we would have to do everything "from scratch," and the challenge of sheer survival might overwhelm us. The trick is thus to see social structures as simultaneously constraining and enabling social action (Giddens 1984).

Society Consists of Reflexive Actors

People in society are aware of themselves, of others, and of their relationships with others. As reflexive actors, we monitor our action and its effects on others. We continue, modify, or halt actions, depending on whether they are achieving their intended effects. According to one school of thought, we are literally actors, because social life is like a theatrical performance in which we try to convince others that we are a certain kind of person (Goffman 1959). To stage effective performances, we must constantly be our own critic, judging and refining our performances. Reflexivity thus means that when we act, we are conscious of our action, we monitor its course, and we make adjustments over time.

To stage such performances, we must undergo socialization. Along the way, we acquire a language that provides us with tools for reflexive thinking. We also acquire a self. Oddly enough, to have a self requires that we first have relationships with others. Through those relationships, we imaginatively see the world from their perspective, which includes seeing ourselves as we imagine we appear to them. It is this ability to see ourselves through the perspective of others—to see ourselves as an object—that defines the self. Reflexive action only becomes possible with a self.

Reflexivity makes ordinary people into practical sociologists. To be a competent person is to be a practical sociologist. We cannot help being sociologists every time we ponder a potential relationship, reconsider a hasty action, or adopt someone else's viewpoint. All such situations call upon and refine the reflexivity that is the hallmark of social action as well as a defining characteristic of the sociological perspective.

Society Is an Interaction of Agency and Structure

Social structures and reflexive actors are intimately connected. Unfortunately, much sociology emphasizes one side of this connection at the expense of the other. Agency-centered views stress the ability of people to make choices out of a range of alternatives in almost any situation. The emphasis on choice implies that people control their own destiny, at least within broad limits. Structure-centered views stress the extent to which people's choices are limited by social structures. The emphasis on structures implies that people's options—if not their lives—are essentially determined by larger social forces over which they have little control. Both approaches have merit, but the challenge is to see structure and agency in a more interconnected way.

Marx once said that people make their own history (acknowledging agency), but under circumstances they do not choose but rather inherit from the past (acknowledging structure). Here's an analogy from the game of pool. Each time you approach the table, you "inherit" a structure left by your opponent when they missed their last shot. Yet, for every layout of balls on the table, there is always a shot that you can attempt, and that action will alter the structure of the table for subsequent shots. In this analogy, structure (the position of balls on the table) both limits and creates opportunities for agency (taking a shot), which in turn alters the structure for the next round of shooting. If pool is not your game, chess is also a good analogy. The point is that agency and structure are two sides of the same coin; each conditions the possibilities of the other as we make our own history in circumstances we don't choose.

The close connection between structure and agency has led one theorist to reject the notion of structure altogether, because it implies something that exists apart from agency. Anthony Giddens (1984) talks about a *process* of structuration. In this view, actors use preexisting structures to accomplish their goals, but they also re-create them as a by-product of their actions. Consider a wedding ceremony. It is a preexisting cultural ritual people use to accomplish the goal of getting married. The by-product of all these individual marriages is the perpetuation of the cultural ritual itself. Generalize this to any situation in which we draw upon an established part of our social world to achieve a goal; in using this part we also sustain (and perhaps transform) it as a part of social structure.

Society Has Multiple Levels

Although society has multiple levels, sociologists often focus on one level at a time. Think about using Google Maps to locate a destination. You can zoom out to get the big picture at the expense of not seeing some important details. Alternatively, you can zoom in on some key details at the expense of not seeing the big picture. Combining these differing views will orient you to your destination, but we must remember it is ultimately all one interconnected landscape.

Sociologists nevertheless distinguish between macro and micro levels of society. When we look at the macro level, we typically include millions of people organized into large categories, groups, or institutions. The macro level is the "big picture" or "high altitude" perspective in which society's largest patterns are evident and individuals are invisible. When we look at the micro level, we might inspect no more than a dozen people interacting in a small group setting. Here, the role of particular individuals is very prominent, and larger social patterns fade into the background.

Some of the best sociology involves understanding not only structure-agency connections but also micro-macro links. Every macro-structure rests on micro-interaction, and every micro-interaction is shaped by macro-structures. The previous example of a wedding also illustrates this point. On the macro level, weddings are a cultural ritual that inducts people into the institution of marriage and the family. However, weddings, marriage, and the family would not exist on the macro level without countless, micro-level interactions. The macro-level institution depends on micro-level actions to sustain it. At the same time, anyone who has ever gotten married will tell you that macro-level, cultural expectations about weddings impose themselves on people as they plan for this supposedly personal event. Every micro-level wedding depends on a macro-level, cultural blueprint for its social significance. The micro and macro levels of society are one interdependent reality rather than two separate things.

Society Involves Unintended Consequences

One of the more profound insights of the sociological perspective concerns unintended and unanticipated consequences of action. Much human action is purposive or goal-directed. People act because they want to accomplish something. Despite this, they sometimes fail to achieve their goals. But whether people achieve their goals or not, their actions always create other consequences that they don't intend or even anticipate. Shakespeare made a profoundly sociological point when he had Juliet fake her own suicide to dramatize her love for Romeo. Unfortunately, the plan never reached Romeo. Juliet neither intended nor anticipated that Romeo would find her unconscious, believe that she was really dead, and take his own life in response. Nor did he intend (or even realize) that she would awaken, discover his real death, and really take her life in response. Talk about unintended consequences!

This principle acknowledges the complexity of the social world and the limits on our ability to control it. It says that despite our best efforts, the effects of social action cannot be confined to one intended path; they always spill over into unexpected areas. The principle is also a cautionary message for those seeking to solve social problems. Such efforts might succeed, but they often bring other consequences that are neither positive nor intended.

Efforts to control crime provide an example. Consider policies to "get tough" on crime through harsher treatment like capital punishment and mandatory sentencing. Because the human beings who serve as judges and juries are reflexive actors who take these facts into account, they are often less likely to convict suspects without overwhelming evidence because of the harshness of the sentence. Thus, the unintended consequence of an attempt to "get tough" on crime might be the opposite, because fewer suspects are convicted than before.

A related idea is the distinction between manifest and latent functions. A manifest function is an outcome that people intend. A latent function is an outcome that people are not aware of; it can complement, but it often contradicts, the manifest function. Crime and punishment provide yet another example. The manifest function of imprisonment is punishment or rehabilitation. The latent function is to bring criminals together where they can meet one another, exchange crime techniques, and become better criminals upon their return to society.

The concept of latent functions is crucial to sociological analysis. Sometimes we observe behavior or rituals that seem irrational, pointless, or self-defeating. This is the time to begin looking for latent functions. What we will often find is that such "irrational" behavior reinforces the identity and sustains the cohesion of the group that performs it. Thus, before we dismiss the tribal rain dance (because "rain gods" don't exist), we must explore its latent function. Even when people don't (manifestly) know what they are (latently) doing, their behavior can be crucial to group cohesion.

Recognizing unintended consequences and latent functions is not just for professional sociologists. Daily living requires managing risk, and ordinary people in everyday life recognize the tricky nature of goal-directed action. The folk wisdom that "the road to hell is paved with good intentions" acknowledges the potential disconnect between goals and outcomes. Such recognition, however, never completely prevents outcomes we neither intend nor expect. These principles give social life some of its most surprising twists, and sociology some of its most fascinating challenges.

No attempt to capture the sociological perspective in a small number of themes can be complete. Other sociologists would doubtless modify this list. But most would recognize these themes as central to thinking sociologically. As such, they provide a foundation for the more detailed investigations to follow.

Sociology's Double Critique

This final theme deserves special emphasis as the foundation of this book. Last but not least, thinking sociologically means looking at the social world in a critical way.

In everyday language, *critical* implies something negative. Being critical is often seen as being harsh, unfair, or judgmental. When we say someone is "critical," we often mean that their behavior is inappropriately mean-spirited. This is a perfectly reasonable use of everyday language, and the point it makes about how people should treat one another is also perfectly reasonable.

In sociological language, *critical* means something else. Doing sociology in a critical way means looking beyond appearances, understanding root causes, and asking who benefits. Being critical is what links knowledge to action and the potential of building a better society. Being critical in the sociological sense rests on the profoundly *positive* belief that we can use knowledge to understand the flaws of the social world and act to correct them.

The sociological perspective contains a double critique. First, mainstream sociology brings an inherently critical angle of vision to its subject. Second, some particular approaches in sociology carry this critique further by building on values that make sociological analysis especially critical of power and domination.

The critical dimension of mainstream sociology derives from the Enlightenment. Despite the flaws noted earlier, the Enlightenment advocated the use of reason, science, and evidence to critically examine religious truth, established doctrine, and political authority. Given its Enlightenment roots, sociology has always cast a critical eye on all types of claims, forms of knowledge, and exercises of power.

It is this quality that Peter Berger (1963) called the "debunking" tendency of sociological consciousness. Debunking means that the sociological perspective never takes the social world at face value and never assumes that it is what it appears to be. The sociological perspective rather looks at familiar phenomena in new ways to get beyond the immediately obvious, publicly approved, or officially sanctioned view. In this way, sociology sees through the facades of social structures to their unintended consequences and latent functions. Sociologically speaking, the problem might not be crime but laws, not revolution but government. Berger concludes that sociology is not compatible with totalitarianism, because the debunking quality of sociology will always be in tension with authoritarian claims to knowledge and power.

Although the world has changed since Berger wrote, the need for debunking is greater than ever. The political fundamentalisms of Cold War and rival superpowers have been replaced by other fundamentalisms that are logical targets for sociology's debunking insights. A world in which more and more people feel they know things with absolute certainty is a world that drastically needs the sociological perspective.

At the same time that some people embrace fundamentalist beliefs, others become suspicious and cynical about everything. This stance ("debunking on steroids") is too much of a good thing. For the ultra-cynical poser, all ideas, values, and beliefs are suspect, and none deserve support. Against this stance, sociology offers nuance and judgment. The sociological perspective recognizes that some ideas, values, and beliefs have more merit, logic, or evidence than others. Careful sociological thinkers make such distinctions. Indeed, the ultra-cynical mind-set itself needs debunking. Cynicism helps people avoid action or evade responsibility. A sociological perspective suggests that such inaction, or evasion, *is* action that tacitly supports dominant powers by refusing to challenge them in any way.

Mainstream sociology does not take the world for granted. Just when we think we have the answers, it poses another level of questions. For all these reasons, sociology in its most generic form has always included a critical angle of vision.

Although mainstream sociology is inherently critical, some versions of sociology take critique to another level by adopting certain values as the basis for their critique. In contrast to mainstream sociology, these approaches are devoted to a critical analysis of how social structures create relations of domination.

This fully critical sociology is best understood in contrast to mainstream sociology. Although mainstream sociology is critical because of its debunking tendency, it also adopts a scientific posture of detachment. Mainstream sociology seeks to be value-free, value-neutral, or objective. Put differently, mainstream sociology deliberately refrains from taking sides that would jeopardize its scientific neutrality. Mainstream sociology recognizes that *as citizens*, sociologists can be political actors. But it insists that in their role as scientific sociologists, they must maintain their objectivity.

Critical sociology differs from mainstream sociology on these issues. It emphasizes that in social science, humans are both the subjects and the objects of study. Notions of objectivity derived from the natural sciences don't necessarily translate into social science. But even if sociology could approximate objectivity, critical sociologists reject such a stance. It is not desirable, because the quest for objectivity diverts sociologists from asking the most important questions and from taking a more active role in the resolution of social problems.

Think of the contrast in this way. Mainstream sociology is primarily committed to one set of Enlightenment values having to do with science and objectivity. Critical sociology is primarily committed to another set of Enlightenment values having to do with freedom and equality. The latter values demand critical scrutiny of any social order that imposes unnecessary inequalities or restrictions on people's ability to organize their lives as they wish. These values require critical analysis of social arrangements that create conflicting interests between people and allow one group to benefit at the expense of another.

Critical sociologists deliberately focus on relations of domination, oppression, or exploitation, because these actions so obviously violate the values of freedom and equality. Critical sociologists are willing to advocate for groups who are victimized by such arrangements. Good critical sociologists realize they cannot speak for such groups. But they can explore how social arrangements make it difficult for some to speak for themselves, and they can underscore the importance of changing those arrangements.

Other issues distinguish mainstream from critical sociology. Mainstream sociology's commitment to science means it maintains a strict divide between scientific questions of what *is* and normative questions of what *ought* to be. Critical sociology wants to transcend this divide by linking critical analysis of how the world is organized now with normative arguments for how the world should be organized in the future. Behind such arguments are hopeful, or even utopian assumptions about alternative worlds that might be constructed. Critical sociology is simultaneously pessimistic about the current state of the world and optimistic about its possible futures. It examines our potential for living humanely, the social obstacles that block this potential, and the means to change from a problematic present to a preferable future.

The debate between mainstream and critical sociology is important and complex, and it will not be resolved by anything said here. But what can be said is that sociology is better because of the debate. Each side provides a corrective to the faults of the other. At the extreme, mainstream sociology becomes an inhumane, sterile approach that reduces human beings to objects of scientific curiosity; it needs a course correction through the humane values of critical sociology. At the extreme, critical sociology becomes an empty, ideological stance that denies the complexities of its own value commitments; it needs a course correction through the scientific caution of mainstream sociology.

Sociology's double critique thus derives from mainstream and critical sociology, respectively. My primary goal in this book is to illustrate critical sociology, but I also include the critical insights of mainstream sociology. I do so because these approaches sometimes speak to different issues, because neither seems adequate on its own, because they are often complementary, and because this best conveys the richness of our discipline itself. In the end, it is less important which side is "right" than that both sides coexist and continually provoke us to be reflexive about our role as sociologists and as actors in the world.

Sociology's double critique is also crucial to rethinking the flaws of the Enlightenment itself. Mainstream sociology's notion of debunking accepted truths grew out of the Enlightenment struggle against religion, but there is no reason it can't also foster critical examination of the Enlightenment itself. Critical sociology's challenge to domination also seems tailor-made to examining and overturning those forms of domination that the Enlightenment ignored, accepted, or promoted. Thus, for all its flaws, the Enlightenment provides tools for its own examination, critique, and transformation.

References

Berger, Peter. 1963. *Invitation to Sociology*. New York: Doubleday.

Berger, Peter, and Thomas Luckmann. 1966. *The Social Construction of Reality*. Garden City, NY: Anchor.

Giddens, Anthony. 1984. *The Constitution of Society*. Berkeley: University of California Press.

Goffman, Erving. 1959. *The Presentation of Self in Everyday Life*. Garden City, NY: Anchor.

Lemert, Charles. 2008. *Social Things*. 4th ed. Lanham, MD: Rowman & Littlefield.

———. 2013. *Social Theory: The Multicultural and Classic Readings*. 5th ed. Boulder, CO: Westview Press.

Mills, C. Wright. 1959. *The Sociological Imagination*. New York: Oxford University Press.

Zeitlin, Irving. 1987. *Ideology and the Development of Sociological Theory*. Englewood Cliffs, NJ: Prentice Hall.

Post-Reading Questions

1. What sort of social developments led to the emergence of sociology as an academic discipline?
2. What does it mean to describe society as a social construction? What does it mean to describe society as an emergent reality?
3. What is social structure? What is structuration? How do social structures impact our daily lives? As an exercise, see if you can name three social structures that have shaped your own experiences in the world.
4. What is human agency? What is the relationship between agency and structure?
5. What does it mean to think sociologically? How is this different from thinking about the world from an individualistic framework?

Using Your Sociological Imagination to Make Connections

Kennedy Devereaux

Kennedy Devereaux, Selection from "Fulfilling the Promise: Infusing Curiosity, Concern, and Passion with Sociological Imagination," *Exploring the Roots of Social Theory and Inquiry: Making Sense of Social Life*, pp. 5–6, 181–187. Copyright © 2018 by Cognella, Inc. Reprinted with permission.

If interest in the systematic study of social life begins with curiosity, skepticism, concern, and passion, it doesn't end there. Curiosity needs to be sated; skepticism and suspicion justified or allayed; social wrongs righted. This requires the acquisition of particular kinds of knowledge and the use of a particular form of imagination—what C. Wright Mills (1959) called the **sociological imagination**.

By the sociological imagination, Mills meant that quality of mind which enables people who possess it to make connections between personal troubles and social issues. Troubles occur within or between individuals sharing the same immediate social environment. Losing a job; doing badly at school; failing at marriage or a relationship; even committing a crime, getting arrested, and being put in prison can certainly be understood in very immediate and personal terms. People lose jobs all the time because they screw up at work or can't get along with their bosses and coworkers. We sometimes do badly at school because we are too lazy to study or would rather party. People sometimes treat their partners with a lack of respect and fail to put the time and attention into a relationship necessary to make it work. Sometimes it really is our fault.

Often, however, it isn't—or isn't completely. When businesses close or stop hiring, when millions of people get laid off and you lose your job, that isn't your fault. When the dropout rates in urban public schools rise and the academic performance of the students who remain drops precipitately, something more is at work than student laziness. When the divorce rate rises dramatically, clearly more is at work than couples failing to make the compromises necessary for a successful marriage. When people decide to drive while drunk or stoned, they place themselves and others at risk. Surely, they should be held accountable for their actions. Yet the need for accountability doesn't explain why some people are held more accountable than others. While people of all races appear to use and sell illegal drugs at about the same rate, black men are imprisoned for drug offenses at rates twenty to fifty times greater than those of white men (Alexander 2012, 7). Sometimes personal problems are connected to public issues.

"An issue is a public matter: some value cherished by publics is felt to be threatened. Often there is a debate about what that value really is and about what it is that really threatens it" (Mills 1959, 8). Murray thinks that the core values, the "founding virtues" that made America great, indeed exceptional—industriousness, honesty, marriage, and religiosity—are being threatened (2012,130). Alexander thinks that the incarceration of poor African American males for drug offenses is not about an increase in crime or drug abuse. It is rather the result of "a stunningly comprehensive and well-disguised system of racialized social control that functions in a manner strikingly similar to Jim Crow" (2012, 4).

Certainly, making connections between personal troubles and social issues requires gathering the relevant facts, and exercising our reasoning capacity to make sense of those facts. But making sense of the social world requires more than facts and reasoning. It requires a quality of mind that will help us "to use information and develop reason in order to achieve lucid summations of what is going on in the world and of what is happening in [ourselves]" (Mills 1959, 5). When we do this, we use our sociological imagination to theorize.

Bibliography

Alexander, Michelle. 2012. *The New Jim Crow: Mass Incarceration in the Age of Colorblindness*, rev. ed. New York: The New Press.
Mills, C. Wright. 1959. *The Sociological Imagination.* New York: Oxford University Press.
Murray, Charles. 2012. *Coming Apart: The State of White America, 1960–2010.* New York: Crown Publishing.

Post-Reading Questions

1. How does the author describe the sociological imagination? What examples of public issues does he provide?
2. Think of an example of a private trouble that may be reflective of a broader public issue. What is the sociological pattern here? How does this pattern extend beyond the individual and impact a larger group in society?
3. How can the sociological imagination be used to promote public sociology? In other words, can you solve social problems by using this tool? If so, how?

Introduction

Race and the Birth of American Sociology

Aldon Morris

Aldon Morris, "Introduction: Race and the Birth of American Sociology," *The Scholar Denied: W. E. B. Du Bois and the Birth of Modern Sociology*, pp. 1–5, 225–227, 251–268. Copyright © 2015 by University of California Press. Reprinted with permission.

There is an intriguing, well-kept secret regarding the founding of scientific sociology in America. The first school of scientific sociology in the United States was founded by a black professor located in a historically black university in the South. This reality flatly contradicts the accepted wisdom.

A broad consensus exists among sociologists that the Chicago school, which emerged in the second decade of the twentieth century, was the first school of American empirical sociology.[1] This hegemonic narrative maintains that the school's primary leader was the premier second-generation University of Chicago sociologist Robert Ezra Park. The Chicago school of sociology, which dominated the field well into the 1930s, was housed in the University of Chicago's prestigious department of sociology, founded in 1892, which included

1. Deegan (2001); Abbott (1999); Fine (1995); Bulmer (1985); Coser (1978); Matthews (1977); Faris (1967); A. Hunter (1980). Even though it is widely accepted that the University of Chicago's department of sociology was America's first and most influential school of sociology, that claim has been challenged. The department at the University of Kansas claims it was the first to open its doors in 1890 and to offer sociology classes; see Sica (1991) and "About Us" at the website of the University of Kansas at http://sociology.ku.edu/about-us (accessed October 30, 2014). Yale, on its website at the page "Welcome to the Yale Sociology Department," maintains that "in 1875, Yale professor William Graham Sumner (1840–1910) offered the first American course titled 'Sociology'" (http://sociology.yale.edu, accessed October 30, 2014). Yet despite these claims, Chicago is widely perceived as the first American sociology department, and there is little debate that it was the most influential.

such other pioneering first-generation sociologists as W. I. Thomas, Charles Henderson, Ernest Burgess, Ellsworth Faris, and the chairman, the innovative Albion Small. These founding faculty members were augmented by the social psychologist George Herbert Mead and the philosopher John Dewey, both housed in Chicago's philosophy department, and colleagues in the geography and political science departments. The dominant narrative claims that this faculty, and especially Park, produced the major theories, concepts, and pathbreaking textbook that guided the emerging field for decades. The Chicago department trained large numbers of graduate students who conducted empirical research, published their scholarship widely, and became leaders in the field, thus spreading the influence of the Chicago school throughout American sociology and the other social sciences. Numerous works of the faculty and students were published by the University of Chicago Press and by the first journal of American sociology, the *American Journal of Sociology*, also published by the University of Chicago Press and edited by University of Chicago sociology professors.

The architects of the Chicago school established deep organizational roots at the University of Chicago. They successfully secured the funds that allowed it to build a formidable infrastructure to support the research activities of faculty and graduate students. Additionally, the city of Chicago served as a social laboratory where empirical research was conducted on the major social processes unfolding in one of the world's great modern cities. Because of these characteristics, the Chicago school dominated the early field of sociology, thus marking the rise of American scientific sociology. This lily-white and elite conception of the origins of American sociology has long been accepted as received wisdom.

Yet although it was only occasionally articulated in the twentieth century, there is a counterview. It argues that in the first years of that century the black sociologist, scholar, and activist W. E. B. Du Bois developed the first scientific school of sociology at Atlanta University, a historically black institution of higher learning located in the heart of Atlanta's black community. This counterview is largely unknown in mainstream academia, for it flies beneath the academic radar, disconnected from the dominant narrative of the origins of American sociology. Nevertheless, it has become more visible and has been developed by a small number of innovative scholars.[2] Even before it was explicitly formulated, a number of earlier accounts documented the importance of Du Bois as a black sociologist and his enduring but usually unacknowledged influence as a pioneer in sociology.[3] This tradition regarding Du Bois's importance as a sociologist has continued in contemporary accounts.[4] Though these earlier works provide only the beginnings of a definitive counternarrative, they nevertheless represent a solid foundation on which to build a comprehensive and accurate account of the emergence of American scientific sociology. Upon this foundation, I will develop an analysis of the myriad factors that gave rise to the Du Bois–Atlanta school.[5]

---

2. E. Wright (2002a, 2002b, 2002c, 2006, 2008); Gabbidon (2007); Zuckerman (2004); Rabaka (2010).

3. Green and Driver (1978); Blackwell and Janowitz (1974); Rudwick (1969); Bracey, Meier, and Rudwick (1971); Broderick (1974).

4. Bell, Grosholz, and Stewart (1996); A. Young et al. (2006); Saint-Arnaud (2009).

5. A legitimate question is why I designate this school as "the Du Bois–Atlanta school of sociology" or as "Du Bois's Atlanta school of sociology." In an e-mail of July 21, 2011, Professor Mary Pattillo writes, "I imagine … you'll justify why it should be called the DuBois School and not the Atlanta School, as would be suggested by what we now have is the Chicago School, not the Park School." I include "Du Bois" in the school's name because Du Bois played the primary role in developing and sustaining it. At Chicago a major sociology department existed with professors, graduate students, and a sociology journal when Park arrived. Thus Park entered a well-established sociology department

Definite political, economic, cultural, and personality factors led white social scientists to suppress Du Bois's scholarship of race and his unique contributions to the developing social sciences at the dawn of the twentieth century. That scholarship stood in direct opposition to the dominant racist views held by most social scientists, especially white sociologists. During this period, the Jim Crow regime, which defined blacks as biologically and culturally inferior, was developing deep roots. Du Bois's sociological arguments stressing that races were socially constructed and blacks were not biologically inferior flew in the face of white racial beliefs. As James McKee has demonstrated, white social scientists concurred with the general white consensus that blacks were created inferior and incapable of functioning as social equals of whites.[6] For them, genetics and culture, rather than social conditions, produced racial inequality. Yet that "scientific" knowledge constituted scientific racism, for it was based on folk concepts rather than careful, systematic, empirical research. The racial analyses of white social scientists, therefore, provided ideological cover for racism.

For Du Bois, externally imposed social conditions constituted the foundations of race oppression and white supremacy. In contrast to white social scientists, Du Bois insisted that the newly emerging social sciences be built on careful, empirical research focused on human action in order to pass the test as genuine science.[7] Because he believed that an authentic social science was possible and that inferior and superior races did not exist, Du Bois was the first social scientist to establish a sociological laboratory where systematic empirical research was conducted to determine the scientific causes of racial inequality. In this manner, Du Bois treated claims of inherent race superiority as hypotheses to be accepted or rejected on the basis of data collected through the best scientific methods available. Given his approach, Du Bois decried any racial findings stemming from racial prejudice and vested interests. Therefore, as the twentieth century opened, Du Bois continued to develop a sociology whose mission was to interject science into the emerging field by relying on data and the execution of scientific research based in empirical methodologies. This book will demonstrate that Du Bois, and his collaborators, did indeed build a sociological school that challenged scientific racism by generating findings suggesting races were socially constructed and that social conditions largely determined racial inequality. From a purely scientific perspective, Du Bois's school of sociology examining race was superior to the "scientific" research of the period—and of decades to come—that was based largely on conjecture, speculation, racist assumptions, and scant empirical data.

Thus there were obvious reasons why white sociologists suppressed Du Bois's scholarship. To embrace Du Bois's sociology, they would need to acknowledge that their theories proclaiming the biological and cultural inferiority of blacks could not be supported scientifically. Such an admission would have placed white social scientists at odds with the racial views of the white majority and those of white elites in particular. That would have been too ideologically jarring for them because they shared the white

---

where he carved out a niche as a lecturer. In contrast, though an embryonic organizational shell of a school and some intellectual activities existed when Du Bois arrived at Atlanta, the tasks of organizing a sociology department, training students, fine-tuning a research organization, and guiding publications awaited him. Without a guiding template, Du Bois singlehandedly developed the pioneering scientific intellectual orientation that guided his school.

6. McKee (1993).
7. Du Bois ([ca. 1905] 2000).

racist consensus and were not willing to distance themselves from the white privileges that sustained their "science."

Additionally, there were deep personal and cultural reasons why white social scientists suppressed Du Bois's scholarship. Early in the twentieth century, whites viewed all African Americans as inferior, even black intellectuals such as Du Bois. White social scientists could not embrace black excellence in science, let alone the superiority of a black scientist. To acknowledge Du Bois's pioneering science, they would have had to admit that Du Bois was a scientific role model deserving white followership. They could not conceive such a view and definitely could not translate it into practice. Thus they suppressed Du Bois's scholarship because it concluded that there were no scientific grounds on which to justify racial oppression and because they could not view Du Bois as an exemplary scholar who pioneered scientific sociology. Because the stakes were exceedingly high for white sociologists, Du Bois's sociology was suppressed, resulting in an impoverished sociology that endured over a century.

On the basis of my findings, I will argue that the Du Bois–Atlanta school deserves credit for founding scientific sociology in America. This book documents the unique contributions that Du Bois's school made to the development of American sociology in terms of scholarship, research, and teaching.

I posit that it was Du Bois who made the most distinctive contribution to American sociology in the first half of the twentieth century. That contribution, rooted in the idea that sociology was an empirical science, consisted of producing community studies and theoretical formulations based on empirical methodology.[8] Though Du Bois's pioneering community studies utilized scientific methodology two decades before Park and his students, this distinctive contribution has nevertheless been attributed to the Chicago school. Moreover, I will provide evidence that Park knew about Du Bois's pioneering studies but failed to accord them the scholarly credit they merited. Even worse, by ignoring Du Bois's groundbreaking scientific work, the Chicago school, mainstream sociology, and social science generally were impoverished theoretically and methodologically for a century—and this is especially true regarding the study of race. Because Park and the Chicago school failed to acknowledge and engage the work of Du Bois and his students, they were able to claim Chicago's primacy. This stance prepared the way for succeeding

8. This book's argument concerns specifically the development of scientific sociology in America beginning in the late nineteenth and early twentieth centuries. In an e-mail of April 7, 2011, Arthur Stinchombe pointed out that a tradition of empirical sociology existed in Europe before Du Bois established his sociology in America. He wrote that "Marx & Engels were good empirical workers on the English industrial revolution, and Marx on the French politics of status groups (e.g. Lumpen Proletariat; petty bourgeoisie), Engels on 'The condition of the English Working Class' … though both mostly used archives rather than ethnography. And of course Weber was 'empirical' in the sense of knowing a hell of a lot of facts about social relations at various times in history in many parts of the world. 'Empirical' doesn't mean only going out in the field and interviewing, though it does indeed include that." I agree. My contention is that prior to Du Bois's work in Philadelphia and Atlanta, American sociologists were not employing empirical methodologies and conducting research on which to develop sociological generalizations. Rather, they relied on armchair theorizing and deductive reasoning to construct various concepts "explaining" social reality. This approach was largely dominant in Europe, though there were notable exceptions, as Stinchcombe argues. In later chapters we will see that American sociologists of the early twentieth century were coming to realize that armchair theorizing was leading to a dead end. Thus there was a need for grounded empirical research if the new discipline was to survive as a legitimate discipline. Du Bois pioneered quantitative and quantitative methods in his sociological scholarship.

generations of scholars to reproduce this fictitious account, thus solidifying the claim that Chicago was the first school of American scientific sociology. The influence of this inaccurate account of the origins of American sociology reflects the wisdom of W. I. Thomas's precept: If people define situations as real, they are real in their consequences.[9]

References

Abbott, Andrew. 1999. *Department and Discipline: Chicago Sociology at One Hundred*. Chicago: University of Chicago Press.

Bell, Bernard, W., Emily R. Grosholz, and James B. Stewart, eds. 1996. *W. E. B. Du Bois on Race and Culture: Philosophy, Politics, and Poetics*. New York: Routledge.

Blackwell, James E., and Morris Janowitz. 1974. *Black Sociologists: Historical and Contemporary Perspectives*. Chicago: University of Chicago Press.

Bracey, John H., August Meier, and Elliott Rudwick. 1971. *The Black Sociologists: The First Half Century*. Belmont, CA: Wadsworth.

Broderick, Frances L. 1974. "W. E. B. Du Bois: History of an Intellectual." In *Black Sociologists: Historical and Contemporary Perspectives*, edited by James E. Blackwell and Morris Janowitz, 3–24. Chicago: University of Chicago Press.

Bulmer, Martin. 1985. "The Chicago School of Sociology: What Made It a 'School'?" *History of Sociology* 5 (2): 61–77.

Coser, Lewis A. 1978. "American Trends." In *A History of Sociological Analysis*, edited by Tom Bottomore and Robert Nisbet, 283–321. New York: Basic Books.

Deegan, M. J. 2001. "The Chicago School of Ethnography." In *Handbook of Ethnography*, edited by P. A. Atkinson, A. J. Coffey, S. Delamont, J. Lofland, and L. Lofland, 11–25. London: Sage Publications.

Faris, Robert E. L. 1967. *Chicago Sociology, 1920–1932*. Chicago: University of Chicago Press.

Fine, Gary A., ed. 1995. *A Second Chicago School?* Chicago: University of Chicago.

Gabbidon, Shaun L. 2007. *W. E. B. Du Bois on Crime and Justice: Laying the Foundations of Sociological Criminology*. Aldershot: Ashgate.

Green, Dan S., and Edwin Driver, eds. 1978. *W. E. B. DuBois on Sociology and the Black Community*. Chicago: University of Chicago Press.

Hunter, Albert. 1980. "Why Chicago? The Rise of the Chicago School of Urban Social Science." *American Behavioral Scientist* 24 (2): 215–27.

Matthews, Fred H. 1977. *Quest for an American Sociology: Robert E. Park and the Chicago School*. Montreal: McGill-Queen's University Press.

McKee, James B. 1993. *Sociology and the Race Problem: The Failure of a Perspective*. Urbana: University of Illinois Press.

Rabaka, Reiland. 2010. *Against Epistemic Apartheid: W. E. B. Du Bois and the Disciplinary Decadence of Sociology*. Lanham, MD: Rowman and Littlefield.

Rudwick, Elliott. 1969. "Note on a Forgotten Black Sociologist: W. E. B. Du Bois and the Sociological Profession." *American Sociologist* 4 (4): 303–6.

Saint-Arnaud, Pierre. 2009. *African American Pioneers of Sociology: A Critical History*. Translated by Peter Feldstein. Toronto: University of Toronto Press.

Sica, Alan. "A Century of Sociology at Kansas." *Footnotes* [American Sociological Association], March 8, 1991.

Thomas, W. I., and Dorothy Thomas. 1928. *The Child in America: Behavior Problems and Programs*. New York: Knopf.

Wright, Earl, II. 2002a. "The Atlanta Sociological Laboratory, 1896–1924: A Historical Account of the First American School of Sociology." *Western Journal of Black Studies* 26 (3): 165–74.

———. 2002b. "Using The Master's Tools: Atlanta University and American Sociology, 1896–1924." *Sociological Spectrum* 22 (1): 15–39.

———. 2002c. "Why Black People Tend to Shout! An Earnest Attempt to Explain the Sociological Negation of the Atlanta Sociological Laboratory Despite Its Possible Unpleasantness." *Sociological Spectrum* 22 (3): 325–61.

———. 2006. "W. E. B. Du Bois and the Atlanta University Studies on the Negro, Revisited." *Journal of African American Studies* 9 (4): 3–17.

———. 2008. "Deferred Legacy! The Continued Marginalization of the Atlanta Sociological Laboratory." *Sociology Compass* 2 (1).

Young, Alford A., Jr., Manning Marable, Elizabeth Higginbotham, Charles Lemert, and Jerry G. Watts. 2006. *The Souls of W. E. B. Du Bois*. Boulder, CO: Paradigm.

Zuckerman, Phil, ed. 2004. *The Social Theory of W. E. B. Du Bois*. Thousand Oaks, CA: Pine Forge Press.

9. Thomas and Thomas (1928, 572).

Post-Reading Questions

1. What was the Chicago School of sociology? Why did it receive more attention than the Atlanta School that W. E. B. Du Bois founded?
2. Where was the first sociological laboratory established? What types of research took place there?
3. Why did many white sociologists at the turn of the twentieth century ignore W. E. B Du Bois's contributions to sociology?

From Public Sociology to Politicized Sociologist

Frances Fox Piven

Frances Fox Piven, Selection from "From Public Sociology to Politicized Sociology," *Public Sociology: Fifteen Eminent Sociologists Debate Politics and the Profession in the Twenty-First Century*, ed. Dan Clawson, et al., pp. 158, 163, 165–166. Copyright © 2007 by University of California Press. Reprinted with permission.

I define the term *public sociology* broadly, as the uses of sociological knowledge to address public and, therefore, political problems. This simple and sweeping definition means, I think, that public sociologists treat public problems as the important part of our research agenda, and it also means that we communicate our findings to the political constituencies who are affected by those problems and can act on them in politics. I am in favor of these uses of sociology. However, I think some self-scrutiny is called for about the social and political influences to which we ourselves are subject when we act as public sociologists.

The current preoccupation with public sociology comes easily to our field. After all, it is, in a way, a return to our roots. Sociology was born in the mid-nineteenth century out of the self-consciousness about the social environment forced on thinkers by the public problems, the disorder, and the disturbances evident in urbanizing and industrializing societies. In the United States, our first sociologists were associated with reform organizations trying to cope with the problems of poverty, deviance, and conflict evident in the growing cities. Later, in response to an insurgent labor movement, we developed a sociology of labor and industrial relations. And later still, as the civil rights, feminist, and antiwar movements gained momentum, we developed sociologies of race, gender, and peace studies. [...]

So, if we are to follow Michael Burawoy's compelling call for public sociology, I think we have to reflect critically on our relations with the public. We should in fact try to reconstruct these relations, by breaking out of the too-comfortable pattern of treating government as our patron and speaking directly to the public. This is easy to say, but the first question it raises is, which public? American society is sharply polarized; indeed, world society is sharply polarized. Bitter conflicts simmer in the United States and rage in the open throughout the world. The corruption of democracy and the ensuing loss of legitimacy by governmental authorities in the United States are, in fact, what make the uses of sociologists and sociology by the American government so problematic. Not so long ago, we took for granted that the American government represented, in a flawed way to be sure, a kind of societal consensus, or at least a majority consensus. However imperfectly, this was a democracy. No attentive person thinks it is that simple now. So, we have to ask, just who is it we serve when we serve government?

If public sociology is to thrive, we have to recognize not one public but many publics, and once we acknowledge the sharp divisions in our society, we have to decide which publics we want to work with. I propose as a guideline that we strive to address the public and political problems of people at the lower end of the many hierarchies that define our society. That means we devote our attention and our knowledge skills to the expressed needs of the poor and the working class rather than to the comfortably well off, to racial minorities and especially African Americans, to women more than men, to those without legal residence instead of those with legal residence and citizenship, to the marginalized and down-and-out of all descriptions. And not just in the United States. We also, when our skills allow, ought to regard the teeming multitudes around the world as our public, especially the hundreds of millions of people elsewhere whose traditional livelihoods are being destroyed by the depredations of international capitalism, which importantly means American capitalism. Their felt problems should become our sociological problems. If we do this, then public sociology becomes a dissident and critical sociology. Maybe there was a time when this was not necessary. Now it is. [...]

But while the universities and colleges offer us some protection, they are far from a perfect environment for nurturing a dissident sociology. Like most institutions, they encourage conformity to whatever it is that went before, to whoever it is that is above us in the hierarchy. So, we have to try to create our own environment, an environment that encourages criticism and dissidence and allows us to devote our intelligence and our time to understanding the problems of the world's majorities. How to do this? Well, if as social subjects we respond to incentives and rewards, we should begin to construct those systems of rewards, and perhaps of sanctions as well. We should use our conferences to honor the best dissident public sociology, and to criticize those sociologists who we think are contributing, by the kind of work they do, to misery and subjugation. We should create alternative journals that publish refereed articles of the best dissident public sociology. Above all, we should make sure we have comrades who support us when we need that support, as we surely will if we are sharp enough and critical enough.

We should also seek out alternative constituencies. We are accustomed to doing research for government agencies. Now we should try to cultivate the relations that will allow us to do research for unions, advocacy organizations, and community groups. And we should explore more participatory research methods with these groups, methods in which the subjects become partners in the design and conduct of the research. Such organizations are not likely to be able to fund the massive research project to which some of us have become accustomed. So be it. We will be able to do good research anyway.

Finally, I think we have to reevaluate the philosophical basis of our endeavors, and do this in writing, with theoretical sophistication. The scientific ideal, the injunction to emphasize the positive science in social science, was always too simple-minded in its treatment of the fact and value distinction. And the best sociology, the sociology of the great thinkers in our field, was, in fact, inspired by the moral and political concerns they confronted in their place and in their time. Now, in our place and in our time, moral and political concerns are overwhelming. Our political system moves toward theocracy, our government undertakes preemptive war and torture and creates concentration camps, our public policies push the planet toward an environmental tipping point, a wholesale assault is under way by the right on critical thinking and science, and wealth concentration spins out of sight while the earnings of most people stagnate and even their pensions are robbed, by the companies they work for, and perhaps by the government as well.

How can we not be critical and dissident public sociologists?

References

Burawoy, Michael. 2005. "2004 Presidential Address: For Public Sociology." *American Sociological Review* 70: 4–28.

Flyvbjerg, Bent. 2001. *Making Social Science Matter: Why Social Science Fails and How It Can Succeed Again.* New York: Cambridge University Press.

Merton, Robert. 1968. "Role of the Intellectual in Public Bureaucracy." In *Social Theory and Social Structure,* R. Merton, enlarged edition, 261–78. New York: The Free Press.

Reed, Adolph. 2004. "Reinventing the Working Class: A Study in Elite Image Manipulation." *New Labor Forum* 13 (Fall): 22.

Schram, Sanford. 1995. *Words of Welfare: The Poverty of Social Science and the Social Science of Poverty.* Minneapolis: University of Minnesota Press.

Scott, James C. 1998. *Seeing Like a State.* New Haven, CT: Yale University Press.

Smelser, Neil. 1988. "Introduction." In *Handbook of Sociology,* ed. N. Smelser, 15. Beverly Hills, CA: Sage Publications.

Toulmin, Michael. 2002. *Return to Reason.* Berkeley: University of California Press.

Post-Reading Questions

1. According to the author, what is the definition of public sociology?
2. What types of publics exist in our society? Why must we recognize and address multiple publics to make a difference?
3. What do you think it means to be critical and dissident sociologists? How does this relate to the mission of public sociology?

UNIT II

IMPORTANT SOCIOLOGICAL THEORIES

Key Terms and Definitions

Review the key terms and definitions below to strengthen your understanding of the readings in this unit.

Anomie: Émile Durkheim's notion that in modern societies, when social norms are not in place, individuals can feel that they lack guidance.

Class Conflict: Inequality and tension between the bourgeoise (capitalist factory owners) and proletariat (ordinary workers). Karl Marx believed that this was the driving force of history.

Communism: A hypothetical social and economic system where there are no distinctions between social classes. In such a system, workers are valued for their time, not their production, and workers share ownership over tools, equipment, and labor, receiving equal compensation to their counterparts.

Conscious Collective: Émile Durkheim's idea that members of a society share certain ideas, values, beliefs, and sentiments in common. This helps to provide a sense of solidarity and togetherness.

The Dialectical Method: Marx's philosophy (which contrasts with Hegelian philosophy) that the economic structure of a society determines its overall ideas and values. Marx believed that the economic structure of capitalism values the rich and discounts the poor, leading to real-world consequences like inequality and poverty.

Hegelian Philosophy: The notion that a society's ideas and values create rational systems. Hegel believed that all ideas and values stem from a thesis (an original position), an antithesis (the opposite of the position), and synthesis (a resolution between the two positions). In this view, the experience an individual has with the economy is based in perception, not material circumstances.

Idealism: Max Weber's philosophy that ideas and values are the foundation upon which a society's economy is built. This is opposite from Karl Marx's dialectical method.

Iron Cage: Max Weber's vision that the rationalization of society under capitalism would lead workers to feel trapped in a situation from which they cannot escape.

Marxism: The viewpoint of Karl Marx that history is driven by class conflict and that the economy influences a society's ideas and values. Under capitalism, this creates inequalities.

Socialism: A social and economic system in which there is social ownership over economic production rather than private control. Like communism, workers are valued for the time, not their production, and workers share ownership over tools, equipment, and labor, receiving equal compensation to their counterpoints. Karl Marx believed that socialism was a pathway to communism (full social and economic equality).

Introduction

Before taking a sociology class, many students enter the classroom with basic familiarity with the political philosopher Karl Marx (1818–1883). Some students are aware that Marx advocated for **communism**, calling for equality among social classes in society. He believed that **socialism**, or shared ownership over economic production, was a step toward communism, which in his vision would lead to full equality in society. In the first reading in this unit, "Voices of Socialism: Karl Marx" by Ralph Miliband, the author describes Karl Marx as a revolutionary. In his famous 1848 book *The Communist Manifesto,* Marx called for members of society to overthrow the economic system of capitalism, which he believed to be inherently unequal. After producing *The Communist Manifesto,* Marx wrote an extensive work in 1867 titled *Capital,* in which he described the functions of the capitalist economy in further detail. In his personal life, Marx faced grave poverty and struggled with illness toward the end of his life. His writing partner, Friedrich Engels, helped to compile Marx's unfinished writings after his death in 1883.

Karl Marx helped advance the discipline of sociology in several ways. He rejected Georg Wilhelm Friedrich Hegel's **Hegelian philosophy**, which suggests that a person's perceptions dictate their experience in the world. Instead, Karl Marx's philosophy, the **dialectical method**, emphasizes that real-world conditions are the root of a person's experiences and that ideas can contradict concrete realities. For example, he saw that capitalism created real imbalances in people's physical resources. Marx believed this determines peoples' experiences more than their ideas and values alone. Ultimately, the author argues that **Marxism** calls to abolish private property and share production. Marx believed that **class conflict** drives all history forward and that revolution was the key to moving past capitalism.

In the second reading, "Rationality's Double-Bind: Max Weber and Modernity's Threat to the Human Spirit" by Charles Lemert, you are introduced to the social thinker Max Weber (1864–1920). Like Karl Marx, Weber was critical of capitalism, but for different reasons. Unlike Karl Marx, Max Weber embraced the philosophy of **idealism**, believing that ideas create the economic structures in society. In his work, the *Protestant Ethic and the Spirit of Capitalism,* Max Weber emphasized that Calvinist Protestants, who believed in predestination, sought to work hard under capitalism in order to find favor in heaven. Weber believed that capitalism would eventually lock workers into an **iron cage**. Because capitalism emphasizes rationality, it prioritizes rules, regulations, and efficiency over a worker's needs. Max Weber believed this to be dehumanizing and difficult to escape.

Finally, in Charles Lemert's "The Reasonable Hope of a Social Bond," you are introduced to another important sociologist, Émile Durkheim (1858–1917). Émile Durkheim's primary concern was how societies maintain a sense of order and balance. He studied how societies remain connected in various periods of history. Unlike Karl Marx, Émile Durkheim did not focus on social conflict but instead focused on social solidarity. Durkheim believed that when people in society lack moral guidance, they may face a sense of **anomie**. He believed that societies maintain a **conscious collective** (sometimes referred to as a collective conscious) that helps to guide their behavior. In other words, members of society share a common orientation about the world that helps them bond to one another.

Each reading in this section sheds light upon the important theories developed by early sociological thinkers. Although each theorist had their own perspective, each contributed to the public good by seeking to understand the underlying operations of society. Karl Marx, Max Weber, and Émile Durkheim had vastly different ideas about what society looks like and how it could be better. Despite this, they shared a public focus, seeking to describe and improve society by exposing the way it operates. In the units to follow, you will learn more about other important figures that help make sociology the discipline it is today.

Voices of Socialism

Karl Marx

Ralph Miliband

Ralph Miliband, "Voices of Socialism: Karl Marx," *Monthly Review*, vol. 66, no. 8, pp. 58–61. Copyright © 2015 by Monthly Review Press. Reprinted with permission. Provided by ProQuest LLC. All rights reserved.

By vocation, Marx was not an economist, or a philosopher, or a sociologist. He was a revolutionary who, being deprived of the opportunity of participating in revolutions in the years after 1848, turned to the detailed analysis of the economic system he wanted to overthrow. Marx never ceased to stress the liberating quality of practical activity; but he himself was compelled by the circumstances of his time to devote most of his life to theoretical work.

Marx was thirty-one years old when he began, in 1849, an English exile which only ended with his death, nearly thirty-five years later. By the time he settled in London, he had already fashioned the new outlook which came, though not by him, to be called Marxism. In the previous half-dozen years, he had freed himself from the constrictions of the Hegelian philosophy he had learnt at the University of Berlin; in Paris, then the home of European socialism, he had assimilated the French revolutionary thought and experience of the previous fifty years; and he had also dug deep into English political economy: the work which he, with the help of Friedrich Engels, two years his junior, did in those few years, already includes all the main moral, economic, and political themes of his system; the *Communist Manifesto* of 1848 is, in effect, the culmination, the summation of an intellectual effort which must rank as one of the most remarkable episodes in the history of ideas.

In the two decades following the defeat of 1848, Marx's main intellectual work was his attempt, as he describes it in the Preface to Volume I of *Capital,* published in 1867, to "lay bare the economic law of motion of modern society." From the foundation of the First International in 1864 until its virtual demise in 1872, Marx was also its leading figure, and it was in its name that he wrote, in 1871, his glowing tribute to the defeated Paris Commune and its tens of thousands of slaughtered defenders.

In all these years in England, Marx and the incomparable Jenny Marx and their children had endured the most bitter poverty, relieved only by Marx's occasional journalism and by Engels's unfailing help. By the early seventies, life had become easier; but Marx was plagued by ill-health, and he had, it would seem, lost the capacity for sustained writing. A mass of work which he had planned or started remained uncompleted, notably Volumes II and III of *Capital*, which Engels put together after Marx's death.

Engels, who survived him by twelve years, witnessed the rising tide of Marxian influence; Marx just missed it. All his life, he was a leader without a movement, a teacher with few disciples, quite unknown outside a narrow circle of socialists, most of whom were opposed to him anyway. In his own lifetime, there were probably fewer people who, in the whole wide world, thought of themselves as "Marxists" than are to be found today in Paris or Rome.

***

On the one hand, there is the Marxism of Engels, Lenin, Luxemburg, Trotsky, and other Marxists. On the other, there is Marx's thought and work. The relation between Marx and Marxism is an interesting question, which has caused much ink to flow, and a lot of blood as well. But Marx, in any case, is not Engels, or Trotsky, or Mao Tse-tung, and there is certainly more than a hyphen which separates Marx from Leninism. In any case, later Marxism must be judged on *its* merits rather than with reference to Marx, the more so as he can, more or less plausibly, be quoted in support of many divergent positions. At the same time, it may at least be possible to distinguish certain fundamental elements which lie at the core of his thought: whatever else authentic Marxism may be deemed to include, it needs to include these.

First of all, there is a certain way of looking at the world: Marx's first concern is with the material, concrete reality which lies hidden, as he believes, behind the religions, the ideologies, the moralities, which men create for themselves and for others out of ignorance, fear, or design. Marx's method, adapted from Hegel, is the dialectical method, or the search for the contradictory features of reality, the awareness of the manysidedness of life and events, the consciousness of movement, conflict, change, impermanence—a method appropriate to a man who told his daughter that his "favorite motto" was "Doubt all things."

Marx's dialectics must be clearly distinguished from the system known, though not to Marx, as "dialectical materialism." This is the dialectics which Engels describes as "the science of the general laws of motion and development of Nature, human society and thought." Marx does not use dialectics in this sense; nor, unlike his followers, did he make any universal claims for his work.

The reality which needs to be uncovered, Marx holds, has above all to do with men's material existence, with their economic life. At the beginning, there is neither the word, nor even the deed, but hunger and need. In their struggle for existence, men enter into certain relationships with each other. For most of history down to the present, these relations have had as their main characteristic the domination of the few over the many, of slave-owner over slave, of feudal lord over serf, of capitalist over wage-earner, the few appropriating the largest possible part of that which the many produce. Modes of exploitation have varied from epoch to epoch—but exploitation itself has endured. Reforms within a system of exploitation are possible, but do not affect its character as a system of exploitation. This can only be done on the basis of the abolition of the private ownership of the means of production.

Class domination and class conflict are two sides of the same coin. Now acute and violent, now latent and subdued, class conflict is the driving force of history, the way in which men make their history; its extreme manifestation is revolution. In class conflict, the state is not neutral. On the contrary, its principal purpose is to offer protection to the economically and socially dominant class. Nor does that class only seek to protect itself by physical force; it also relies on its control of the "mental means of production" and upon the socially soporific influence of ideologies of resignation and accommodation, of which religion is only one expression.

Marx was a remarkably flexible thinker, save in one respect—his absolute certainty that capitalism was no more permanent than the social systems which had gone before it. Its supersession, he said, was not only desirable but inevitable, above all because there lay at its heart a "contradiction" which could only be resolved by its abolition; with the development of capitalism, "the monopoly of capital becomes a fetter upon the mode of production, which has sprung up and flourished along with, and under it. Centralization of the means of production and socialization of labor at last reach a point where they become incompatible with their capitalist integument. This integument is burst asunder. The knell of capitalist private property sounds. The expropriators are expropriated."

Marx did not exclude the possibility that the proletarian revolution he announced might be peaceful, but it is quite clear that he expected it to be violent. It is equally clear that revolution, for him, is above all the business of the class-conscious proletariat, whose dictatorship it installs. The "dictatorship of the proletariat," in Marx, is not the rule of an elite or a party on behalf of the people: it is rule by the people, their actual running of society. The model depends upon the existence of the class-conscious proletariat as a dominant force: in the absence of such a force, it undergoes fundamental modifications.

The abolition of capitalism does not usher in the "truly human" society; it only makes it possible. As for the character of that truly human, classless, society, Marx consistently refused to speculate on it: it is for those who will make that society to define its features. But the vision which underlies his whole work, from the early 1840s to the end, is the vision of human liberation, of which material fulfilment is the condition but not the sum. Ultimately, this is what Marx, the mature Marx as well as the "young Marx," is about—life against existence.

***

There are many loose threads in Marx's work: his economic analysis, his theory of capitalist crisis, his theory of the state and of classes, his model of social change, the relation between "material base" and "superstructure," in brief, all the most important aspects of his work yield large questions rather than neat solutions. This, however, is not Marx's weakness but his strength, save to religious minds. For the questions to which he compels attention, and which his work illuminates, are at least as relevant now as when he asked them; and so is the challenge he poses.

The Victorian era was a great era for explorers. Marx was the greatest and boldest of them all. No one has so far provided a better point of entry into the jungle of social analysis. But having entered, those who follow him are on their own, and must make their own way.

***

But by destroying the circumstances surrounding that metabolism [between humanity and nature] ... it [capitalist production] compels its systematic restoration as a regulative law of social production, and in a form adequate to the full development of the human race.

—Marx, *Capital*, vol. 1

Post-Reading Questions

1. Why did Karl Marx reject capitalism? Which social and economic systems did he believe should exist instead?
2. What were the reasons that Karl Marx rejected Hegel's philosophy? What did he propose instead?
3. How does capitalism produce class conflict today? Do you think that today's workers will incite revolution if inequality continues?

Rationality's Double-Bind

Max Weber and Modernity's Threat to the Human Spirit

Charles Lemert

Why Do Rational Rules Result in a Double-Bind?

Max Weber was born 1864, when Marx was still writing his greatest book, *Capital, I*. By the time Weber had published his doctoral thesis, *The History of Commercial Partnerships in the Middle Ages* (1889), Marx's social theory was very well known. Historians of economic and social history as well as the early sociologists could not help but take seriously Marx's theory of the economic foundations of society. Weber was no exception. Yet even a passing glance at Weber's earliest scholarly work makes it clear that we are dealing here with a very different sort of thinker from Marx. But the difference should not be exaggerated. Weber was not nearly so engaged in politics and, when he was, his politics were not nearly so radical. Still, like all of the social theorists of the classical era, Weber was deeply troubled by the contradictions of modern life. In the end, his version of modernity's riddle proved less easily solved than Marx's.

Weber, even more than Marx, was the personification of the German scientific scholar in a day when Germany set the universal standard for scientific work. He mastered languages easily. His thesis required Latin, Italian, and Spanish, as well as his native German. He worked closely with original sources buried in archives. Yet, even *The History of Commercial Partnerships in the Middle Ages* was not as remote from the concerns of the modern age as one might suppose. Commercial partnerships—or, formally organized business groups—were a very early instance of "rational-legal" administration—that is: rule by reasonable laws, as opposed to force. Weber's first book (which, it is safe to say, has been read by no more than a few hundred scholars) was, in effect, a first step toward the ideas that made his *Protestant Ethic and the Spirit of Capitalism* (1904–1905) one of social theory's most widely read books.

> **Spirit of capitalism,** Weber's expression for the this-worldly ascetic disposition that drove the capitalist entrepreneur; one of Weber's translators has aptly described the disposition as an "ethical orientation"; see also **this-worldly asceticism.**

Why has Weber's *Protestant Ethic and the Spirit of Capitalism* been so interesting to so many for so long? In part because it poses a question that Marx did not ask (and probably could not have). Marx had come to conclude that the modern world was just as corrupt in its own way as any that came before. Weber, however, was more puzzled by the evidence that so much that was good in modernity had turned remarkably bad.

"But fate decreed that the cloak should become an iron cage. … No one knows who will live in this cage in the future." Few figures of speech are as appropriate as the one Weber chose to convey the double-bind of the modern world as an iron cage. Industrial capitalism, at the end of the nineteenth century, was built of iron and steel. By the turn of the nineteenth century, when Weber was writing on capitalism, the cotton mills had given way to the manufacture of steel that made the railroad and the machine-based factory possible. The factory system was truly cast in iron, which, of course, meant that it was ever-more mechanized than even the first cotton mills. Weber, unlike Marx, was not preoccupied with the evil of the factory system. He appreciated the benefits of the new industrial order. But he was unlike Marx in that he believed that modernity, including the culture that stood behind capitalism, was a threat to humanity—to, that is, the essential human spirit, which, since the Enlightenment, had become one of early modern culture's foremost ideals.

"The Puritan wanted to work in a calling; we are forced to do so." When we speak today of people having a good work ethic, we speak in the language of Max Weber—who understood both the good and the evil aspects of hard work. For Marx, work in the factory system estranged the worker from herself and from her fellow workers, but the alienation was attributed to the external structures of the mode of production. For Weber, the evil of the modern world—though a consequence of exterior economic conditions—was *interior,* a vital element in the ethical attitudes of modern people. For him, modernity induced in people an attitude toward work that caused many to work without ceasing and for little human benefit. The dark side of the work ethic is, as we now know very well, an inner drive so powerful as to become a pathological compulsion, even an obsession. While Marx emphasized the negative pressures of modern life on the workers, Weber saw them as more universal—as bad for the bourgeois industrialist as for the worker. Plus which, while Marx interpreted the evil of capitalism as a straightforward social problem, Weber saw it in a more paradoxical way. The good and the bad of the modern world were, for Weber, literally a double-bind—an interior contradiction that could *not* be overcome by reason or revolution, as Marx thought. In other words, for Weber, no matter which way modern man turned he could not escape the paradox that the benefits of hard work were also deadly.

For Weber, modernity meant "a departure from an age of full and beautiful humanity, which can no more be repeated in the course of our cultural development than can the flower of the Athenian culture of antiquity." For Marx, the past was no more than prelude to the present. And in this comparison the most important difference between the two is apparent. Weber felt that culture was a powerful force in itself, while Marx thought that culture was no more than the inverted image of economic structures. Hence Marx's famous figure of speech describing social reality as a *camera obscura*—a lens that pictured the modern world as if it were good, when the reality was just the opposite. Weber's *iron cage* is a figure of another kind, describing a problem ever more complicated.

Differences aside, both Weber and Marx were imbued with a nineteenth-century way of thinking about materialism and idealism as opposing attitudes. Marx, the materialist, believed that ideas and culture were no more than the false images of material reality. Weber, the idealist, believed that, as important as economic matters were, one cannot think about the modern realities without a theory of culture. Weber did not reject economic, or material, factors in his thinking. He was first and foremost an economic historian as the subject of his 1889 thesis indicates. Yet, the fame attributed to him for *Protestant Ethic and the Spirit of Capitalism* owes to the way he politely but firmly criticized the materialists by offering historically sound evidence in support of his important question, which was, roughly put: *There is no doubt that capitalism is now, early in the twentieth century, a "tremendous cosmos" that dominates modern life. But where did the capitalists come from?*

Weber's question, compared to Marx's, is the kind of question more likely to be asked by a man of science than by one whose politics are at the fore. While Weber was quite serious about politics, his politics were always separate from his science (as they were not in Marx's case). One of his most famous public statements on the subject, *Politics as a Vocation* (1918), was less about politics as such than about the kind of interior, ethical attitude that leads an individual to engage in politics. At the end of this essay he said famously: "Politics is a strong and slow boring of hard boards." He meant that it is very hard and tedious work that can succeed in the long run only when the work is done by those with a passion for politics. Interestingly, this was much the same view he expressed in a lecture on science, delivered in conjunction with the one on politics.

In *Science as a Vocation* (1918), Weber said that the scientist must be willing to work very long hours, making countless calculations, against the risk that nothing will come of it. "Ideas occur to us when they please, not when it pleases us." He meant here also that the work can succeed only if the scientist is willing to gamble hours of labor against the odds that she will not discover a new idea. In fact, Weber felt so strongly that he added: "In the field of science only he who is devoted *solely* to the work at hand has 'personality.'" He meant, in other words, that when it comes to science (and politics and by implication other kinds of work) the meaning of an individual's work (and by implication his life) derives from the passionate devotion to the work itself without any assurance of success.

What would prompt people to live and work in such a way? Weber's answer is central to his distinctive view of the modern individual. What distinguishes the modern individual from others is the expectation that her work, whatever it is, can have meaning—that (to use the word in the title of the essays on science and politics) she has a *vocation*, which is to say: a *calling*. Obviously, the expression comes from traditional religious practices and that too is crucial to Weber's thinking. In premodern or elementary cultures, it was normally the religious man—the priest or shaman—who enjoyed the benefits of a calling that set him apart from ordinary men and women and thus endowed him with the "personality" whereby he could do the priestly work with authority. In modern times, Weber thought, it is much more commonly believed that workers work for meaning—not all of course (because even in the modern world there remain very unmodern and traditional values). This is one of the ways that Weber began to answer the question Marx could not: *Where did the capitalists come from?* They came from a change in the basic, personal values by which individuals organized their lives.

BEN FRANKLIN, THE IDEAL TYPE

"The most trifling actions that affect a man's credit are to be regarded. The sound of your hammer at five in the morning, or eight at night, heard by a creditor, makes him easy six months longer; but if he sees you at a billiard-table, or hears your voice at tavern, when you should be at work, he sends for his money the next day. ..."

One of the fundamental elements of the spirit of modern capitalism, and not only of that but of all modern culture: rational conduct on the basis of the idea of the calling, was born ... from the spirit of Christian asceticism. One has only to re-read the passage from [Ben] Franklin [just quoted] in order to see the essential elements of the attitude which was there called the spirit of capitalism are the same as ... the Puritan worldly asceticism, only without the religious basis which by Franklin's time had died away. ... The Puritan wanted to work in a calling; we are forced to do so. For when the asceticism was carried out of monastic cells into everyday life, and began to dominate worldly morality, it did its part in building the tremendous cosmos of the modern economic order.

—Max Weber, *Protestant Ethic* (1904–5)

Thus, another distinctive feature of Weber's social theory. He was more confident than Marx that the individual retained a sense of the inner meaning of his or her life, even under the severely dehumanizing conditions brought on by the new world of capitalism. At the same time, he too saw, as did Marx, that the human spirit was threatened by the modern world. Without Marx's theory of false consciousness, however, Weber could not quite determine the cause of this unthinkable situation.

Vocation, or **calling,** the idea that work is endowed with meaning—whether divine, in the case of traditional religions, or historical, in the case of modern professional or entrepreneurial workers.

[...] Weber's sociology was, however, a well-thought-out and creative science; but it was also a social ethic. He not only described the modern ethic, he believed in it; and thus worried when it became clear that its effect had terrible consequences. Thus, Weber's stirring warning at the end of *Protestant Ethic and the Spirit of Capitalism*. Like Marx and most social theorists, Weber worried about the fate of the human individual.

Unlike Marx, Weber worried too much—to the point where he was unable to make settled decisions on some important matters. For one, though it is obvious Weber was a man of reason, he did not or could not use reasonable methods that would encapsulate the world as a whole. Weber's social theory was every bit as subtle as Marx's; yet, Marx's theory, being less troubled by paradox, was better able to make definite judgments as to the essential nature of the modern world. For example, Marx was a decided materialist. To him the structures of economic production explained everything. Being clear on the general point allowed Marx to cut quickly to a main idea. Weber, by contrast, would not let himself be too clear about a historically murky situation. Sometimes a good theory gives up the power of clear idea for the reality of social facts. Weber, thus, was not a materialist but neither was he a pure idealist. He was, if not both exactly, able to see both sides, as is clear from the goal of *The Protestant Ethic* to correct, without contradicting, Marx's theory of capitalism by adding in the cultural element of the ethic of the entrepreneur. This Weber did *without* reducing his theory of the modern world to a subjectivism (as in many ways Marx reduced his to an objectivism).

WEBER'S IRON CAGE, AGAIN

For when asceticism was carried out of monastic cells into everyday life, and began to dominate worldly morality, it did its part in building the tremendous cosmos of the modern economic order. This order is now bound to the technical and economic conditions of machine production which to-day determine the lives of all the individuals who are born into this mechanism, not only those directly concerned with economic acquisition, with irresistible force. Perhaps it will so determine them until the last ton of fossilized coal is burnt. In Baxter's view the care for external goods should only lie on the shoulders of the "saint like a light cloak, which can be thrown aside at any moment." But fate decreed that the cloak should become an iron cage.

—Max Weber, *Protestant Ethic* (1904–5)

Objectivism, an exaggeration of the objective social structures that overcomes the role of subjective meanings; **subjectivism,** the opposite kind of mistake.

[...] Though Weber's theory of charismatic authority applies to secular figures, such as Hitler, the ideal type is a religious prophet such as Moses. The problem is that the prophet is as likely to be evil as good. Moses led the Hebrew people into a promised land. Hitler led them to the gas chambers. There are no assurances that the prophet will, over time, lead people well because, as with the traditional despot, there are no limits on his or her power. Still, when you ask Weber where modern people can look for relief from the iron cage, there are not very many answers. If the iron cage destroys human qualities such as the thirst for freedom, as Weber thought, then one strong prospect for help may be the wish that a prophet will come along to break history open and keep hope alive. Though such a one comes along every now and again, charismatic heroes are hardly a realistic basis for serious political work. Weber's politics, like Marx's, failed to provide for the necessary element that could turn the social evil of modernity into good. Marx could not account for how the oppressed worker can overcome alienation to join the revolution, just as Weber could not account for how modern reason could keep humanity from the iron cage that reasonable rationality creates.

Weber's double-bind is his version of the riddle of modernity. The benefits of rationality—of reason in all its practical forms—seldom outweigh the dehumanizing effects of rigid rules, of obsessive work, of technical ethics without gods, of culture without substance, and so on. Weber, perhaps, fell too deeply into pessimism. Between him and Marx, however, you have two sides of the riddle. Marx's social theory was vastly more comprehensive, critical, and definitive; yet his politics were almost naïve in their belief that revolutionary reason in the hands of the proletariat can free men from their chains. Weber's social theory is vastly more complicated, circumspect, and historically subtle; but his moral politics left no room for human freedom that could find a way out of the iron cage.

Post-Reading Questions

1. What does it mean to say that Max Weber is an idealist? How does this shape his view of capitalism?
2. What is Max Weber's idea of the iron cage? In his view, how does capitalism create an iron cage for workers?
3. How do Max Weber's views of society and capitalism differ from Karl Marx's perspectives?

The Reasonable Hope of a Social Bond

Émile Durkheim and Modern Man's Trouble with Conflict

Charles Lemert

Charles Lemert, Selection from "The Reasonable Hope of a Social Bond: Emile Durkheim and the Modern Man's Trouble with Conflict," *Thinking the Unthinkable: The Riddles of Classical Social Theories*, pp. 77–81, 83–84, 85, 90–91, 95–96. Copyright © 2007 by Taylor & Francis Group. Reprinted with permission.

How, Without Religion, Can Industrial Society Overcome Social Conflict?

The resilience of the individual human spirit can be a wonder to behold. Time and again, people, even children, face and get beyond the most tragic of experiences. Most of the thousands who lost their loved ones in the 9/11 attack on New York's World Trade Center somehow put their lives back together. Victims of holocausts, if they survive the chambers and machetes, very often carry on with great dignity. Many people in New Orleans whose homes were washed away came back, intent upon rebuilding their former lives as best they could with so little hope or help.

Yet, a paradox remains. While individuals as individuals are sometimes able to defy the odds of arbitrary disasters to rejoin life and limb, the same individuals when caught up in powerful social groups seem less able to resist the effects of *social* conflict. Achilles almost single-handedly defeated the Trojans in battle, but fatally exposed his heel to the twin gods of social uncertainty—grief and rage. Extreme social disorder to the point of conflict and violence can be debilitating, even fatal. Depression, grief, rage, and other emotional assaults on the individual's resiliency are always rooted in some or another structural dislocation in the exterior life.

Late in the nineteenth century, conflict preoccupied the attentions of European social theorists. It is not that before the late nineteenth century there was no conflict. Conflict and violence are normal tragic features of life in groups. But as industrial society came to dominate, so too arose the paradox of modern social life—conflict grew both more severe *and* more unexpected. Both Weber and Marx, in different ways, were alert to this contradiction of the modern. Modernity offered itself as the most reasonable form of social order, and the most enlightened, even well intended; yet conflict was more, not less, severe as it had been in times gone by. Not only that, but, in addition to conflict being at odds with expectations, in the new industrial cities class conflict was especially dramatic because the number of working people affected was so great and the opposing sides of the barrier to progress lived in such tight quarters. Numbers in tight proximity breed contemptible familiarities that aggravate tensions between the unequal sides. It is one thing to be told, and to believe, that modernity is the better civilization; something else to see, each day, that it was not true and that you have been dealt the bad hand. Marx's idea that the oppressed workers would certainly revolt when the contradictions became severe enough was at least partly based on the social logic that when the good society is put out of reach of the poor, the poor lose their stake in the social whole, which makes them ready to tear it down, cut off heads, and burn it up.

This sort of conflict had grown more and more evident since the urban revolt in France in 1789 that defined modernity. The French Revolution, and its reverberations across the subsequent century, was, more than any other single event, the reason both Marx and Weber took seriously the contradictions of the capitalist social order. They were struck by the incongruity between surface appearances and underlying reality—between modernity's promise of progress and the brutal conditions of actual working life, in Marx's case; between the evident good of rationality in its several forms and the ways it led, against expectations, to the iron cage, in Weber's. They were chief among the early social theorists willing to struggle with the contradictions of modern society; and this is why their riddles were, for the time, particularly astute.

Émile Durkheim (1858–1917), a contemporary of Weber's, also put conflict at the fore of his political and scientific thinking. But Durkheim differed from Marx and Weber in that he was less inclined to think that modern societies could not resolve the debilitating effects of social conflict. Accordingly, Durkheim—every bit as much the scholar as was Weber and, in his own more guarded way, just as engaged in politics as was Marx—was unlike both in not tolerating contradiction very well. Contradictions are for those more critical of modernity than Durkheim was. To be sure, he was critical of the modern order, but he generally hedged his bets against his confidence in the power of the social bond to promote the good.

ANOMIE, ETHICS, AND ESTRANGEMENT

We repeatedly insist ... upon the state of juridical and moral anomie in which economic life actually is found. Indeed in the economic order, occupational ethics exist only in the most rudimentary state. There is a professional ethic of the lawyer and the judge, the soldier and the priest, etc. But if one attempted to fix in a little more precise language on what ought to be the relations of employer and employee, of worker and manager, of tradesmen in competition, to themselves or to the public, what indecisive formulas would be obtained! ... The most blameworthy acts are so often absolved by success that the boundary between what is permitted and what is prohibited, what is just and what is unjust, has nothing fixed about it, but seems susceptible to almost arbitrary change by individuals. An ethic so unprecise and inconsistent cannot constitute a discipline. The result is that all this sphere of collective life is, in large part, freed from the moderating action of regulation.

—Émile Durkheim, *Notes on Occupational Groups*
(1902)

At the heart of Durkheim's life work are a concept and a concern that set him apart: *anomie* and *ethics*. The first, anomie, is Durkheim's best-known concept. It served to describe the condition of social disorder that, he thought, beset any society that fails to provide the individual with guidance. The second, ethics, was a concern (much like Weber's) as to the moral state of modern societies. Durkheim (unlike Weber) was confident that sociology could help society discover a social ethic suitable to the needs of a society that desperately, he believed, required relief from anomie's dangers.

Durkheim was most clear in his concepts and concerns, and in the way they could solve social problems. Like Marx (more so even than Weber), Durkheim believed that in the modern industrial order the structured relations among workers and those between workers and owners were a cause of social conflict. But unlike Marx, he did not think that workers acting together in their own interests could solve the problem. Thus, for Durkheim, industrial conflict was the one area where ethical guidance and moral order are most needed but least available. Whereas Marx saw the conflict of the industrial order as due to the inherent evil of capitalism, and Weber saw it arising from the excess of modernity's rational order, Durkheim understood conflict as a failure of the social to hold the moral bond in place. In one sense it was the same conflict as Marx's class conflict. No one thinking about the then new world order late in the nineteenth century could have missed it. The difference, however, is that for Durkheim class conflict was the result not of a structural failure of the economic system but of the lack of a universal social ethic able to moderate the actions of individuals in the workplace. Thus, in a way, but a small way, Durkheim was somewhat closer to Weber in believing that ethics were the innermost dilemma of the modern world.

Anomie, literally: the absence of norms; generally, Durkheim's term for the dire condition that arises in the individual when society fails to provide norms or rules to regulate behavior.

Sociology, according to Durkheim, the science of **social things.**

Social things, a concept implicit to Durkheim's idea that sociology is the science of social facts, which are "things in themselves" not reducible to other orders of human life such as (and especially) the psychological.

With Durkheim, the ethical emerges as a socially necessary element in society. The question of modern ethics obviously played a major role in Weber's thinking, but he was more the scholarly sociologist of modern ethics, less the personal adherent. Durkheim was somewhat more the believer whose scholarship was moved by his values. He believed that one of the most important functions of the social group was to provide the moral bond that would regulate the passions of the individual. Left to themselves, individuals go wild, making trouble for the collective life not to mention for themselves. So strongly did Durkheim believe this that he simply did not think the individual was able, on his own, to manage his personal life without the moral support of the group. He stopped just shy of seeing the individual—by which he meant, oddly, modern *man*—as a threat to himself and thus to modern societies without good moral regulations. Regulations are rules, literally. Weber thought they could be good or bad. Durkheim thought them largely good.

People think as they dream, in one language at a time. But with Durkheim it might be said that the primary language was overlaid on another of a different, more primitive, kind. The one, of course, was French. The second was, if not Hebrew exactly, the cultural language of the rural Jewish community in which he grew up. Durkheim wrote and thought social theory in French. But his social theory was permanently influenced by the religious community, long after he left the village in the east of France, where his father, as his fathers before him, had been rabbis. French and the moral vocabulary of his small-town Jewish community conspired to fix one of Durkheim's most particular ideas. He believed what he had seen in childhood—that the individual was lost without the community and, conversely, that the community was the primal source of the moral order that makes the individual human.

Durkheim's experience formed an idea that the French language allowed him to turn into a theory of the social bond. Here his most elegant phrase was *conscience collective*. From French he took this singular expression that conveys the theoretical dilemma to which he devoted his life work. *Conscience collective*—or, in English, "collective consciousness"—has two meanings. The individual's *consciousness* is of the same origin as what in English we call his *conscience*—and neither is psychological. For Durkheim, men—and he meant men, in particular—are at risk without the moral conscience of the community (and, of course, more broadly of the wider society). But, again, the happy conspiracy between French and Jewish cultures is crucial in that it is possible to express an aspect of Jewish culture particularly well in the French language because *conscience* has its double meaning. The social bond of collective consciousness *is* the moral bond of collective life.

> **Conscience collective,** the untranslatable French phrase that means in English both "collective consciousness" and "collective conscience," thus aptly conveying Durkheim's idea that consciousness and moral conscience are two sides of the social benefits of the social bond; consciousness of the social is itself moral; *we think together; therefore we know.*

Collective representations, stories, poetry, symbols, myths and legends, songs, wisdom, sciences, rituals, and the like whereby a social group expresses its *conscience collective* (not always consciously); in modern usage, **culture,** more or less.

Moral bond, in Durkheim, a fundamental aspect of all social orders whereby the moral element is less a matter of rules and prescriptions than, in the Latinate word, the shared *mores,* or customs, of a social group collectively.

As it was for Weber, religion was important to Durkheim's social theory. But Durkheim came at the subject very differently. For Weber, the key historical individual of modern religion was the Protestant, who became the capitalist entrepreneur on the basis of a firmly individualist ethic. Weber's ethic of modernity, the rational spirit of capitalism, was as intensely individualistic as Durkheim's moral bond was social. Accordingly, with Durkheim, social theory explores a completely different aspect of modern social ethics.

[...] A cardinal rule of modern culture in the West is that knowing is mental and that mental is psychological. Durkheim challenges this rule in his idea that we think collectively, by which he meant two things at once: that concepts are produced by the collective consciousness, and that the categories with which we think come from shared social experience. The two points are closely related, of course, but their difference can be seen in the following way.

It is hard to think in modern scientific ways without a concept of *causes*. Modern science, for the most part, attempts to explain events by demonstrating their causes—as in the case of Weber, who sought to demonstrate that capitalism, the economic system, was in some important degree caused by the prior existence of capitalists who possessed the rationalizing ethic. *Causality* is one of the basic categories of thinking itself; and it is impossible to use the concept of *cause* without other categories, among them *time*. Causality is a measure of how events at one moment in time are associated with events in a subsequent time. To borrow an example from Weber, Capitalism cannot cause Protestantism because the modern idea of time is that time always moves ahead. But Protestantism could cause Capitalism because, at least, if the event to be explained, C, occurs in the nineteenth century, then if P is to be a cause it must occur sometime before that—namely, in the sixteenth century. But temporal sequences are not enough; there must also be an aspect of space. If P is a cause of C, then it must be that P and C can be shown to have occurred in close proximity to each other—in, that is, roughly the same social spaces. Thus, Weber's argument was based on the evidence that C, Capitalism, arose first and most powerfully, in the same regions where P, Protestantism, had been prominent—the Northeast of the United States, the Protestant regions of Germany, Switzerland, and England, among other places. Thus, it is evident that the idea of causal thinking, in modern science, depends on concepts like *causality, time,* and *space,* which are among the categories through which moderns think.

WE THINK TOGETHER; THEREFORE WE KNOW

The nature of the concept ... bespeaks its origin. If it is common to all, it is the work of the community. Since it bears the mark of no particular mind, it is clear that it was elaborated by a unique intelligence, where all others meet each other, and after a fashion, come to nourish themselves. If it has more stability than sensations or images, it is because the collective representations are more stable than the individual ones; for while an individual is conscious even of the slight changes which take place in his environment, only events of a greater gravity can succeed in affecting the mental status of a society. Every time that we are in the presence of a *type* of thought or action which is imposed uniformly upon particular wills or intelligences, this pressure exercised over the individual betrays the intervention of the group. Also, ... the concepts with which we ordinarily think are those of our vocabulary. Now it is unquestionable that language, and consequently the system of concepts which it translates, is the product of a collective elaboration. What it expresses is the manner in which society as a whole represents the facts of experience. The ideas which correspond to the diverse elements of language are thus collective representations.

—Émile Durkheim, *Elementary Forms of the Religious Life* (1912)

[...] Thus, returning directly to a Durkheimian interpretation of the Weber example, it is not possible to have capitalism if people can only think of time as cyclical. Capitalism is about profits that may come in the future if one acts rationally in the present. Profits are not harvested in a good season provided by the gods or the spirits, so much as *made* by hard work, discipline, and good calculations over time. Durkheim was making an ironic point. In modern culture, the prevailing assumption in the West is that thinking is something done by the individual mind. But, in Durkheim's theory, even the modern thinker must think *with* others; that is: individuals think only because they are pressed by the social force of their languages and cultures to think in a definite way. Even the thought that "only individuals think" is a thought made possible by the assumptions taught and enforced by a common culture. Or, in another example, the very idea of the spirit of capitalism (and, thereby, of capitalism itself) cannot occur in cultures that are not modern because the modern social bond trains individuals to think in terms of the causal effects of hard work over time. We moderns require a culturally specific idea of time as progress, just as the Lakota required a cyclical idea of time that accounts for the seasons when the buffalo return. Concepts like *profit* or *progress* or *growth* are recognized by moderns because moderns understand (or think they understand) that time moves across social space, but forward. The concepts may be economic, but there can be no economic concepts without the ability to think as one's social group requires one to think. For Durkheim, thinking works much like language itself. If the group you are with at the time speaks only Chinese, all the English in the world will not get you very far. If you want to get with Chinese people, speaking their language is required. A foreigner may learn the language by herself, but the requirement to learn it is a social fact that, in effect, forces the learning on her. Even if members of the Chinese group speak some English, joining them fully puts on the pressure to learn; likewise, if one wants to get by in a modern economic system with the moral tools of the agrarian past—acquire the tools or leave. The differences between modern industrial and elementary nomadic societies are certainly economic, but economic survival in each requires very different ideas by which to calculate the time of profits or the buffalo.

[...] Durkheim's writings appear to some to be all too finely scientific and even remote. Still, he was not obscure because the science was meant to serve a very human purpose—to heal the wounds of modern life, a mission already evident in the first of his three great books. *The Division of Labor in Society* (1893), Durkheim's doctoral thesis, took up the very nature of modern societies. In fact, the original French edition bore the revealing subtitle *A Study of the Social Organization of Advanced Societies*.

Division of Labor is an admirably disciplined comparison of the structural differences between modern and premodern societies—a theme found in all the classic social theorists. With Marx, the difference appeared in his analytic contrast between the capitalist mode of production and premodern ones, like feudalism; and with Weber the contrast between modern and premodern appeared in his harkening back to traditionalism as the standard against which modern rationality was measured. Durkheim's terms for the distinction of present from past were *mechanical* and *organic*—a real difference, but also a bit confusing. As is often the case, when a good theorist gets confusing he is being pulled by his theory. For Durkheim in *Division of Labor,* the premodern social form was *mechanical* solidarity, while the modern (meaning, industrial) one was *organic* (meaning, natural or living) solidarity. The confusion, of course, arises from the metaphors. For the first-time reader it is easy to suppose that the premodern social form would be the more organic and the modern the more machine-like. Durkheim may have had it the other way around because, again, he valued the social benefits of the rural, premodern community and was determined to reproduce them in the large, industrial society.

In either case, his theory of the social bond's importance caused him to see things as he saw them—and there was, in his mind, a good reason to use the expression *mechanical solidarity* for the preindustrial society. Premodern social orders, such as feudal or early-modern rural villages, or the more elementary tribal encampments of hunters and gatherers, were mechanical in the sense that all the parts were fused together. A mill requires a power source, usually moving water, circulating paddles that would translate the force of the water into a steady motion that would turn, say, the grindstone that milled the grain into bulk lots. The basic parts—the paddles, the mill, the grindstone—were each necessary but they worked only if they remained fixed in a place where all the working elements were present. If any one of them broke down, or the water source dried up, the whole would stop, eventually to rot away. The functioning of one part depended on the working of all others.

[...] Durkheim's credit today is backed by the investments he made in public life. Ever the serious scientist, Durkheim was also the public intellectual—and a serious one. Unlike so many clowns of the academic circus today who mouth platitudes as to the urgency of public intellectual work while never in their lives having ventured into the open air of public controversy, Durkheim emerged in his Paris years as a prominent public figure in France. But nowhere was his public presence more telling than in his work on education. He wrote on the subject and also, from his first days in Paris, he taught professional teachers. More important, Durkheim was almost single-handedly the major influence on the reconstruction of France's public educational system. Why this? Because, his sociology helped him identify the threat of conflict and the need for a renewal of ethical principles. He knew that religion could no longer play that role. What could? Education! The schools were the new *schuls*. He did not say such a thing, but it is said today, more or less. Education transmits knowledge of several kinds—science, math, reading, yes; but also basic knowledge of the civic values of a nation. American children must study American history. Very often what they are taught is bogus crap. But even when they are taught partial or false truths, they are taught something that has the effect of pulling them together; even more so in France, where the teachings include a very high level of training in the glories of French culture. Let us agree that schools everywhere make incomplete, even dishonest, presentations of a nation's values. The fact remains that no matter how foolish those civic values are, they do serve to hold things in place, for better or worse. Not all social values prevent social conflict as Durkheim had hoped, but they do, to some degree, tie people together in ways that at least modulate some conflicts. Durkheim was right to use his sociology to serve a social purpose and he was right, also, that education would be the institution in thoroughly modern societies where, if there are common values, they would be passed down best in the schools, even the worst of schools. No one of sane mind would want to rely on the garden-variety politician or preacher to instruct children in the common good. Not where I live.

Durkheim's riddle is, therefore, much less of a mind-breaker than those of Marx and Weber. Yet, it was a riddle. *How, indeed, will industrial and postindustrial societies overcome conflict?* The class conflict of the early industrial era was, sadly, nothing compared to the record of violence and war in the bloody twentieth century, the most violent in human history. Social violence feeds on social differences. This Durkheim understood. This was a fact of modern social things. How, then, can the effect of the differences be softened? The puzzle lies in the fact that—as noble and workable as the ideal of moral bonding may be—nobility does not cut this mustard. Class conflicts are one thing and they have yet to be healed by moral bonding. In our day, the conflicts are greater by far in kind and ferocity. This, too, because of a fundamental inequality in the access of people to what goods there may be in the world. But what has emerged as an alternative to education, including moral education? Alongside the evil perversion of the very idea of moral values by the many religious rights we have seen the rise of what, in Durkheim's mind, was a method of repression.

In *Division of Labor* he argued that it was the premodern mechanical societies that repressed the deviants and the organic societies that sought to rehabilitate them. This, in effect, is the difference between dead-heading the flowering bush and watering the garden of common life. In the successors to the modern societies Durkheim studied, social conflict has increasingly come to be managed by incarcerations of various kinds. Prisons, the military, vocational schools, child guidance centers, detention halls and summer schools, welfare offices, short buses—all are branches of the carceral society's apparatus for controlling the deviants; and few of them retain a true rehabilitative program. What schools there are for the children of the poor, including the children of guest workers, are anything but the bright, shining cathedrals of the social whole. They are the steerage class on a ship going nowhere in particular.

Durkheim's riddle was less the mind-breaker because he had, for his day, the more practical solution. What remains in our day of the Durkheimian riddle is, however, plainly visible to those who would see it. If the modern world is good because its knowledge is better, then why is there no reasonable moral bond to be found among its manifold inventions and unthinkable wealth?

Post-Reading Questions

1. What is Émile Durkheim's position on society? How does it differ from Karl Marx's perspective of class conflict?
2. What is anomie? According to Émile Durkheim, how does this contribute to the way that people function in society?
3. What is the conscious collective? In Durkheim's vision of society, how are people in society united by this force?

UNIT III

GENDER AND SEXUALITY

Key Terms and Definitions

Review the key terms and definitions below to strengthen your understanding of the readings in this unit.

Black Feminist Epistemology: Knowledge that centers the voices of Black females, providing a unique lens into their struggles and victories amid societal oppression.

Critical Social Theory: A form of social theory that seeks to illuminate and explain collective experiences of societal oppression and injustice. This form of social theory has the purpose of promoting social justice and making society's institutions more equitable for all.

Gender: The social meanings ascribed to people in society based around assumptions about biological sex. These social meanings are often portrayed in a binary fashion, categorizing people as either male or female. However, a variety of gender identities and expressions fall outside of the gender binary.

Gender Wage Gap: The persistent difference in pay between women and men, whereby women earn roughly eighty cents per every dollar that a man earns. This pay gap increases when considering race, as women of color earn even less than white males.

Heterosexuality: A category for sexual and nonsexual behavior that was invented in 1892 and eventually became a commonplace way to differentiate people who have opposite-sex attraction or relationships. This is a category that carries privilege in society.

The Human Capital Approach: A theory that explains the gender wage gap between women and men by examining differences in education and experience between groups.

Matrix of Domination: The overlapping ways that we experience social advantages and/or disadvantages due to aspects of our identity like gender, race, social class, and other aspects of identity.

The Occupational Segregation Approach: A theory that explains the gender wage gap between women and men by analyzing their location in separate occupational fields.

Sex: The biological characteristics assigned to females, males, and Intersex individuals at birth, during puberty, or at other times in the life course as well as the social meanings that these categories produce.

Sexuality: A wide range of sexual ideas and practices that includes a person's sexual identification, expression, and relationships.

Standpoint Theory: A feminist perspective that prioritizes the knowledge that arises from individual experiences and collective realities. For example, we hold unique standpoints on the world because of our gender, race, social class, and other aspects of identity.

Introduction

In the first reading, titled "Sexuality, Heterosexuality, and Gender Hierarchy: Getting Our Priorities Straight" by Stevi Jackson, the author explains the meanings of **gender**, **sex**, **sexuality**, and **heterosexuality** and describes the intersections between these categories. Jackson defines **gender** as a social structural phenomenon that creates a separation between women and men. This binary conception of **gender** is an attempt to obscure the existence of nonbinary genders. The author regards **sexuality** as a wide range of physical or erotic interactions that people have. She then defines **heterosexuality** as the dominant way in which society defines "normative" sexual and nonsexual behavior related to gender. Ultimately, this reading reveals how each of these categories is socially constructed in ways that afford some people privilege and cause other people to face various disadvantages in society.

In "Black Feminist Thought: Black Feminism, Knowledge, and Power," Patricia Hill Collins outlines the ways in which Black women have been excluded from academia. Black women are by no means a uniform group, but they have the collective experience of facing prejudice and discrimination in society. Collins argues that because of this, Black women are uniquely positioned to use **critical social theory** to analyze society. By redefining Black womanhood, Black women have made major contributions to society and opened a new worldview. Black women's experiences in the **matrix of domination** reveal deep inequalities. For example, racial segregation in housing and the concentration of many Black women in low-wage work has given them unique collective knowledge and wisdom amid oppression. However, unfortunately, the voices of Black women are still very often excluded from academic dialogues. By centering the voices of Black women, all of us can learn from a unique vantage point. Collins argues that we must embrace **Black feminist epistemology** to understand how this group faces unique challenges and victories in society. By using **standpoint theory**, we can better understand how each of us has a unique set of experiences based on our social identities.

The final reading in this unit, "Origins of the Gender Wage Gap" by Yasemin Besen-Cassino, outlines the **gender wage gap** that exists between women and men in American society. The author notes that to understand the gender wage gap better, it is important to examine work experiences that happen at a young age. The author uses two theories in her analysis: **the human capital approach** and **the occupational segregation approach**. The author explains that the human capital approach does not fully explain the gender wage gap. In recent decades, women outpace men in completing college, and yet women continue to be paid less relative to men. However, some women do tend to have less labor market experience, which can be due to parental leave, childcare, and domestic responsibilities. The occupational segregation approach looks at the type of work that women tend to perform. Even during the teenage years, young women and men tend to work in fields that follow stereotypical gender roles. Young women also work fewer hours and receive less pay. Ultimately, the author's research shows that the gender age gap starts early and widens with age. Even though young women and men work for the same general reasons, they do not have the same labor market experiences.

Sexuality Heterosexuality and Gender Hierarchy

Getting Our Priorities Straight

Stevi Jackson

Stevi Jackson, Selection from "Sexuality, Heterosexuality and Gender Hierarchy: Getting Our Priorities Straight," *Thinking Straight: The Power, the Promise, and the Paradox of Heterosexuality*, ed. Chrys Ingraham, pp. 16–19, 35–36. Copyright © 2005 by Taylor & Francis Group. Reprinted with permission.

[...] Conceptual Ground-Clearing

Underlying many of the debates about gender, sexuality, and heterosexuality are differences in the ways these terms are defined. There are differences, too, in the ways in which the social or cultural construction of gender and sexuality are understood. Hence, before going any further, I will say a little about how I use such contested terms as "sex," "gender," "sexuality," and "heterosexuality," how I understand the relationship between them, and how I conceptualize the process of social construction. Having clarified my concepts, I will survey some influential accounts of the gender–sexuality articulation and explore their implications for the analysis of heterosexuality.

I define gender as a hierarchical social division between women and men embedded in both social institutions and social practices. Gender is thus a social structural phenomenon, part of the social order, but it is also lived out by embodied individuals who "do gender" in their daily lives, constantly (re)producing it through habitual, everyday interaction. Gender, as I understand it, is an entirely social and cultural phenomenon, in no way resting on a pre-existing biological base. So-called "biological sex differences" cannot be taken for granted as given, since the recognition of them is itself a social act.[footnote]Kessler and McKenna, 1978; Delphy, 1993[/footnote] It is gender that enables us to "see" biological sex: it "transforms an anatomical difference (which is itself devoid of significance) into a relevant distinction for social practice."[footnote]Delphy, 1984: 144[/footnote] While gender is a binary division, the categories it produces are not homogeneous since we live not only in a gendered world, but also one in which class, racial, national, and other distinctions intersect with gender.

If gender is used to denote all aspects of the distinction and division between women and men (and boys and girls), then "sex" can be reserved for carnal or erotic activities. "Sexuality" is a broader term referring to all erotically significant aspects of social life and social being. This usage helps to resolve the ambiguities of everyday discourse. "Sex" and "sexual" are peculiarly imprecise terms since they can refer both to differences between women and men (the "two sexes" or "the sexual division of labor") and to specifically erotic relations and practices (to "have sex" or "sexual fantasies"). This semantic slippage is no chance effect, but the product of specific cultural assumptions. At birth we are classified as one of two "sexes" (girl or boy) on the basis of assumptions made about parts of our body designated as "sex organs"; we are then expected to grow into adults who "have sex" with the "opposite sex," thus deploying our "sex organs" in the proper way. In this way, femininity and masculinity are defined as "natural" and heterosexuality is privileged as the only "normal" and legitimate form of sexuality. Theoretically and politically, we need to challenge these assumptions, to break the chain that binds (socially defined) anatomy into gender and sexuality. Conceptually, we need to know what we are talking about: if we speak of "gender relations," we know we refer to all aspects of social life, while "sexual relations" more often means specifically physical, erotic interaction.

Sexuality and gender are empirically interrelated, but analytically distinct. Without an analytical distinction between them, we cannot effectively explore the ways in which they intersect; if we conflate them, we are in danger of deciding the form of their interrelationship in advance. If, on the other hand, we ignore the empirical linkage between them, there is a danger, evident in much current theorizing, of abstracting sexuality from the social, of analyzing it as if it were separated from other socioeconomic structures and processes, uncontaminated by material inequalities. We should recognize that sexuality, as well as gender, is fully social; sexual practices, desires, and identities are embedded within complex webs of nonsexual social relations.

Heterosexuality is the key site of intersection between gender and sexuality, and one that reveals the interconnections between sexual and nonsexual aspects of social life. As an institution, heterosexuality includes nonsexual elements implicated in ordering wider gender relations and ordered by them. As I have noted elsewhere,[1] it entails who washes the sheets as well as what goes on between them. Thus, heterosexuality is not precisely coterminous with heterosexual sexuality. While heterosexual desires, practices, and relations are socially defined as "normal" and normative, serving to marginalize other sexualities as abnormal and deviant, the coercive power of compulsory heterosexuality derives from its institutionalization as more than merely a sexual relation.

How we conceptualize the interconnections between gender, sexuality and heterosexuality depends on how we understand the process of social construction. Social constructionism is not a single perspective, but a cluster of differing approaches deriving from varied theoretical roots. First, there are different degrees of social constructionism,[2] differences in the extent to which some form of sexual drive or biological

1. Jackson, 1996a, b, 1999a, b
2. Vance, 1989

difference is presupposed, and hence differences in *what* is understood as socially constructed. Here I consider it risky to assume that any aspect of sexuality or gender is innate, since this can entail placing aspects of our gendered and sexual practices beyond critique. There are also different approaches to the question of *how* gender and sexuality are constructed. Here I conceive of social construction as a multilayered or multifaceted process, requiring attention to a number of levels of social analysis. Not all of these receive the attention they should.

It is sometimes assumed that the more radically antiessentialist positions, those that hold that there is no essential pre-given basis for either gender or sexuality, derive from postmodern theorizing. This misconception results in the erasure of earlier sociological accounts of the construction of sexuality[3] and the first feminist critiques of sex–gender distinction.[4] Newer forms of social constructionism, which take such writers as Foucault and Butler as originators, are often not very social at all. Indeed, they are often emptied of the social and are better characterized as cultural constructionism. Of course the social world includes the cultural, it includes the realms of discourse and symbolic representation, but the cultural is not all there is to the social. The distinctively social has to do with questions of social structure but also situated social practices. It is concerned with meaning, both at the level of our wider culture and as meanings emerge from or are deployed within everyday social interaction. It includes subjectivity since our sense of who we are in relation to others constantly guides our actions and interactions and, conversely, who we are is a consequence of our location within gendered, class, racial and other divisions, and the immediate social and cultural milieux we inhabit.

In my recent work I have, in keeping with this picture of the social, identified four intersecting levels or facets of social construction:[5] (1) the structural, in which gender is constructed as a hierarchical social division and heterosexuality is institutionalized, for example, by marriage, the law, and the state; (2) the level of meaning, encompassing the discursive construction of gender and sexuality and the meanings negotiated in everyday social interaction; (3) the level of routine, everyday social practices through which gender and sexuality are constantly constituted and reconstituted within localized contexts and relationships; and (4) at the level of subjectivity through which we experience desires and emotions and make sense of ourselves as embodied gendered and sexual beings.

What cultural—as opposed to social—constructionism does is to exclude the first level, that of structure, altogether. It then deals with meaning primarily at the level of culture and discourse, but ignores the meanings emergent from and deployed within everyday social interaction. Sometimes practices are included—as in Butler's (1990) discussion of performativity—but rarely are these practices located in their interactional or wider social setting. Finally, subjectivity is usually theorized through psychoanalysis, which completely abstracts it from its social context; alternative perspectives linking the self and the social are rarely even considered. What I am suggesting is that an understanding of gender and sexuality as fully social, as contingent upon the material conditions of our existence, must take account of all

3. For example, McIntosh, 1968; Gagnon and Simon, 1974
4. See Kessler and McKenna, 1978; Delphy, 1984; Stanley, 1984. Elsewhere I have attributed this to the "cultural turn" in feminist and social theory (Jackson 1999b, 2000), which has also had the effect of diminishing the scope of social constructionist accounts.
5. Jackson, 1999a, b, 2000

these processes through which they are constructed. I am not proposing here some total theory of social construction wherein all these levels are welded together as a seamless whole. Such an endeavor would be ill advised and likely to produce another form of reductionism. Moreover, it is difficult, if not impossible, to focus on all these levels at once. We do, however, need to be aware that when we concentrate on one facet of social construction, we have only a partial view of a multifaceted process.

I will return to this framework later [...], but for now it forms the backdrop to my reading of past and current debates on gender and heterosexuality and informs my evaluation of others' perspectives.

[...]

References

Delphy, Christine. 1984. *Close to home: A materialist analysis of women's oppression*. London: Hutchinson.

–––. 1993. Rethinking sex and gender, *Women's studies international forum*, 16(1): 1–9.–––.

1994. Changing women in a changing Europe: is difference the future for feminism? *Women's studies international forum*: 27(2): 187–201.

Gagnon, John and William Simon. 1974. *Sexual conduct*. London: Hutchinson.

Jackson, S. 1996a. *Christine Delphy*. London: Sage.

–––. 1996b. Heterosexuality and feminist theory, in D. Richardson (ed.) *Theorising heterosexuality: Telling it straight*. Buckingham: Open University Press.

–––. 1999a. *Heterosexuality in question*. London: Sage.

–––. 1999b. Feminist sociology and sociological feminism: Recovering the social in feminist thought, *Sociological research online*, 4(3), http://www.socresonline.org.uk/socresonline/4/3/jackson.html

–––. 2000. For a sociological feminism, in J. Eldridge, J. MacInnes, S. Scott, C. Warhurst and A. Witz (eds.) *For sociology*. Durham: Sociology Press.

Kessler, S.J. and W. McKenna. 1978. *Gender: An ethnomethodological approach*. New York: Wiley

McIntosh, M. 1968. The homosexual role, *Social problems*, 16(2): 182–192.

Stanley, L. 1984. Should "sex" really be "gender" or "gender" really be "sex"?, in R. Anderson and W. Sharrock (eds.) *Applied sociology*. London: Allen & Unwin.

Vance, C.S. 1989. Social construction theory: problems in the history of sexuality, in D. Altman et al. (eds.) *Which homosexuality?* London: Gay Men's Press.

Post-Reading Questions

1. How does the author define gender, sex, sexuality, and heterosexuality? How are these categories socially constructed?
2. In which ways do these categories, as defined by society, limit peoples' options for identity and expression?
3. As a society, how can we expand the social meanings of gender, sex, and sexuality to account for the diversity that exists in these categories? How can our society become more inclusive when it comes to gender, sex, and sexuality?

Black Feminist Thought

Black Feminism, Knowledge, and Power

Patricia Hill Collins

Black Feminist Thought as Critical Social Theory

Even if they appear to be otherwise, situations such as the suppression of Black women's ideas within traditional scholarship and the struggles within the critiques of that established knowledge are inherently unstable. Conditions in the wider political economy simultaneously shape Black women's subordination and foster activism. On some level, people who are oppressed usually know it. For African-American women, the knowledge gained at intersecting oppressions of race, class, and gender provides the stimulus for crafting and passing on the subjugated knowledge[1] of Black women's critical social theory (Collins 1998, 3–10).

As an historically oppressed group, U.S. Black women have produced social thought designed to oppose oppression. Not only does the form assumed by this thought diverge from standard academic theory—it can take the form of poetry, music, essays, and the like—but the *purpose* of Black women's collective thought is distinctly different. Social theories emerging from and/or on behalf of U.S. Black women and other historically oppressed groups aim to find ways to escape from, survive in, and/or oppose prevailing social and economic injustice. For African-American women, critical social theory encompasses bodies of knowledge and sets of institutional practices that actively grapple with the central questions facing U.S. Black women as a collectivity. The need for such thought arises because African-American women as a *group* remain oppressed within a U.S. context characterized by injustice. This neither means that all African-American women within that group are oppressed in the same way, nor that some U.S. Black women do not suppress others. Black feminist thought's identity as a "critical" social theory lies in its commitment to justice, both for U.S. Black women as a collectivity and for that of other similarly oppressed groups.

Historically, two factors stimulated U.S. Black women's critical social theory. For one, prior to World War II, racial segregation in urban housing became so entrenched that the majority of African-American women lived in self-contained Black neighborhoods where their children attended overwhelmingly Black schools, and where they themselves belonged to all-Black churches and similar community organizations. Despite the fact that ghettoization was designed to foster the political control and economic exploitation of Black Americans (Squires 1994), these all-Black neighborhoods simultaneously provided a separate space where African-American women and men could use African-derived ideas to craft distinctive oppositional knowledges designed to resist racial oppression.

As mothers, othermothers, teachers, and churchwomen in essentially all-Black rural communities and urban neighborhoods, U.S. Black women participated in constructing and reconstructing these oppositional knowledges. Through the lived experiences gained within their extended families and communities, individual African-American women fashioned their own ideas about the meaning of Black womanhood. When these ideas found collective expression, Black women's self-definitions enabled them to refashion African-influenced conceptions of self and community. These self-definitions of Black womanhood were designed to resist the negative controlling images of Black womanhood advanced by Whites as well as the discriminatory social practices that these controlling images supported. In all, Black women's

---

1. My use of the term *subjugated knowledge* differs somewhat from Michel Foucault's (1980) definition. According to Foucault, subjugated knowledges are "those blocs of historical knowledge which were present but disguised," namely, "a whole set of knowledges that have been disqualified as inadequate to their task or insufficiently elaborated: naive knowledges, located low down on the hierarchy, beneath the required level of cognition or scientificity" (p. 82). I suggest that Black feminist thought is not a "naive knowledge" but has been made to appear so by those controlling knowledge validation procedures. Moreover, Foucault argues that subjugated knowledge is "a particular, local, regional knowledge, a differential knowledge incapable of unanimity and which owes its force only to the harshness with which it is opposed by everything surrounding it" (p. 82). The component of Black feminist thought that analyzes Black women's oppression partially fits this definition, but the long-standing, independent, African-derived influences within Black women's thought are omitted from Foucault's analysis.

participation in crafting a constantly changing African-American culture fostered distinctively Black and women-centered worldviews.

Another factor that stimulated U.S. Black women's critical social theory lay in the common experiences they gained from their jobs. Prior to World War II, U.S. Black women worked primarily in two occupations—agriculture and domestic work. Their ghettoization in domestic work sparked an important contradiction. Domestic work fostered U.S. Black women's economic exploitation, yet it simultaneously created the conditions for distinctively Black and female forms of resistance. Domestic work allowed African-American women to see White elites, both actual and aspiring, from perspectives largely obscured from Black men and from these groups themselves. In their White "families," Black women not only performed domestic duties but frequently formed strong ties with the children they nurtured, and with the employers themselves. On one level this insider relationship was satisfying to all concerned. Accounts of Black domestic workers stress the sense of self-affirmation the women experienced at seeing racist ideology demystified. But on another level these Black women knew that they could never belong to their White "families." They were economically exploited workers and thus would remain outsiders. The result was being placed in a curious *outsider-within* social location (Collins 1986), a peculiar marginality that stimulated a distinctive Black women's perspective on a variety of themes (see, e.g., Childress 1986).

Taken together, Black women's participation in constructing African-American culture in all-Black settings and the distinctive perspectives gained from their outsider-within placement in domestic work provide the material backdrop for a unique Black women's standpoint. When armed with cultural beliefs honed in Black civil society, many Black women who found themselves doing domestic work often developed distinct views of the contradictions between the dominant group's actions and ideologies. Moreover, they often shared their ideas with other African-American women. Nancy White, a Black inner-city resident, explores the connection between experience and beliefs:

> Now, I understand all these things from living. But you can't lay up on these flowery
> beds of ease and think that you are running your life, too. Some women, white women,
> can run their husband's lives for a while, but most of them have to ... see what he tells
> them there is to see. If he tells them that they ain't seeing what they know they *are* seeing,
> then they have to just go on like it wasn't there! (in Gwaltney 1980, 148)

Not only does this passage speak to the power of the dominant group to suppress the knowledge produced by subordinate groups, but it illustrates how being in outsider-within locations can foster new angles of vision on oppression. Ms. White's Blackness makes her a perpetual outsider. She could never be a White middle-class woman lying on a "flowery bed of ease." But her work of caring for White women allowed her an insider's view of some of the contradictions between White women thinking that they are running their lives and the patriarchal power and authority in their households.

Practices such as these, whether experienced oneself or learned by listening to African-American women who have had them, have encouraged many U.S. Black women to question the contradictions between dominant ideologies of American womanhood and U.S. Black women's devalued status. If women are allegedly passive and fragile, then why are Black women treated as "mules" and assigned heavy cleaning chores? If good mothers are supposed to stay at home with their children, then why are U.S. Black women on public assistance forced to find jobs and leave their children in day care? If women's highest calling is to become mothers, then why are Black teen mothers pressured to use Norplant and

Depo Provera? In the absence of a viable Black feminism that investigates how intersecting oppressions of race, gender, and class foster these contradictions, the angle of vision created by being deemed devalued workers and failed mothers could easily be turned inward, leading to internalized oppression. But the legacy of struggle among U.S. Black women suggests that a collectively shared, Black women's oppositional knowledge has long existed. This collective wisdom in turn has spurred U.S. Black women to generate a more specialized knowledge, namely, Black feminist thought as critical social theory. Just as fighting injustice lay at the heart of U.S. Black women's experiences, so did analyzing and creating imaginative responses to injustice characterize the core of Black feminist thought.

Historically, while they often disagreed on its expression—some U.S. Black women were profoundly reformist while more radical thinkers bordered on the revolutionary—African-American women intellectuals who were nurtured in social conditions of racial segregation strove to develop Black feminist thought as critical social theory. Regardless of social class and other differences among U.S. Black women, all were in some way affected by intersecting oppressions of race, gender, and class. The economic, political, and ideological dimensions of U.S. Black women's oppression suppressed the intellectual production of individual Black feminist thinkers. At the same time, these same social conditions simultaneously stimulated distinctive patterns of U.S. Black women's activism that also influenced and was influenced by individual Black women thinkers. Thus, the dialectic of oppression and activism characterizing U.S. Black women's experiences with intersecting oppressions also influenced the ideas and actions of Black women intellectuals.

The exclusion of Black women's ideas from mainstream academic discourse and the curious placement of African-American women intellectuals in feminist thinking, Black social and political theories, and in other important thought such as U.S. labor studies has meant that U.S. Black women intellectuals have found themselves in outsider-within positions in many academic endeavors (Hull et al. 1982; Christian 1989). The assumptions on which full group membership are based—Whiteness for feminist thought, maleness for Black social and political thought, and the combination for mainstream scholarship—all negate Black women's realities. Prevented from becoming full insiders in any of these areas of inquiry, Black women remained in outsider-within locations, individuals whose marginality provided a distinctive angle of vision on these intellectual and political entities. [...]

Black Feminist Epistemology

Because U.S. Black women have access to the experiences that accrue to being both Black and female, an alternative epistemology used to rearticulate a Black women's standpoint should reflect the convergence of both sets of experiences. Race and gender may be analytically distinct, but in Black women's everyday lives, they work together. The search for the distinguishing features of an alternative epistemology used by African-American women reveals that some ideas that Africanist scholars identify as characteristically "Black" often bear remarkable resemblance to similar ideas claimed by feminist scholars as characteristically "female." This similarity suggests that the actual contours of intersecting oppressions can vary dramatically and yet generate some uniformity in the epistemologies used by subordinate groups. Just as U.S. Black women and African women encountered diverse patterns of intersecting oppressions yet generated similar agendas concerning what mattered in their feminisms, a similar process may be at work regarding the epistemologies of oppressed groups. Thus the significance of a Black feminist epistemology may lie in its ability to enrich our understanding of how subordinate groups create knowledge that fosters both their empowerment and social justice.

This approach to Black feminist thought allows African-American women to explore the epistemological implications of transversal politics. Eventually this approach may get us to a point at which, claims Elsa Barkley Brown, "all people can learn to center in another experience, validate it, and judge it by its own standards without need of comparison or need to adopt that framework as their own" (1989, 922). In such politics, "one has no need to 'decenter' anyone in order to center someone else; one has only to constantly, appropriately, 'pivot the center' " (p. 922).

Rather than emphasizing how a Black women's standpoint and its accompanying epistemology differ from those of White women, Black men, and other collectivities, Black women's experiences serve as one specific social location for examining points of connection among multiple epistemologies. Viewing Black feminist epistemology in this way challenges additive analyses of oppression claiming that Black women have a more accurate view of oppression than do other groups. Such approaches suggest that oppression can be quantified and compared and that adding layers of oppression produces a potentially clearer standpoint (Spelman 1988). One implication of some uses of standpoint theory is that the more subordinated the group, the purer the vision available to them. This is an outcome of the origins of standpoint approaches in Marxist social theory, itself reflecting the binary thinking of its Western origins. Although it is tempting to claim that Black women are more oppressed than everyone else and therefore have the best standpoint from which to understand the mechanisms, processes, and effects of oppression, this is not the case.

Instead, those ideas that are validated as true by African-American women, African-American men, Latina lesbians, Asian-American women, Puerto Rican men, and other groups with distinctive standpoints, with each group using the epistemological approaches growing from its unique standpoint, become the most "objective" truths. Each group speaks from its own standpoint and shares its own partial, situated knowledge. But because each group perceives its own truth as partial, its knowledge is unfinished. Each group becomes better able to consider other groups' standpoints without relinquishing the uniqueness of its own standpoint or suppressing other groups' partial perspectives. "What is always needed in the appreciation of art, or life," maintains Alice Walker, "is the larger perspective. Connections made, or at least attempted, where none existed before, the straining to encompass in one's glance at the varied world the common thread, the unifying theme through immense diversity" (1983, 5). Partiality, and not universality, is the condition of being heard; individuals and groups forwarding knowledge claims without owning their position are deemed less credible than those who do.

Alternative knowledge claims in and of themselves are rarely threatening to conventional knowledge. Such claims are routinely ignored, discredited, or simply absorbed and marginalized in existing paradigms. Much more threatening is the challenge that alternative epistemologies offer to the basic process used by the powerful to legitimate knowledge claims that in turn justify their right to rule. If the epistemology used to validate knowledge comes into question, then all prior knowledge claims validated under the dominant model become suspect. Alternative epistemologies challenge all certified knowledge and open up the question of whether what has been taken to be true can stand the test of alternative ways of validating truth. The existence of a self-defined Black women's standpoint using Black feminist epistemology calls into question the content of what currently passes as truth and simultaneously challenges the process of arriving at that truth.

Toward a Politics of Empowerment

One way of approaching power concerns the dialectical relationship linking oppression and activism, where groups with greater power oppress those with lesser amounts. Rather than seeing social change or lack of it as preordained and outside the realm of human action, the notion of a dialectical relationship suggests that change results from human agency. Because African-American women remain relegated to the bottom of the social hierarchy from one generation to the next, U.S. Black women have a vested interest in opposing oppression. This is not an intellectual issue for most African-American women—it is a lived reality. As long as Black women's oppression persists, so will the need for Black women's activism. Moreover, dialectical analyses of power point out that when it comes to social injustice, groups have competing interests that often generate conflict. Even when groups understand the need for the type of transversal politics, they often find themselves on opposite sides of social issues. Oppression and resistance remain intricately linked such that the shape of one influences that of the other. At the same time, this relationship is far more complex than a simple model of permanent oppressors and perpetual victims.

Another way of approaching power views it not as something that groups possess, but as an intangible entity that circulates within a particular matrix of domination and to which individuals stand in varying relationships. These approaches emphasize how individual subjectivity frames human actions within a matrix of domination. U.S. Black women's efforts to grapple with the effects of domination in everyday life are evident in our creation of safe spaces that enable us to resist oppression, and in our struggles to form fully human love relations with one another, and with children, fathers, and brothers, as well as with individuals who do not see Black women as worthwhile. Oppression is not simply understood in the mind—it is felt in the body in myriad ways. Moreover, because oppression is constantly changing, different aspects of an individual U.S. Black woman's self-definitions intermingle and become more salient: Her gender may be more prominent when she becomes a mother, her race when she searches for housing, her social class when she applies for credit, her sexual orientation when she is walking with her lover, and her citizenship status when she applies for a job. In all of these contexts, her position in relation to and within intersecting oppressions shifts.

As each individual African-American woman changes her ideas and actions, so does the overall shape of power itself change. In the absence of Black feminist thought and other comparable oppositional knowledges, these micro-changes may remain invisible to individual women. Yet collectively, they can have a profound impact. When my mother taught me to read, took me to the public library when I was five, and told me that if I learned to read, I could experience a form of freedom, neither she nor I saw the magnitude of that one action in my life and the lives that my work has subsequently touched. As people push against, step away from, and shift the terms of their participation in power relations, the shape of power relations changes for everyone. Like individual subjectivity, resistance strategies and power are always multiple and in constant states of change.

Together, these two approaches to power point to two important uses of knowledge for African-American women and other social groups engaged in social justice projects. Dialectical approaches emphasize the significance of knowledge in developing self-defined, group-based standpoints that, in turn, can foster the type of group solidarity necessary for resisting oppressions. In contrast, subjectivity approaches emphasize how domination and resistance shape and are shaped by individual agency. Issues of consciousness link the two. In the former, group-based consciousness emerges through developing oppositional knowledges such as Black feminist thought. In the latter, individual self-definitions and behaviors shift in tandem with a changed consciousness concerning everyday lived experience. Black feminist thought encompasses both meanings of consciousness—neither is sufficient without the other. Together, both approaches to power also highlight the significance of multiplicity in shaping consciousness. For example, viewing domination itself as encompassing intersecting oppressions of race, class, gender, sexuality, and nation points to the significance of these oppressions in shaping the overall organization of a particular matrix of domination. Similarly, personal identities constructed around individual understandings of race, class, gender, sexuality, and nation define each individual's unique biography.

Both of these approaches remain theoretically useful because they each provide partial and different perspectives on empowerment. Unfortunately, these two views are often presented as *competing* rather than potentially *complementary* approaches. As a result, each provides a useful starting point for thinking through African-American women's empowerment in the context of constantly changing power relations, but neither is sufficient. Black feminism and other social justice projects require a language of power that is grounded within yet transcends these approaches. Social justice projects need a common, functional vocabulary that furthers their understanding of the politics of empowerment.

Thus far, using African-American women's experiences as a lens, this text has examined race, gender, class, sexuality, and nation as forms of oppression that work together in distinctive ways to produce a distinctive U.S. matrix of domination. Whether viewed through the lens of a single system of power, or through that of intersecting oppressions, any particular matrix of domination is organized via four interrelated domains of power, namely, the structural, disciplinary, hegemonic, and interpersonal domains. Each domain serves a particular purpose. The structural domain organizes oppression, whereas the disciplinary domain manages it. The hegemonic domain justifies oppression, and the interpersonal domain influences everyday lived experience and the individual consciousness that ensues.

When it comes to power, the challenges raised by the synergistic relationship among domains of power generate new opportunities and constraints for African-American women who now desegregate schools and workplaces, as well as those who do not. On the one hand, entering places that denied access to our mothers provides new opportunities for fostering social justice. Depending on the setting, using the insights gained via outsider-within status can be a stimulus to creativity that helps both African-American women and our new organizational homes. On the other hand, the commodification of outsider-within status whereby African-American women's value to an organization lies solely in our ability to market a seemingly permanent marginal status can suppress Black women's empowerment. Being a permanent outsider-within can never lead to power because the category, by definition, requires marginality. Each individual must find her own way, recognizing that her personal biography, while unique, is never as unique as she thinks.

When it comes to knowledge, Black women's empowerment involves rejecting the dimensions of knowledge that perpetuate objectification, commodification, and exploitation. African-American women and others like us become empowered when we understand and use those dimensions of our individual, group, and formal educational ways of knowing that foster our humanity. When Black women value our self-definitions, participate in Black women's domestic and transnational activist traditions, view the skills gained in schools as part of a focused education for Black community development, and invoke Black feminist epistemologies as central to our worldviews, we empower ourselves. C. Wright Mills's (1959) concept of the "sociological imagination" identifies its task and its promise as a way of knowing that enables individuals to grasp the relations between history and biography within society. Resembling the holistic epistemology required by Black feminism, using one's point of view to engage the sociological imagination can empower the individual. "My fullest concentration of energy is available to me," Audre Lorde maintains, "only when I integrate all the parts of who I am, openly, allowing power from particular sources of my living to flow back and forth freely through all my different selves, without the restriction of externally imposed definition" (1984, 120–21). Developing a Black women's standpoint to engage a collective Black feminist imagination can empower the group.

Black women's empowerment involves revitalizing U.S. Black feminism as a social justice project organized around the dual goals of empowering African-American women and fostering social justice in a transnational context. Black feminist thought's emphasis on the ongoing interplay between Black women's oppression and Black women's activism presents the matrix of domination and its interrelated domains of power as responsive to human agency. Such thought views the world as a dynamic place where the goal is not merely to survive or to fit in or to cope; rather, it becomes a place where we feel ownership and accountability. The existence of Black feminist thought suggests that there is always choice, and power to act, no matter how bleak the situation may appear to be. Viewing the world as one in the making raises the issue of individual responsibility for bringing about change. It also shows that while individual empowerment is key, only collective action can effectively generate the lasting institutional transformation required for social justice.

References

Brown, Elsa Barkley. 1989. "African-American Women's Quilting: A Framework for Conceptualizing and Teaching African-American Women's History." *Signs* 14 (4): 921–29.

Childress, Alice. [1956] 1986. *Like One of the Family: Conversations from a Domestic's Life*. Boston: Beacon.

Christian, Barbara. 1989. "But Who Do You Really Belong to—Black Studies or Women's Studies?" *Women's Studies* 17 (1–2): 17–23.

Collins, Patricia Hill. 1986. "Learning from the Outsider Within: The Sociological Significance of Black Feminist Thought." *Social Problems* 33 (6): 14–32.

–––. 1998. *Fighting Words: Black Women and the Search for Justice*. Minneapolis: University of Minnesota Press.

Gwaltney, John Langston. 1980. *Drylongso, A Self-Portrait of Black America*. New York: Vintage.

Hull, Gloria T., Patricia Bell Scott, and Barbara Smith, eds. 1982. *But Some of Us Are Brave*. Old Westbury, NY: Feminist Press.

Lorde, Audre. 1984. *Sister Outsider*. Trumansberg, NY: Crossing Press.

Mills, C. Wright. 1959. *The Sociological Imagination*. New York: Oxford University Press.

Spelman, Elizabeth V. 1988. *Inessential Woman: Problems of Exclusion in Feminist Thought*. Boston: Beacon.

Squires, Gregory D. 1994. *Capital and Communities in Black and White: The Intersections of Race, Class, and Uneven Development*. Albany: State University of New York Press.

Walker, Alice. 1983. *In Search of Our Mother's Gardens*. New York: Harcourt Brace Jovanovich.

Post-Reading Questions

1. What experiences might Black women in the United States share? In what areas might their experiences differ?
2. What is Black feminist epistemology? Why is it important to examine, not just for group members, but for everyone?
3. What is standpoint theory? How might we benefit by looking at the subjective experiences that people have in the world?

Origins of the Gender Wage Gap

Yasemin Besen-Cassino

Yasemin Besen-Cassino, Selections from "Origins of the Gender Pay Gap," *The Cost of Being a Girl: Working Teens and the Origins of the Gender Wage Gap*, pp. 26–32, 34–37, 163–190. Copyright © 2017 by Temple University Press. Reprinted with permission.

The gender wage gap has been a persistent component of labor markets and women's lives. There has been lot of progress in closing the pay gap, with it narrowing substantially in the 1970s and 1980s, but the progress slowed substantially starting in the 1990s (Blau and Kahn 2006; Gottfried 2013). According to the U.S. Census Bureau, based on median annual earnings of year-round, full-time workers, the female-to-male pay ratio rose from 59.7 percent to 68.7 percent between 1979 and 1989 (Blau and Kahn 2005). Despite this rapid progress in the 1970s and 1980s, the ratio has been stagnant for the past few decades, and the progress seems to have plateaued since the 1990s (Blau and Kahn 2006; Reskin 1993; Reskin and Roos 2002). A small portion of the gender wage gap still remains unexplained. To explain this persistently unexplained portion, many scholars are searching for alternatives to study where and when inequalities emerge (Fortin 2008), especially looking at prelabor values and gender identities: masculinities and femininities and appropriate ways of doing gender (Kimmel 2000; Schilt and Wiswall 2008). In this [reading], I look at very early work experiences to understand how boys and girls learn to do gender (West and Zimmerman 1987) and potentially trace the origins of the gender wage gap. Since people enter the labor market at a young age, working in both freelance and employee-type jobs, early work experience can shed light on this persistent inequality. Is there a time of equality in the workforce? When does the first gender wage gap emerge? What factors contribute to the early gender inequality in pay?

To begin with, this [reading] deals with two of the dominant theories of the gender pay gap: the human capital approach and the occupational segregation approach. The human capital approach focuses on men's and women's individual characteristics in explaining the pay gap (Altonji and Blank 1999; Becker 1964; Blau and Kahn 2006; Brown and Corcoran 1997; Fuller and Schoenberger 1991; Goldin 1990; Groshen 1991; Mincer 1962; Paglin and

Rufolo 1990; Schilt and Wiswall 2008; Wood, Corcoran, and Courant 1993). According to this view, the pay differences between men and women can be explained by individual characteristics, such as differences in education and experience on the job (Bose and Bridges-Whaley 2011; Gottfried 2013). While this view has been popular in previous decades, some of the explanations are really no longer applicable. For example, this view argued that women were paid less than men because women are not as educated, do not have as many advanced degrees, or have lower graduation rates. However, while this might have been true in previous decades, today women outnumber men in college attendance and graduation. Over the past forty years, women's educational attainment has outpaced men's substantially (Haveman and Beresford 2012). Heather A. Haveman and Lauren S. Beresford (2012), based on their analysis of 2011 data from National Center for Education Statistics, show that in 1970–1971, women accounted for only 43 percent of all bachelor's degrees. By 2009, women earned 57 percent of all bachelor's degrees. Haveman and Beresford observe a similar trend in higher degrees, as well. Women earned 40 percent of all master's degrees in 1970–1971, whereas by 2008–2009, they accounted for 60 percent of master's degrees. In 1970–1971, women earned only 14 percent of all doctoral degrees, but by 2008–2009, they earned 52 percent of all doctorates.

Along with the rapid gains in educational attainment at all levels, the subjects, majors, and areas of specialization pursued by women have changed quickly as well (Haveman and Beresford 2012). Women have become more likely to seek out bachelor's and master's degrees in business, from 9 percent of business BAs and 4 percent of MBAs in 1970–1971 to 49 percent of business BAs and 45 percent of MBAs in 2008–2009 (Haveman and Beresford 2012). Even in science, technology, engineering, and mathematics (STEM) fields, there have been important changes, with STEM majors increasing from 18 percent female in 1970 to 38 percent in 2004 (Haveman and Beresford 2012; see also National Science Foundation 2007). There are some differences in specialization, with women being underrepresented in mathematically heavy subfields of finance and STEM fields (Bertrand, Goldin, and Katz 2010; Carrell, Page, and West 2009; Prokos and Padavic 2005). Despite significant educational gains, the pay gap persists (Charles 2003; Charles and Bradley 2009).

The human capital approach also argues that unequal pay is due to differences in experience (Gottfried 2013). As with the claims about differential levels of education, such claims are less compelling than they might once have been, as women have made substantial progress in increasing their job experience (Bose and Bridges-Whaley 2011). Forty years ago, only 41 percent of women (as opposed to 76 percent of men) were employed, but by 2009, 54 percent of women and 65 percent of men worked, closing the work experience gap (Haveman and Beresford 2012). One important factor contributing to the experience gap is the fact that women are also more likely to work part time (Goldin 1990; Jacobs 1989; Gatta and Roos 2005; Roos and Gatta 1999). Typically, part-time jobs offer little to no benefits and few opportunities for advancement, and they contribute little to women's careers. However, women often take these part-time jobs to balance child care and domestic duties.

Women may also have fewer years of job experience, which are due to labor market interruptions linked to parental leave, child care, and domestic duties (Bertrand, Goldin, and Katz 2010). Haveman and Beresford (2012) break the workforce into four age cohorts: twenty-five to thirty-four, thirty-five to forty-four, forty-five to fifty-four, and fifty-five to sixty-four. Among the youngest men, the median amount of job experience was 2.8 years, increasing to 5.2 years in the next age group, 8.2 years in the one after that, and 10.1 in the oldest age group. For women of all age groups, the median experience level was lower: 2.6 years, 4.7 years, 7 years, and 9.8 years, respectively—all lower than their male counterparts in the relative age groups (Haveman and Beresford 2012). There has been a rapid shift in the past few decades in attitudes toward working: today, attitudes toward working women and working mothers are overwhelmingly positive (Brewster and Padavic 2000), in a major shift from where they stood in the 1980s. However, even today, there remains a bias against mothers with small children working full-time (Treas and Widmer 2000). Especially with limited parental leave policies and in the absence of governmental programs that could help to balance work and family commitments, many women take time off from work or opt for reduced hours (Collinson and Collinson 2004; Jacobs and Gerson 2004). Jerry A. Jacobs and Kathleen Gerson (2004) find that women experience more work-family conflict than men do. Especially with recent changes in parenting and the increasing movement toward intensive mothering, more of the responsibility of parenting falls on the shoulders of women, where they are expected to be involved in all activities of the children. Women are more likely to be expected to tend to the everyday lives of their children rather than delegating to babysitters and nannies (Epstein 2004; P. Stone 2008). Expectations that mothers will chauffeur their children to structured activities, manage bake sales, volunteer at their children's schools, and coach sports teams make it increasingly difficult to find workplaces that will accommodate the demands of intensive parenting (Lareau 2003; Lareau and Weininger 2008). As a result, many highly educated working women leave the workforce or interrupt their careers to focus on intensive mothering (Belkin 2003; P. Stone 2008; Story 2005), either by choice or for lack of options.

In addition to childcare responsibilities, women also perform more housework than men do (Bianchi 2011; Bianchi et al. 2000; Bianchi et al. 2012; Sayer 2005). Today, among dual-earner couples, the division of chores is nowhere near equal: it is divided approximately two thirds to one third, with women performing two thirds of the house chores and men performing only one third (Coltrane and Adams 2001). In addition to the inequality in the division of chores, even individual tasks are gendered. For example, men are more likely to do more masculine tasks, such as mowing the lawn and barbecuing, while women are more likely to sew and iron. The tasks that men perform are typically not as time sensitive as women's tasks, either. For example, men are able to mow the lawn any day within the week based on their work schedule and availability, whereas everyday cooking, which is typically performed by women, has more immediate deadlines and more time pressures (Bittman et al. 2003; Coltrane 2010; Coltrane and Adams 2001). Similarly, typically masculine tasks, such lawn care, snow removal, and car repairs, can be subcontracted to others (sometimes even children can take over such tasks), while traditionally female tasks, such as everyday cooking, are much less likely to be performed by others. Overall, despite changes and progress, the bulk of the house chore responsibilities still fall on women, even when men and women work comparable hours. Because women are more likely to multitask and be responsible for house chores, they are more likely to be distracted, which may result in in lower workplace productivity.

Overall, this view argues that the pay gap can be explained through individual differences between men and women, resulting in lower productivity for women because they have fewer years of schooling, fewer credentials, and fewer years of experience (Corcoran and Duncan 1979; Duncan 1996; Goldin and Polachek 1987; Oaxaca 1973; Polachek 1981). Mary Corcoran and Greg J. Duncan (1979) for example, make use of the Panel Study of Income Dynamics to find that 44 percent of the observed gender wage gap is accounted for by differences in human capital. Solomon W. Polachek (1981), however, argues that even the measurement of human capital is a measure highly biased to privilege men and advocates for measurements to correct for such biases.

Alternatively, the occupational segregation approach argues that the wage gap is explained not through individual characteristics but through occupational factors. In other words, men and women do not get paid the same, not because they are different but because they work in different jobs (Gottfried 2013). In the past few decades, much progress has been made in occupational segregation, mostly with women entering traditionally male occupations (Reskin and Hartmann 1986; Reskin and Roos 2002), but relatively few men have entered women's jobs. Several studies have confirmed that sex segregation has very strong negative effects on wages (England, Hermsen, and Cotter 2000; Tomaskovic-Devey and Skaggs 2002).

Despite the difference in the two perspectives, these models have one thing in common: they focus on the *adult* work force, while work experiences often start much earlier. As noted previously, the majority of high school students work sometime during the school year, and they are even more likely to work during the summer (Staff, Schulenberg, and Bachman 2010). By the time they graduate from high school, most students have worked at some point either during the school year or the summer, so the gender wage gap potentially starts long before what has traditionally been measured. Wage differentials among teenagers, despite the prevalence of their work, have received scant academic attention. Two early studies point to boys and girls working in widely divergent sectors of the economy (Medrich et al. 1982; see also Goldstein and Oldham 1979), leading the authors to speculate that such different work arrangements may mirror differences of chore divisions at home. Lynne White and David Brinkerhoff (1981) find that boys and girls tend to work in different sectors, but their limited dataset includes young people between the ages of two and seventeen, a group dominated by people too young to have jobs of any kind. Simply because of the limitations of their data, they are unable to pinpoint what types of jobs young people work at and when the wage gap begins to emerge. In the early 1980s, Ellen Greenberger and Laurence Steinberg, in their article "Sex Differences in Early Labor Experience: Harbinger of Things to Come" (1983), explore gender inequality in the workplace for young workers. In their study, which remains the most comprehensive study of gender inequality in early labor markets, they point to gender differences in employment, sectors, and wages. They find that "the earliest experiences of boys and girls in the formal labor force mirrors sex differentials in the adult labor force. From virtually the moment youngsters go to work outside the home, they enter a labor force where the work of males and females is quite distinct" (Greenberger and Steinberg 1983, 481–482).

Based on their analysis, first, they find that adolescent girls work fewer hours in their first jobs than adolescent boys do and that adolescent girls have lower hourly wages. However, they offer only descriptive differences and do not delve into explanations of why such gender differences would exist, instead calling for more systematic studies of gender differences: "More systematic studies of children's early work are needed, however to clarify when boys' and girls' labor force participation begins, when boys' and girls' work moves in different directions, and when sex differences in hours of employment and hourly wages begin to emerge. The latter issue is virtually unexplored to date" (Greenberger and Steinberg 1983, 469). Unfortunately, despite the call for more studies to explain the gender wage gap in early years, data limitations have prevented many scholars from exploring these early inequalities in the past few decades.

This [reading] aims to fill this gap in the literature and delve into gender differences in the teenage workforce. I situate my analysis at the intersection of these dominant theories, to help trace the origins of this persistent problem and also naturally control for many methodologically problematic confounds. Like a natural laboratory, focusing on these very young workers will help eliminate a wide range of confounds, including house chores, child care, and many other human capital explanations. Teenagers in this age group are not married and do not have children, and they do not have domestic or child-care duties.

The National Longitudinal Survey of Youth (NLSY97 [...]) provides ample data on income and employment variables along with demographic information on youth. For comparison purposes and easier interpretation, the dataset is aggregated by age to enable analysis and explore changes over time. It is also separated into three cohorts: twelve- to thirteen-year-olds, fourteen- to fifteen-year-olds, and sixteen- to nineteen-year-olds. This dataset is particularly valuable not only in terms of the detailed, nationally representative data it provides on the employment characteristics of youth but also because of its inclusion of twelve- to fifteen-year-olds, most of whom are traditionally omitted from analysis of youth labor.

Typical accounts portray youth employment as "gender utopia" in terms of labor-force participation rates, a place where men and women seem to be, for once, on completely equal footing. If we focus solely on labor-force participation rates, in fact, we observe no significant differences (Figure 10.1). In none of the three age cohorts is there a substantial difference between boys and girls in terms of their labor-force participation rates. Among the twelve-to thirteen-year-olds, 36 percent of girls and 37 percent of boys work, among the fourteen- to fifteen-year-olds, 47 percent of girls and 51 percent of boys work, and among the sixteen- to nineteen-year-olds, 66 percent of girls and 65 percent of boys are employed. Such marginal differences mean that we can treat the labor participation rates, at least, as being approximately equal. Unlike when Greenberger and Steinberg (1983) found that boys were more likely to work than girls, for the past few decades, boys and girls have had comparable labor-force participation rates. This well-known finding, perhaps, leads to the perception of the youth labor market as a place of gender equality.

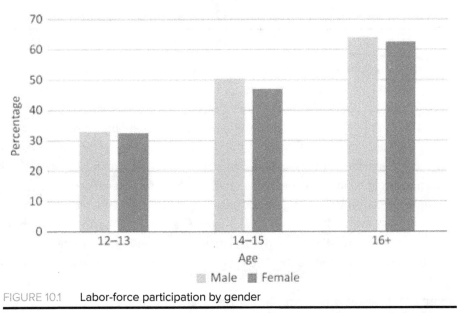

FIGURE 10.1   Labor-force participation by gender

However, a lack of differences in the likelihood of youths working does not imply equality in all aspects of youth employment. While boys and girls of a certain age are equally likely to work, it is still possible that they receive differential pay for their work or are segregated into different types of jobs. [...]

The Making of the Gender Wage Gap

The overall analysis of the data shows a difference in the types of jobs taken by boys and girls, especially a marked concentration of girls in freelance jobs and boys in employee-type jobs, but we have yet to show that this is the cause of the gender wage gap. First, there is no evidence to suggest differential pay for different types of jobs among the youth. The vast majority of youth employed in employee-type jobs receive the minimum wage, and there is no reason to believe that freelance jobs pay more to one gender than the other.

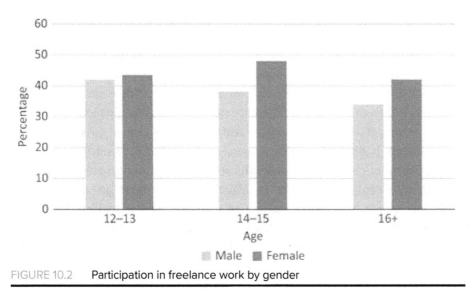

FIGURE 10.2   Participation in freelance work by gender

Second, the disproportionate employment of girls in freelance jobs cannot alone be the cause of the gender wage gap, as child labor laws restrict youth under 16 from employment. Therefore, the samples of twelve- to thirteen-year-olds and fourteen- to fifteen-year-olds are predominantly employed in freelance-type jobs (although exceptions do exist for agricultural workers, work in family businesses, and some other situations, they do not apply to most children). If the disproportionate employment of girls in freelance-type jobs explained the gender wage gap, we would not observe the significant pay differential for the fourteen- to fifteen-year-old cohort that we do, as relatively few of the teenagers work in employee-type jobs. Moreover, while the concentration of girls and boys in traditionally gendered jobs increases, this does not map onto the earliest signs of the gender wage gap. Even among the twelve- to thirteen-year-old cohort, where girls actually earn slightly more than their male counterparts, there is a concentration of girls and boys in traditionally gendered jobs. The extent to which job choice results in the discrepancy in pay needs to be tested.

The purpose of this analysis is to account for the effect of gender on income by controlling for all the possible confounding factors. Even though the number of hours does not differ for boys and girls, it is important to control for it as a confounding variable. In addition to the average number of hours worked per week, the regression analysis includes several variables representing structural explanations for the wage gap applicable to youth, such as the type of job (freelance versus employee-type), and demographic-control variables traditionally included in similar analyses, such as race (white or Asian versus nonwhite or Asian), age (as youth typically earn more as they become older), the socioeconomic status of the household (measured through household income, as a percentage of the local poverty level), and, of course, the gender of the respondent. The model uses all of these to explain the income of the respondent, logged in order to minimize the impact of outliers. Simply put, the existence of a difference in wages based on gender, rather than on hours worked or any other explanation, should be evident from a significant coefficient attached to the variable representing the gender of the respondent.

All of the predictor variables in the model have statistically significant effects on youth income. In interpretation of the table coefficients, it is important to note that all reflect changes in logged, rather than actual, income. The details of the model are presented in the methodological notes. The most important finding of this regression is in the coefficient attached to the gender of the respondent. Accounting for all the explanations applicable to the youth in our sample, including the number of hours worked and the nature of the job, girls can expect to earn about $93 less per year solely by virtue of their gender. While this may not seem like a great deal of income, it is very large relative to the mean earnings of a girl in the sample, which come out to only $606.76 per year. Thus, at these young ages, girls are making almost 13 percent less than boys, solely because of their gender.

Other factors in the model were used solely for control purposes to identify the pure effect of gender, but they also provide interesting comparisons by which we can better comprehend the magnitude of the effects of gender on income. It is interesting to see that the effects of race result in an average difference between white and nonwhite workers of $63, one-third less than the effect of gender.

The heteroskedastic maximum-likelihood regression also allows for the substantive interpretation of the causes of the variance in our model. [...] As predicted, the variance in the model increases with age and income—the latter bolstering the assertion of depressed model fit due to reporting error in the dependent variable—but decreases with the interaction of the two, a striking result, especially given the relative strengths of the coefficients. This can be interpreted to mean that as youth become more like adults—as they age and earn more money—the relationship of their demographic characteristics to their earnings becomes more predictable. It may be only this variance that allows for the equality of pay in the youngest cohorts, and it fades away rapidly with increases in age and earnings. But, interestingly, a further analysis of the heteroskedasticity patterns shows an interesting clustering of older, higher-income youth—most of whom are boys, with the marked omission of girls.

So far, the analysis has identified the effect of gender on the earnings of youth, controlling for all possible explanations and demographic characteristics. However, it is important to show how these factors translate into the gender wage gap. While the maximum likelihood estimation identifies the direct effect of gender, it is also evident that the gender results in unequal earnings through the concentration of girls in freelance jobs. As presented in Figure 10. 3, the total average gender wage gap in the youth sample is $130, 71 percent of which is accounted by the pure effect of gender. In addition to this, 10 percent of this difference is accounted for by the differential concentration of girls in freelance jobs. Therefore, we can say that overall, this model accounts for 81 percent of the gender wage gap. [...]

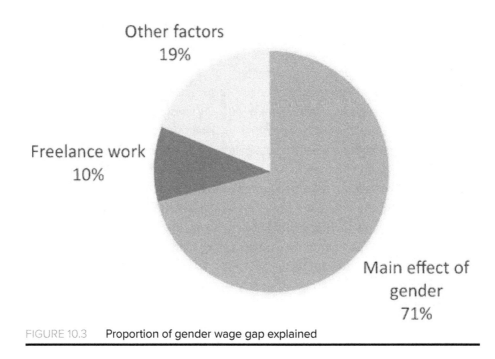

FIGURE 10.3   Proportion of gender wage gap explained

Note: Total gender wage gap = Average wage of boys ($737.57) – Average wage of girls ($606.76) = $130.81; Portion explained by main effect of gender = Dollar value attached to coefficient for gender = $93.01; Portion explained by freelance work = (Expected value of freelance for girls (0.4775) – Expected value of freelance for boys (0.4244)) × Dollar value attached to coefficient for freelance ($245.01) = $13.01; Portion explained by other factors = Total gender wage gap ($130.81) – Portion explained by main effect of gender ($93.01) – Portion explained by difference in likelihood of freelance work ($13.01) = $24.75.

References

Altonji, Joseph G., and Rebecca M. Blank. 1999. "Race and Gender in the Labor Market." In *Handbook of Labor Economics*, vol. 3C, edited by O. Ashenfelter and D. Card, 3143–3259. Amsterdam: Elsevier.

Becker, Gary. 1964. *Human Capital*. New York: National Bureau of Economic Research.

Belkin, Lisa. 2003. "The Opt-Out Revolution." *New York Times*, October 26. Available at http://www.nytimes.com/2003/10/26/magazine/the-opt-out-revolution.html.

Bertrand, Marianne, Claudia Goldin, and Lawrence F. Katz. 2010. "Dynamics of the Gender Gap for Young Professionals in the Financial and Corporate Sectors." *American Economic Journal: Applied Economics* 2 (3): 228–255.

Bianchi, Suzanne M. 2011. "Family Change and Time Allocation in American Families." *The Annals of the American Academy of Political and Social Science* 638:21–44.

Bianchi, Suzanne M., Melissa A. Milkie, Liana C. Sayer, and John P. Robinson. 2000. "Is Anyone Doing the Housework? Trends in the Gender Division of Household Labor." *Social Forces* 79:191–228.

Bianchi, Suzanne M., Liana C. Sayer, Melissa A. Milkie, and John P. Robinson. 2012. "Housework: Who Did, Does or Will Do It, and How Much Does It Matter?" *Social Forces* 91 (1): 55–63.

Bittman, Michael, Paula England, Liana Sayer, Nancy Folbre, and George Matheson. 2003. "When Does Gender Trump Money? Bargaining and Time in Household Work." *American Journal of Sociology* 109:186–214.

Blau, Francine D., Marienne A. Ferber, and Anne E. Winkler. 2006. *The Economics of Women, Men, and Work*. 5th ed. Upper Saddle River, NJ: Prentice Hall.

Blau, Francine D., and Lawrence M. Kahn. 2005. "Changes in the Labor Supply Behavior of Married Women: 1980–2000." National Bureau of Economic Research Working Paper no. 11230. Available at http://www.nber.org/papers/w11230.pdf.

———. 2006. "The Gender Pay Gap: Going, Going ... but Not Gone." In *The Declining Significance of Gender*, edited by F. D. Blau, M. J. Brinton, and D. B. Grusky, 37–67. New York: Russell Sage Foundation.

Bose, Christine, and Rachel Bridges-Whaley. 2011. "Sex Segregation in the United States Labor Force." In. *Feminist Frontiers*, 8th ed., edited by L. Rupp and Verta Taylor, 233–251. Boston: McGraw-Hill.

Brewster, Karin L., and Irene Padavic. 2000. "Change in Gender-Ideology, 1977–1996: The Contributions of Intracohort Change and Population Turnover." *Journal of Marriage and Family* 62:477–487.

Brown, Charles, and Mary Corcoran. 1997. "Sex-Based Differences in School Content and the Male-Female Wage Gap." *Journal of Labor Economics* 15 (3): 431–465.

Carrell, Scott E., Marianne E. Page, and James West. 2010. "Sex and Science: How Professor Gender Perpetuates the Gender Wage Gap." *Quarterly Journal of Public Economics* 125 (3): 1101–1144.

Charles, Maria. 2003. "Deciphering Sex Segregation: Vertical and Horizontal Inequalities in Ten National Labor Markets." *Acta Sociologica* 46 (4): 267–287.

Charles, Maria, and Karen Bradley. 2009. "Indulging Our Gendered Selves? Sex Segregation by Field of Study in 44 Countries." *American Journal of Sociology* 114 (4): 925–976.

Collinson, David L., and Margaret Collinson. 2004. "The Power of Time: Leadership, Management and Gender." In *Fighting for Time: Shifting the Boundaries of Work and Social Life*, edited by C. F. Epstein and A. L. Kalleberg, 219–246. New York: Russell Sage Foundation.

Coltrane, Scott. 2010. "Gender Theory and Household Labor." *Sex Roles* 63:791–800.

Coltrane, Scott, and Michele Adams. 2001. "Men's Family Work: Child-Centered Fathering and the Sharing of Domestic Labor." In *Working Families: The Transformation of the American Home*, edited by R. Hertz and N. Marshall, 72–99. Berkeley: University of California Press.

Corcoran, Mary, and Greg J. Duncan. 1979. "Work History, Labor Force Attachments, and Earning Differences between the Races and Sexes." *Journal of Human Resources* 14 (1): 3–20.

Duncan, Kevin C. 1996. "Gender Differences in the Effect of Education on the Slope of Experience-Earnings Profiles: NLSY, 1979–1988." *American Journal of Economics and Sociology* 55 (4): 457–471.

England, Paula, Joan M. Hermsen, and David A. Cotter. 2000. "The Devaluation of Women's Work: A Comment on Tam." *American Journal of Sociology* 105:1741–1751.

Epstein, Cynthia Fuchs. 2004. "Border Crossings: The Constraints of the Time Norms in Transgressions of Gender and Professional Roles." In *Fighting for Time: Shifting Boundaries of Work and Social Life*, edited by Cynthia Fuchs Epstein and Arne L. Kalleberg, 317–340. New York: Russell Sage Foundation.

Fortin, Nicole M. 2008. "The Gender Wage Gap among Young Adults in the United States: The Importance of Money versus People." *Journal of Human Resources* 43 (4): 884–918.

Fuller, Rex, and Richard Schoenberger. 1991. "The Gender Salary Gap: Do Academic Achievement, Internship Experience, and College Major Make a Difference?" *Social Science Quarterly* 72:715–726.

Gatta, Mary L., and Patricia A. Roos. 2005. "Rethinking Occupational Integration." *Sociological Forum* 20 (3): 369–402.

Goldin, Claudia. 1990. *Understanding the Gender Gap: An Economic History of American Women*. New York: Oxford University Press.

Goldin, Claudia, and Solomon Polachek. 1987. "Residual Differences by Sex: Perspectives on the Gender Gap in Earnings." *American Economic Review* 77 (2): 143–151.

Goldstein, Bernard, and Jack Oldham. 1979. *Children and Work: A Study of Socialization*. New Brunswick, NJ: Transaction Books.

Gottfried, Heidi. 2013. *Gender, Work, and Economy: Unpacking the Global Economy*. Cambridge, MA: Polity.

Greenberger, Ellen, and Laurence D. Steinberg. 1983. "Sex Differences in Early Labor Force Experience: Harbinger of Things to Come." *Social Forces* 62 (2): 467–486.

Groshen, Erica L. 1991. "The Structure of the Female/Male Wage Differential. Is It Who You Are, What You Do, or Where You Work?" *Journal of Human Resources* 26 (3): 457–472.

Haveman, Heather A., and Lauren S. Beresford. 2012. "If You're So Smart, Why Aren't You the Boss? Explaining the Persistent Vertical Gender Gap in Management." *Annals of the American Academy of Political and Social Science* 639:114–130.

Jacobs, Jerry. 1989. *Revolving Doors*. Stanford, CA: Stanford University Press.

Jacobs, Jerry A., and Kathleen Gerson. 2004. *The Time Divide*. Cambridge, MA: Harvard University Press.

Kimmel, Michael. 2000. *The Gendered Society*. New York: Oxford University Press.

Lareau, Anette. 2003. *Unequal Childhoods*. Oakland: University of California Press.

Lareau, Anette, and Elliot B. Weininger. 2008. "Time, Work, and Family Life." *Sociological Forum* 23:419–454.

Medrich, Elliott A., Judith A. Roizen, Victor Rubin, and Stuart Buckley. 1982. *The Serious Business of Growing Up: A Study of Children's Lives Outside of School*. Berkeley: University of California Press.

Mincer, Jacob. 1962. "On-the-Job Training: Costs, Returns and Some Implications." *Journal of Political Economy* 70 (5): 50–79.

National Science Foundation. 2007. "Science and Engineering Degrees: 1966–2004." Available at https://wayback.archive-it.org/5902/20160210223704/http://www.nsf.gov/statistics/nsf07307/pdf/nsf07307.pdf.

Oaxaca, Ronald. 1973. "Male-Female Wage Differentials in Urban Labor Markets." *International Economic Review* 14 (3): 693–709.

Paglin, Morton, and Anthony M. Rufolo. 1990. "Heterogeneous Human Capital, Occupational Choice, and Male-Female Earnings Differences." *Journal of Labor Economics* 8 (1): 123–144.

Polachek, Solomon W. 1981. "Occupational Self-Selection: A Human Capital Approach to Sex Differences in Occupational Structure." *Review of Economics and Statistics* 63 (1): 60–69.

Prokos, Anastasia, and Irene Padavic. 2005. "An Examination of Competing Explanations for the Pay Gap among Scientists and Engineers." *Gender and Society* 19 (4): 523–543.

Reskin, Barbara F. 1993. "Sex Segregation in the Workplace." *Annual Review of Sociology* 19:241–270.

Reskin, Barbara, and Heidi I. Hartmann. 1986. *Women's Work, Men's Work, Sex Segregation on the Job*. Washington, DC: National Academy Press.

Reskin, Barbara, and Patricia Roos. 2002. *Job Queues, Gender Queues: Explaining Women's Inroads into Male Occupations*. Philadelphia: Temple University Press.

Roos, Patricia A., and Mary Lizabeth Gatta. 1999. "The Gender Gap in Earnings: Trends, Explanations, and Prospects." In *Handbook of Gender and Work*, edited by Gary Powell, 95–123. Thousand Oaks, CA: Sage.

Sayer, Liana C. 2005. "Gender, Time, and Inequality: Trends in Women's and Men's Paid Work, Unpaid Work, and Free Time." *Social Forces* 84:285–303.

Schilt, Kristen, and Matthew Wiswall. 2008. "Before and After: Gender Transitions, Human Capital, and Workplace Experiences." *B.E. Journal of Economic Analysis and Policy* 8 (1): 1–28.

Staff, Jeremy, John E. Schulenberg, and Jerald G. Bachman. 2010. "Adolescent Work Intensity, School Performance, and Academic Engagement." *Sociology of Education* 83:183–200.

Stone, Pamela. 2008. *Opting Out? Why Women Really Quit Careers and Head Home*. Oakland: University of California Press.

Story, Louise. 2005. "Many Women at Elite Colleges Set Career Path to Motherhood." *New York Times*, September 20. Available at http://www.nytimes.com/2005/09/20/us/many-women-at-elite-colleges-set-career-path-to-motherhood.html.

Tomaskovic-Devey, Donald, and Sheryl Skaggs. 2002. "Sex Segregation, Labor Process Organization, and Gender Earnings Inequality." *American Journal of Sociology* 108 (1): 102–128.

Treas, Judith, and Eric D. Widmer. 2000. "Married Women's Employment over the Life Course: Attitudes in Cross-national Perspective." *Social Forces* 78: 1409–1436.

West, Candace, and Don Zimmerman. 1987. "Doing Gender." *Gender and Society* 1:13–37.

White, Lynn K., and David B. Brinkerhoff. 1981. "The Sexual Division of Labor: Evidence from Childhood." *Social Forces* 60 (1): 170–181.

Wood, Robert G., Mary E. Corcoran, and Paul N. Courant. 1993. "Pay Differentials among the Highly Paid: The Male-Female Earnings Gap in Lawyers' Salaries." *Journal of Labor Economics* 11 (3): 417–441.

Post-Reading Questions

1. What is the human capital approach to understanding the gender wage gap? What are the strengths and weaknesses of this approach?
2. What is the occupational segregation approach to the gender wage gap? What are the strengths and weaknesses of this approach?

UNIT IV

RACE AND ETHNICITY

Key Terms and Definitions

Review the key terms and definitions below to strengthen your understanding of the readings in this unit.

Assimilation: The process whereby a minoritized ethnic group's cultural practices dissolve over generations and melds into the way of the life of the ethnic majority. Often, in the context of the United States, this connotes a gradual shift toward the norms and practices of native-born white Americans.

Critical Social Theory: A form of social theory that seeks to illuminate collective experiences of societal oppression and injustice. This form of social theory has the purpose of promoting social justice and making society's institutions more equitable for all.

Ethnic Disadvantage Theory: A theory that posits that immigrants, especially those who are marginalized by race and ethnicity, even after assimilating over time, may continue to face social disadvantages due to structures of ethnocentrism and racism in society.

Ethnicity: Cultural differences like nationality, religion, and language (as well as other beliefs, values, and practices) that set people apart from one another.

Hart–Cellar Act: An immigration law passed in 1965 that eliminated a discriminatory quota system that favored immigrants from certain countries. This opened the door to immigration to the United States from Asia, Africa, Southern and Eastern European countries, and other nations.

Identity Development Models: A set of theories in psychology (including the MEIM model, racial identity schema, and AAID models) that emphasizes how people come to internalize their ethnic and racial identities over the course of their development, leading to positive psychological outcomes. These theories are sometimes criticized for their focus on individual development and for their lack of attention to the social consequences of structural ethnocentrism and racism.

Intersectionality: A feminist theory that focuses on how multiple aspects of identity such as race, ethnicity, gender, sexuality, and social class simultaneously shape daily lived experiences. One of the assumptions of this theory is that If we study only one aspect, such as a person's race, without considering their gender, sexuality, or social class, we fail to grasp the full extent of people's social experiences.

Nativism: A cultural backlash against immigrants (or those perceived as immigrants), wherein these groups are regarded as inferior to native-born residents by members of the dominant culture.

Race: Physical markers such as skin color, eye shape, and hair texture that are identified to be socially meaningful in society.

Racialization: When people in society or institutions extend racial meaning to an individual, group, or social practice. This can happen in a neutral, positive, or negative manner, depending on the context.

Segmented Assimilation Theory: The theory that some recent immigrants may achieve upward mobility and integrate into society, whereas others may face societal oppression and fall into a cycle of downward mobility.

Social Construction: The process by which social meanings are created through human interaction.

Introduction

In "Intersectionality in and of Race: Identity Construction Re/Considered," Alina S. Wong describes how racial and ethnic categories in the United States are **social constructions**. The terms **race** and **ethnicity** are frequently used interchangeably but have a distinct sociological difference. Race describes physical markers that are identified to be socially meaningful in society. Ethnicity, on the other hand, refers to cultural differences like nationality, religion, and language (as well as other beliefs, values, and practices) that set people apart from one another. Biologists, DNA experts, and scholars of race have articulated time and again that there is very little biological basis for race. In other words, the meaning that members of society place on physical markers like skin color, eye shape, and hair texture is socially, but not biologically, significant. In fact, scientists have found that there is *more* DNA variation between people of the same race than between people of different races. Yet race has deep, long-standing but shifting social meaning. People in society and institutions have used racial markers to denote differences between people for many generations. We know that not all races are treated equally in society, and people of color face prejudice, discrimination, institutional exclusion, and other forms of oppression. Meanwhile, people who are designated as white maintain many social privileges, whether or not they are aware of these advantages. Certain ethnic groups, some of whom are considered white, and others who are not, have also faced prejudice, discrimination, and social exclusion. For example, Jewish people across the world have faced centuries of prejudice, discrimination, and genocide. In the United States, Native Americans have faced prejudice, discrimination, forced assimilation, and massacre. Japanese Americans were forced to live in internment camps in the United States during World War II.

Alina S. Wong uses two theories, **intersectionality** and **critical social theory**, to analyze the way race operates in society. In doing so, she describes the way ethnicity and race are socially constructed for Chinese American and Filipinx American college students. In her study, she conducts in-depth interviews with students from two public universities to collect her data. Wong believes that **identity theory models** are insufficient in explaining the way race and ethnicity operate in these settings. Under these models, the argument is that once a person becomes aware of their ethnicity and/or racial affiliation, this identity becomes fixed, and they have mostly positive psychological outcomes. In contrast to this idea, Wong's research indicates that the racial and ethnic identities of college students are constantly shifting and evolving. Participants in her study simultaneously identified as Asian American and as part of a specific ethnic group (e.g., Chinese American or Filipinx American). Many of them focused on the American aspects of their identity. Ultimately, the author concludes that these identities provide a sense of belonging but also establish a means of resistance against racial and ethnic oppression.

The second reading in this unit, "Immigration and Growing Diversity" by John Iceland, outlines the history of immigration to the United States. He reveals the various social debates that have emerged about immigration throughout history. Iceland reviews the ways in which immigration is changing the racial and ethnic landscape of society, the degree to which groups have assimilated to the culture, and how immigration in the United States differs from other nations. Our immigration history begins with the occupation of the United States by Europeans, followed by the involuntary migration of African American slaves, and the influx of voluntary migration after this point, much of which was fueled by people escaping extremely difficult circumstances abroad. The author notes that by the end of the nineteenth century, some resistance to immigration began to surface, much of which was fueled by racism. For example, in the mid-1800s, restrictions were placed on immigration to the United States from China and Japan. After WWII, immigration opened again, and in 1965, the **Hart–Cellar Act** removed the previous discriminatory quota system. The quota system limited immigration from Southern and Eastern Europe, Asia, and Africa. This immigration opening changed the racial landscape of the United States, making our country more racially and ethnically diverse than ever before. It is projected that this pattern will continue, eventually leading to non-Hispanic whites becoming the numeric minority.

Iceland details how previous waves of immigrants largely assimilated to US cultural norms over the generations but argues that **assimilation** does not imply cultural acceptance. He suggests that according to **ethnic disadvantage theory**, even after assimilating, recent waves of immigrants who are marginalized by race or ethnicity may continue to face social disadvantages in society due to structures of ethnocentrism and racism in society. Another theory, **segmented assimilation theory**, suggests that some recent immigrants may achieve upward mobility and integrate into society, while others may face societal oppression and fall into a cycle of downward mobility. Finally, the author argues that the United States must provide a viable pathway to citizenship for undocumented immigrants. With such a policy, undocumented immigrants have a better chance of social inclusion and economic gains.

In the third reading, titled "Latino Post-Millennials Create America's Future" by David Hayes-Bautista, the author highlights how Latinx individuals are often miscast as "illegal immigrants" by dominant members of society. They have also undergone **racialization** and faced **nativism** propelled by powerful members of society. He provides a historical overview of the long-standing presence of Latinx people in the United States and its territories to negate this misconception. Hayes-Bautista reveals that the majority of Latinx people in the United States are native-born and have an established presence here. The author also anticipates that the new generation of Latinx individuals in the United States will have a large influence on future political elections and will increasingly shape civil society in major ways for the foreseeable future.

Intersectionality in and of Race

Identity Construction Re/Considered

Alina S. Wong

Within academic discourse, race is widely understood as a social construction through which racial categories were created as a tool of racism (Apple, 1993; Goldberg, 1993; Hall, 1992; McCarthy & Crichlow, 1993; Omi & Winant, 1994; Werbner, 1997). Racial categorizations in the United States (historically coded as White, Black, Asian, His-panic, and Native) were created to uphold a system of White privilege such that White Americans—including White American ethnicities, values, religions, skin color, and so on—were considered ideal and normative, whereas other racialized Americans were deemed lacking at best and dehumanized at worst (Alexander, 2010; Omi & Winant, 1994). "Race" as a divisive category contributed to notions of superiority and inferiority, and as rationalizations for colonization, enslavement, discrimination, and criminalization (Apple, 1993; Spade, 2010).

Over time, these racial categories were codified into racial identities, with both positive and detrimental consequences. As the biological foundations for race were eroded, cultural justifications replaced them. This shift occurred partly because of powerful movements fought by communities of color to claim agency in defining their own identities, and to refuse negative portrayals and stereotypes. However, this move from racial categorization to racial identity also allowed dominant ideology to continue to place responsibility for discrimination, unequal access, and exclusion on the individual. If race was not biological, then behaviors and outcomes were choices. Portrayals of Mexicans as lazy, Black youth as drug dealers and gang members, or Asian Americans as irrevocably foreign created such strong stereotypes that mainstream society attributed inequity as a consequence of culture. Oppressed communities have been active in response, creating resistance movements, studying our own histories, and refusing dominant White narratives. This is the sociopolitical context in which racial identities are constructed, contested, and claimed.

I use intersectionality and critical theory to reconsider how race and racial identities are constructed in the United States, particularly by Chinese American and American college students. Research on identity and student development indicates that late adolescence is a crucial time for individuals to garner a sense of self, especially with regard to racial and ethnic identities (Torres, Jones, & Renn, 2009). With concerns about students' well-being and academic performance, scholars have studied the collegiate experiences of students of color, including Asian Americans.[1] This work provided insight into the experiences of students of color and how their college realities differed from dominant White narratives (Morrison, 2010). Yet, there has been little consideration of *being* raced and racialized. What is it to be Asian American? How do you know if you are, and what does it mean to have or claim such an identity? And what choice, if any, does one have in the matter?

In this [reading], I discuss the multiple constructions of Asian American identities and communities as well as how intersectionality and critical theory allow for more holistic understandings of racial identities than do traditional identity development models—such as Phinney's Multi-Ethnic Identity Model (MEIM) (Phinney, 1992, 1996a, 1996b; Phinney & Alpuria, 1997), Helms's racial identity schema (Alvarez, 2002; Alvarez & Helms 2001; Alvarez & Yeh, 1999), and Kim's Asian American Identity Development (AAID) (Kim 1981, 2001). Considering colleges and universities as spaces infused with and reflective of dominant racial discourses, I explored the processes of racial identity construction—how students define and construct their sense of self—in a qualitative study using in-depth interviews with Chinese American and Filipin@ American college students. Students' narratives demonstrated how identities are constantly in flux and under construction, and how identities are internally formed through personal experiences while simultaneously influenced by social relationships and politics. What it means to be Asian American (and Chinese American and Filipin@ American) was a dynamic and iterative process of negotiation and renegotiation, of definition and redefinition. As the participants discussed, racial identity is in the lived experiences of being raced and living as racialized beings. As Hall (1992) noted,

> Thus, identity is actually something formed through unconscious processes over time, rather than being innate in consciousness at birth. ... Thus, rather than speaking of identity as a finished thing, we should speak of *identification*, and see it as an on-going process. (p. 288)

The theoretical frameworks and interventions used in this study are significant departures from the traditional ways that racial identity has been studied in higher education. Using intersectionality and critical theory is helpful to better understand students' lived realities, and to recognize the ways that discourse around race and racial identities is part of systemic oppression and institutionalized racism. Such an approach challenges the dominant racial discourse in higher education research and practice. I hope to offer space for a radical reimagining of how racial identities are conceived, studied, and liberated.

---

1. Other common references include Asian American and Pacific Islander [AAPI], Asian Pacific American [APA], and Asian/Pacific Islander American [A/PIA] to be inclusive of Pacific Islanders who are often grouped together with U.S. citizens, permanent residents, and immigrants of Asian descent. I use Asian American and AAPI throughout.

Theoretical Considerations: Intersectionality

Building on critical theory, critical race theory, and feminist theory, intersectionality (Dill & Zambrana, 2009) offers a framework to understand identity in context, to examine power structures and social contexts in research on identity. Intersectionality suggested that to understand how identities are formed, research must take into account how an individual sense of self interacts with power and social status (Jones, 2009), reminding us that we live in hegemonic power structures that place our bodies and minds in raced, gendered, classed, and sexualized hierarchies. Intersectionality is characterized by four "theoretical interventions": centering the experiences of people of color; exploring individual and group identities; interrogating power, inequality, and oppression; and working in praxis to connect research and practice toward social justice (Dill & Zambrana).

Using intersectionality as an analytic lens also broadens conversations about identity to include both race and racism. Because intersectionality considers how individual and collective identities are formed within and by systems of power, conversations about race necessarily involve an examination of racism as part of one's identity. Intersectionality provides a unique approach to understanding Asian American identities, and the processes through which students construct and make meaning of them. "The point is not to deny the importance—both material and discursive—of categories but to focus on the process by which they are produced, experienced, reproduced, and resisted in everyday life" (Weber, 1998, p. 1783). Students understood the racist policies and discourses that had created the category of "Asian American," yet also claimed it as a holistic identity of empowerment and transgression. Asian American students lived in one and several racial and cultural spaces simultaneously; not fragments of Asian and American but rather something unique and whole. [...]

Praxis: Intersections of Theory, Research, and Lived Experience

I endeavored to understand how Asian America is constructed and what it means to be Asian American—that is, Asian American *as* and *in* process. This discussion is part of a larger study that also looked at the salient college experiences and relationships that influence students' sense of self. Here I focus on how students expressed themselves as racial beings.

I conducted a qualitative study using in-depth interviews of third- and fourth-year Chinese American and Filipin@ American students at two selective, public universities. I included 20 participants: 5 Filipin@ American and 5 Chinese American students from Michigan University (MU) and California University (CU).[2] They are similar in size and selectivity, but both institution and location vary greatly in the representation of Asian Americans. California has one of the largest populations of Asian Americans in the United States. At the time of the interviews, CU included 44% Asian Americans. I chose MU because it has similar institutional characteristics, but is dissimilar in student racial diversity, state demographics, and geographic location. Asian American students accounted for 12% of MU students at the time the interviews were conducted.

---

2. I assigned pseudonyms to institutions and participants.

I chose Chinese American and Filipin@ American students because they are the two largest Asian American communities. According to the 2000 census, Asian Americans comprised 4.3% of the U.S. population, with 22.6% Chinese and 18.3% Filipin@ (U.S. Bureau of the Census, 2002). Their immigration histories of the nineteenth century are similar, although their sociocultural experiences differ. I also wanted to capture the experiences of two ethnicities with distinct cultural histories and relationships with the United States. I focused on two ethnic groups to recognize the different experiences of Asian American ethnic groups.

I used a purposeful sample of third- and fourth-year students identified through student organizations, faculty, staff, and peers. There were eight male students (five Filipin@ American and three Chinese American). All male students were included for gender balance. I randomly selected female participants (five Filipin@ American and seven Chinese American). Interviews ranged from 40 to 120 minutes, and were audio recorded and professionally transcribed. Participants were all first- or second-generation U.S. citizens—five were born outside the United States, and most immigrated at a young age (one student emigrated from China during high school). Only two students at MU were nonresidents, and all of the CU students had grown up in the state. All students were gendered and one male student self-identified as gay. Many majors were represented, and parental educational attainment and professions were also very diverse. All interviews were conducted in English.

I applied a phenomenological perspective (Lester, 1999; Magrini, 2012; Patton, 2001; van Manen, 1990) to a quasi-traditional thematic analysis, using an emic, iterative approach, research memos, and reflections, with three rounds of coding. Exploratory coding was first conducted by hand, with written reflections following the reading of each transcript. The second layer was done by reading and coding each transcript in AtlasTI, and the third round was conducted by using AtlasTI to focus and organize participants' narratives. I contacted all participants for member checking. Seven responded (three from MU and four from CU—two Chinese American, and five Filipin@ American students). They provided feedback on my interpretations and agreed with my portrayal of their institutions and identities. I also conducted peer debriefing with two undergraduate students at another institution (a White woman and a Chinese American woman), a Korean American woman who was a student affairs practitioner and works with cultural organizations, and a White male student affairs practitioner with experience in qualitative research.

Relationships of power between researcher and participants should be considered, particularly because talking about race and identity is difficult and complex. It was important that students felt a level of safety and comfort with me. In most instances, I was afforded "insider" status because of similar racial or ethnic backgrounds. This affected our interactions and their comfort in discussing personal and sometimes difficult topics. Some students said they would not have participated in the study or been as comfortable had I not been Asian American. Interestingly, as I did not know the students before their participation, most made assumptions about my identity upon seeing my last name in an e-mail. [...]

Both-And: Simultaneous Identities

Students demanded space to construct their unique identities as Asian Americans, distinct from—and simultaneous to—their identities as Chinese American and Filipin@ American. Claiming these multiple identities allowed students to make meaning of their own identities and experiences. Without disregarding their cultural heritage and family histories (which students most commonly referred to as their Chinese American or Filipin@ American identities) students were able to develop an independent and dynamic identity that honored their ancestries *and* recognized their current social contexts. Their identities reflected students' individual experiences while connecting them to each other and with a broader sociopolitical history.

In all of these narratives, students located themselves and their homes in the United States. While many did explore their roots in China, Taiwan, and the Philippines, they recognized the ways that their experiences, identities, and perspectives were uniquely American. Carmen was finding new freedoms and choices in her immediate context. Her Chinese American identity, which was grounded in her perspectives and desire for a sense of belonging, was in process and, unlike some of the other students', was a very conscious process of integrating her changing views and present contexts while trying to leave behind the ideas that no longer resonated with her ways of being.

For Ruby, being Filipin@ American was a very personal experience, one that was difficult to describe. Ruby had a difficult family dynamic, and it was her mother's extended family and Filipin@ American church in Chicago that helped them through.

> When I say Filipin@ American, it's grounded more in this very personal identity. So when I think Filipin@ American, you know, I'm thinking of my family, and I'm thinking of, like, all these experiences. So, yeah, Filipin@ American community is just like this personal cultural, it's like a glue to me. It's just very personal. I don't know if I could put words to it.

Ruby also identified as Asian American, and these identities were neither interchangeable nor separate. For Ruby, being Filipin@ American was part of her personal and family history, while her Asian American identity included her in a larger collective.

> I think when I was younger and I didn't fully understand, it was very easy for me to say that's Asian. That's American. But I think ever since I started college, I don't think about that very much. ... The focus has shifted to what does it mean for me to be Asian American. And so instead of, like, separating things into these two categories like Asian and American, I'm sort of bringing together what makes me Asian American. I feel like I'm getting a pretty good hold of, I'm very comfortable with who I am as an Asian American.

Sam identified strongly as Asian/Pacific Islander American "with a slash between the *A* and the *P*, that's really important" because he felt part of the pan-AAPI coalition and he recognized the diversity within Asian America. He also held a Chinese American identity. Like Tanya and Eddie at CU, he looked to his family's roots in China (language, cultural practices, etc.) to understand his heritage while acknowledging that his identity was greatly informed by being born and living in the United States. This was not a conflict for him, but a blending of cultures. He created a space for himself between "two worlds" as he found he did not see his experiences reflected in mainstream American or Chinese cultures. He also described them as "two identities fused into one as a Chinese American. So they are, they can be very distinct, but I think they are kind of pushed together, forced together like in second-generation folks. I think being Chinese American is one way to be an American."

Beth shared Sam's multilayered approach to understanding her identity. Beth was born in China but immigrated to the United States when she was two and a half.

> [Racially], I guess I would say Asian. Ethnically, I would say Chinese. [Culturally], I say
> Chinese. Chinese American. I guess 'cause I kind of feel like a merging of two different
> worlds in my life. You know, I'm ethnically Chinese, but my upbringing has been Chinese
> in America, so I feel like in my life, [I'm] Chinese American.

Beth had a strong understanding of race as a social construction, and that "Asian" as a racial identity didn't exist in the same way in other places as it did in the United States. She had also talked about racial identities and dynamics through her community engagement and social justice work. This informed her thinking of race as a construction, ethnicity as heritage, and culture as common collective experiences.

Angela also understood how racial politics and constructions of "American" identities affected her. Angela immigrated from Taiwan at 14 and had a very strong identity as Chinese American. She lived with her father first in upstate New York and later in Georgia as he changed jobs. Her mother was still in Taiwan. Angela talked about her childhood and feeling pressure to assimilate to White American norms from her peers and her father.[3] Angela's Chinese American identity developed organically from her experiences.

> [Racially, I identify as] Chinese American [now]. Just being Chinese in America. It's just,
> like, Chinese American is part of being American. Because this is really how I am, and I
> feel comfortable, and I don't think anyone should have to prescribe to a certain image to
> be American. And that image is usually, you know, rich, White Americans.

Holding on to simultaneous identities without privileging one over the other was challenging for some participants, particularly Filipin@ American students at CU. While many of them understood how they identified with other Asian Americans, they could not always reconcile the distinctive experiences of Filipin@s and Filipin@ Americans in terms of colonization, immigration, class inequities, and ethnic hierarchies. While students claimed power to construct their own identities and cultural experiences, they did not always feel a part of that larger collective they created. They understood it, but were not in it. This complicated negotiation between their constructed realities and lived experiences added another dimension to understanding Asian American identities.

Mary commented, "Somewhere in there I want to fit in, like, that I do have an Asian American identity, as well, but I think at the forefront of my identity is me being Filipin@ American." Like Mary, Henry felt that "racially, I'm Asian American," but talked mostly about being Filipin@ American. Other Filipin@ American students at CU often felt marginalized by or excluded from Asian America; indeed, Leslie and Rosa identified themselves as "brown" while describing Asian Americans as "yellow." Although Leslie honored the importance of coalition, she felt the experiences of Filipin@ Americans were distinct from those of other ethnic groups.

> [Asian American] is more, like, an overarching, like, umbrella term, but for me, I know
> it doesn't apply to me. [W]hen I was growing up, like, I was, like, I'm not Asian, I'm Pacific
> Islander. ... [F]or me, it's, like, ... I felt like Asian American had this own identity. And for
> me, I didn't feel like I really was a part of it.

---

3. In the process of member checking, Angela reflected that she had actually found liberation in claiming a Chinese American identity as she had experienced emotional abuse from her father. Naming herself as Chinese American gave her space to develop her own values and sense of self, distinct from, though in relation to, her family.

For Rosa, a senior Asian American studies major and education minor, recognizing the colonial history of the Philippines, as well as the oppression of Filipin@s and Filipin@ Americans within Asian America, was very important. She struggled to reconcile the unique experiences of Filipin@ Americans within such a generalized group. Like Rosa, Christopher did not identify as Asian American, but did understand being part of a broader coalition.

As intersectionality suggests the importance of the interplay between individuals and systems, this study highlights the dynamic and constructed nature of Asian American and racial identities. These students reclaimed Asian American identity as it had been perceived and defined previously to make sense of their racial identities as lived experiences. As discussed, not all students who might be identified as Asian American chose to own such an identity. This did not exclude them from participating in Asian American communities, however, nor did it erase their contributions to Asian American identities. It does demonstrate the multifaceted and changing meanings of being Asian American and the need for complicating understandings of race, ethnicity, and culture even further.

Intersectionality as Intervention: Antiessentialism and Antiracism in Higher Education

Chinese American and Filipin@ American students created space to construct their own identities and give voice and meaning to their own experiences, as changing and evolving ways of being, and as means for resistance. The complicated and multilayered dialogue among racial, ethnic, and cultural identities—and the various ways they are taken up, ignored, owned, defined, and changed—in simultaneous processes points to the sophisticated imaginations of today's students. Participants noted that although they were empowered to determine their racial identities, they were shaped by the racist structures around them.

In higher education research, identity development models are commonly used to study Asian American students. Although these models are intended to explain how students develop a positive sense of self, they begin with the assumption that Asian Americans are born into fixed identities. The MEIM, racial identity schema, and AAID considered racial identity as ancestry (counted as a statistical variable), participation and behaviors (based on a set of values and activities identified by the researchers), or conflict (construed as the clashing of collective Asian values and individualistic European/American values). These approaches only reify the racial categories created to divide and discriminate against different groups because they conceptualize race and culture as static, fixed, and inherent. Identity development models are predicated upon essentialist notions of identity. That they are Asian American is a foregone conclusion, so the focus is on how they come to know themselves as Asian American in positive ways. Such an approach does not give space for creating meaning around being Asian American. As McCarthy and Crichlow (1993) note,

> By essentialism, we refer to the tendency in current mainstream and radical writing on race to treat social groups as stable or homogeneous entities. Racial groups such as "Asians," "Latinos," or "blacks" are therefore discussed as though members of these groups possessed some innate and invariant set of characteristics that set them apart from each other and from "whites." ... [C]urrent tendencies toward essentialism in the analysis of race

relations significantly inhibit a dynamic understanding of the operation of race and race-
based politics in education and society. (p. xviii)

Moreover, "Asian" and "Asian American" are products of White European/American imaginations, however claimed or reclaimed by individuals and communities. Traditional methods and models of racial identity development do not consider both the colonization and decolonization of bodies in the construction of racial identities. As Hall (1992) discussed, what may be of greater concern is not identity but rather identification. How one chooses—if one chooses—to identify as Asian American is grounded in the individual's construction of Asian American identities and communities. As indicated in this study, students had multiple ways of understanding, expressing, and taking up their Asian American identities, if they did so. This prismatic conceptualization of race occurred not only between individuals, but also within individuals who saw themselves and others differently, depending on relationships, contexts, and consequences. College remains an important context and time for students to explore their social identities, including race. What is needed in higher education research, as Werbner (1997) called for, is a more careful reading of how students understand and construct notions of self. Intersectionality and critical theories—such as cultural studies, queer theory, gender performance theory, critical race theory, and postcolonialism—provide innovative approaches to learning from students' lived realities and subjective experiences. Rather than adding to or combining identity models to examine multiple and simultaneous identities, scholars must find ways to incorporate intersectionality into identity studies. For example, Eddie's understanding of himself as Chinese American is predicated upon his experiences as cisgender, male, heterosexual, and middle class—including his frustrations with wanting but being unable to date a Chinese American woman. How Eddie understood being Chinese American is intimately tied to systems of racism, sexism, and patriarchy.

As student affairs practitioners, we must also consider how students are being supported and challenged in their affective growth and in cocurricular spaces. Traditional multicultural programming models also rely on essentialized concepts of culture and cultural practice.

[M]any schools attempt to achieve multicultural education by initiating multicultural student organizations. These clubs can serve educational purposes, providing opportunities for dialogue across difference and the development of political consciousness among students.... Instead, these clubs tend to host dances, organize cultural festivals, or sponsor international food fairs. Although students may learn valuable lessons through the cross-cultural collaboration necessary to coordinate "cultural" events, they are concurrently helping to maintain inequity by focusing on surface-level programming instead of authentic equity concerns. Equally important, we soften multicultural education when we invest in student organizations instead of addressing the hostile climates that make them necessary. (Gorski, 2006, p. 172)

As Gorski notes, while heritage months, holiday celebrations, and similar events provide much-needed attention and visibility, they do not challenge institutionalized racism and systemic oppression. Further, when communities must compete for funding, space, and audiences, oppressed groups are pitted against each other, losing sight of their motivations for doing this work in the first place. As a practitioner myself, I choose instead to refocus programming and student organizations on relationships and community building, emphasizing *how* we do our work together and *why* we do our work. Students may still choose to plan heritage months or events to build awareness around a particular community or issue. Administrators, practitioners, and faculty must support them in their endeavors and encourage them to consider what impact they hope to have on the campus community. I also ask students to focus on what they would like to learn in the process of planning these programs to stress that in *doing*, they are *becoming* and *constructing* what it means to be.

The struggle for power and agency in defining one's own identities is an act of cultural resistance that challenges the hierarchies of current U.S. society and alters how race may be seen and understood. By centering themselves in the American landscape and demanding that their histories and experiences be included on their college campuses and in the United States, the Asian American students in this study re/claim the power to construct themselves and what it is to be Asian American.

References

Alexander, M. (2010). *The new Jim Crow: Mass incarceration in the age of color-blindness*. New York: New Press.

Alvarez, A. N. (2002). Racial identity and Asian Americans: Supports and challenges. In M. E. McEwen, C. J. Kodama, A. N. Alvarez, S. Lee, & C. T. H. Liang (Eds.), *New directions for student services, no. 97. Working with Asian American college students* (pp. 33–43). Danvers, MA: Wiley.

Alvarez, A. N., & Helms, J. E. (2001). Racial identity and reflected appraisals as influences on Asian Americans' racial adjustment. *Cultural Diversity and Ethnic Minority Psychology, 7*(3), 217–231.

Alvarez, A. N., & Yeh, C. T. (1999). Asian Americans in college: A racial identity perspective. In D. S. Sandhu (Ed.), *Asian and Pacific Islander Americans: Issues and concerns for counseling and psychotherapy* (pp. 105–119). Commack, NY: Nova Science Publishers.

Apple, M. (1993). Series editor's introduction to race, identity, and representation in education. In C. McCarthy & W. Crichlow (Eds.), *Race, identity, and representation in education* (pp. vii–ix). New York: Routledge.

Brah, A. (2000). Difference, diversity, differentiation: Processes of racialisation and gender. In L. Back & J. Solomos (Eds.), *Theories of race and racism: A reader* (pp. 431–446). New York: Routledge.

Dill, B. T., & Zambrana, R. E. (2009). *Emerging intersections: Race, class, and gender in theory, policy, and practice*. New Brunswick, NJ: Rutgers University Press.

Goldberg, D. (1993). *Racist culture: Philosophy and the politics of meaning*. Cambridge, MA: Blackwell.

Gorski, P. C. (2006). Complicity with conservativsm: The de-politicizing of multicultural and intercultural education. *Intercultural Education, 17*(2), 163–177. doi:10.1000/14675980600693830

Grossberg, L. (1993). Cultural studies and/in new worlds. In C. McCarthy & W. Crichlow (Eds.), *Race, identity, and representation in education* (pp. 89–105). New York: Routledge.

Hall, S. (1992). The question of cultural identity. In S. Hall, D. Held, & T. McGrew (Eds.), *Modernity and its futures* (pp. 273–316). Cambridge, UK: Polity.

Jones, S. R. (2009). Constructing identities at the intersections: An autoethnographic exploration of multiple dimensions of identity. *Journal of College Student Development, 50*, 287–304. doi:10.1353/csd.0.0070

Kim, J. (1981). *Processes of Asian American identity development: A study of Japanese American women's perceptions of their struggle to achieve positive identities as Americans of Asian ancestry*. (Unpublished doctoral dissertation). University of Massachusetts, Amherst.

Kim, J. (2001). Asian American identity development theory. In C. L. Wijeyesinghe & B. W. Jackson III (Eds.), *New perspectives on racial identity development: A theoretical and practical anthology* (pp. 67–90). New York: New York University Press.

Lester, S. (1999). *An introduction to phenomenological research*. Taunton, UK: Stan Lester Developments. Retrieved from http://www.sld.demon.co.uk/resmethy.pdf

Macey, D. (2000). *The Penguin dictionary of critical theory*. London, UK: Penguin Books.

Magrini, J. (2012). Phenomenology for educators: Max van Manen and human science research. *Philosophy Scholarship*, Paper 32. Retrieved from http://dc.cod.edu/philosophypub32

McCarthy, C., & Crichlow, W. (1993). Introduction: Theories of identity, theories of representation, theories of race. In C. McCarthy & W. Crichlow (Eds.), *Race, identity, and representation in education* (pp. xiii–xxix). New York: Routledge.

Mohanty, C. T. (1989–1990). On race and voice: Challenges for liberal education in the '90s. *Cultural Critique, 18*(14), 179–208.

Morrison, G. (2010). Two separate worlds: Students of color at a predominantly White university. *Journal of Black Studies, 40*, 987–1015. doi: 10.1177/0021934708325408

Omi, M., & Winant, H. (1994). *Racial formation in the United States: From the 1960s to the 1990s*. New York: Routledge.

Patton, M. (2001). *Qualitative research and evaluation methods*. Thousand Oaks, CA: Sage.

Phinney, J. S. (1992). The multigroup ethnic identity measure: A new scale for use with diverse groups. *Journal of Adolescent Research, 7*, 175–176.

Phinney, J. S. (1996a). Understanding ethnic diversity: The role of ethnic diversity. *The American Behavioral Scientist, 40*(2), 143–152.

Phinney, J. S. (1996b). When we talk about American ethnic groups, what do we mean? *American Psychologist, 51*, 918–927.

Phinney, J. S., & Alpuria, L. (1997). *Ethnic identity in older adolescents from four ethnic groups.* Paper presented at the biennial meeting of the Society for Research in Child Development, Baltimore, MD. (ERIC Document Reproduction Service No. ED 283058)

Roman, L. G. (1993). White is a color! White defensiveness, postmodernism, and anti-racist pedagogy. In C. McCarthy & W. Crichlow (Eds.), *Race, identity, and representation in education* (pp. 71–88). New York: Routledge.

Spade, D. (2010). *Normal life: Administrative violence, critical trans politics, and the limits of the law.* Brooklyn, NY: South End.

Torres, V., Jones, S. R., & Renn, K. A. (2009). Identity development theories in student affairs: Origins, current status, and new approaches. *Journal of College Student Development, 50*(5), 577–596.

U.S. Bureau of the Census. (2002). *Annual population estimates 2000–2002.* Retrieved from https://www.census.gov/popest/data/historical/2000s/vintage_2002/

van Manen, M. (1990). *Researching lived experience: Human science for an action sensitive pedagogy.* New York: State University of New York Press.

Weber, L. (1998). A conceptual framework for understanding race, class, gender, and sexuality. *Psychology of Women Quarterly, 22*, 13–32. Retrieved from EBSCO database

Werbner, P. (1997). Introduction: The dialects of cultural hybridity. In P. Werbner & T. Modood (Eds.), *Debating cultural hybridity: Multicultural identities and the politics of anti-racism* (pp. 1–28). London: Zed Books.

Post-Reading Questions

1. Do some outside research: according to sociological sources, what are some of the differences between race and ethnicity?
2. In the research study, what were some of the different ways that Chinese American and Filipinx American college students perceived their social identities?
3. What is intersectionality? How can this perspective help us to understand race and ethnicity better?

Immigration and Growing Diversity

John Iceland

The United States is often said to be a land of immigrants—and with good reason. Immigration from a wide variety of other countries has continuously changed the character of this country. The initial wave of colonial settlement from England and around it—along with the large number of involuntary immigrants from Africa sold into slavery—eventually gave way to immigration from the rest of northern and western Europe in the early to mid-1800s. The stream of immigration then shifted to eastern and southern Europe by the end of the nineteenth century. Immigration slowed to a trickle after the passage of restrictive laws in the 1920s, aided and abetted by two world wars and a deep depression, before once again accelerating in the last decades of the twentieth century. During this last wave, immigrants came from an even broader array of countries spanning the globe—millions from Asia, Latin America, and Africa.

For a land of immigrants, however, the subject of immigration has long been a source of considerable political contention in the United States. Debates have generally centered around two issues: (1) the extent to which immigrants are assimilating and (2) the overall social and economic impact of immigration on the nation. New groups of immigrants from differing origins have long been viewed with suspicion by a substantial portion of the native-born population. Many have worried that immigrants weaken the character of the country or that they are too different from the native born to assimilate or, worse yet, indifferent to assimilating altogether. Others have fretted that immigrants are a drain on the economy, or that they bring crime and social disorganization to our nation's cities and communities, or that they take jobs away from native-born Americans. These debates on immigration have echoed across generations.

For example, many nativists reacted with alarm to the increasing immigration of Catholics from Germany and Ireland in the early eighteenth century. Catholics, who were associated with the pope and other monarchies of Europe, were viewed by some as an internal threat who might undermine the republic. As historian Roger Daniels recounts:

> When relatively large numbers of Irish and German Catholic immigrants, many of them desperately poor, began to arrive in the late 1820s and early 1830s, what had been a largely rhetorical anti-Catholicism became a major social and political force in American life. Not surprisingly, it was in eastern cities, particularly Boston, where anti-Catholicism turned violent, and much of the violence was directed against convents and churches. Beginning with the burning down of the Ursuline Convent just outside Boston by a mob on August 11, 1834, well into the 1850s violence against Catholic institutions was so prevalent that insurance companies all but refused to insure them.[1]

By the end of the century, when immigrants from southern and eastern Europe were pouring in, the targets of the nativists changed, though many of the underlying concerns were the same. As Daniels again relates:

> But lurking behind and sometimes overshadowing these [religious and economic] objections to continued immigration was a growing and pervasive racism, a racism directed not against non-white races, but against presumed inferior peoples of European origin. ... According to one of its founders [of an immigration restriction league], the question for Americans to decide was whether they wanted their country "to be peopled by British, German and Scandinavian stock, historically free, energetic, progressive, or by Slav, Latin and Asiatic races (this latter referred to Jews rather than Chinese or Japanese), historically down-trodden, atavistic and stagnant."[2]

As immigration from non-European countries picked up steam after changes in immigration policy enacted in 1965, many commentators again raised the alarm of immigration's effect on the character of the nation. Writing in 1995, immigration policy critic Peter Brimelow argued that the 1965 law resulted in immigration that is "dramatically larger, less skilled, and more divergent from the American majority than anything that was anticipated or desired ... is probably not beneficial to the economy ... is attended by a wide and increasing range of negative consequences, from the physical environment to the political ... [and] is bringing about an ethnic and racial transformation in America without precedent in the history of the world—an astonishing social experiment launched with no particular reason to expect success." Indeed, he asks, "Is America still that interlacing of ethnicity and culture we call a nation—and can the American nation-state, the political expression of that nation, survive?" Given that his book is titled *Alien Nation: Common Sense about America's Immigration Disaster*, one may not be surprised to find out that Brimelow offers a pessimistic answer to this question.[3]

The rest of this [reading] addresses issues raised in these immigration debates by tackling the following basic questions: To what extent is immigration changing the racial and ethnic composition of the country? Are immigrants being successfully integrated into society? What is the economic and social impact of immigration? How does America's experience with immigration compare with those of other countries?

1. Daniels 2002, 266.
2. Daniels 2002, 275–76.
3. Brimelow 1995, 9 and 232.

A review of the research on these issues can give us a better sense of the types of policies the United States should consider pursuing, keeping in mind that policy is usually driven by a diverse set of constituents with sometimes competing goals.

Immigration Policy and Current Immigration Patterns

From the founding of the country until about 1875 the United States had an open-door immigration policy. The Naturalization Act of 1790 allowed immigrants to acquire citizenship after several years of residence in the United States, and there were no legal restrictions on the number of immigrants or on places of origin. From time to time throughout the nineteenth century there was serious opposition to immigration—or at least to immigrants from certain origins—but these efforts did not have a significant impact on national policy. As noted above, the feeling was sometimes quite vehement, resulting in periodic violence against certain groups, such as Roman Catholics from Ireland.[4]

By the end of the nineteenth century there was considerable debate about the number of immigrants from southern and eastern Europe. In addition, on the West Coast many opposed immigration from China and Japan, as these immigrants were seen as undercutting the economic prospects of the native born.[5] In all cases, racism undoubtedly played a role, for these groups were often considered inferior to the native stock, and the extent to which they could assimilate into American society was also questioned. After the passage of mainly minor laws that barred the entry of convicts and prostitutes in 1875, Congress passed the Immigration Act of 1882, which prohibited immigration from China.[6] Japanese immigration was later limited in 1907 with the "Gentleman's Agreement," in which Japan was pressured to agree not to issue passports to Japanese citizens interested in immigrating to the United States, and the United States agreed to accept the presence of Japanese immigrants already in the country.

The Immigration Act of 1921 was the first law to put a ceiling on the overall number of immigrants allowed entry into the United States, followed by the even tougher Immigration Act of 1924. The 1924 law limited the number of immigrants from any country to 2 percent of the number of people from that country who were already living in the United States in 1890. By using 1890 as the base year for the quotas, the law had the effect of reducing the number of immigrants from southern and eastern Europe, who came in large numbers to the United States especially after that time. Levels of immigration plummeted after these legislative acts and remained low also in part because of the Great Depression in the 1930s and World War II in the early 1940s.[7]

Immigration policy generally became less restrictive in a number of small ways during and after World War II. Perhaps in part a reaction to the racist excesses of Nazism, overt racism in the United States increasingly fell out of favor. In general, many Americans felt that more effort should be made to harmonize policies with basic American ideals of liberty and equality of opportunity.[8] President Franklin Delano

4. Daniels 2002, 267–69.
5. Martin and Midgley 2006, 12. See also Daniels 2002, 271.
6. Martin and Midgley 2006, 12.
7. Daniels 2002, 287.
8. Daniels 2002, 329.

Roosevelt, for example, passed an executive order in 1941 that forbade racial discrimination by defense contractors. The Chinese exclusion laws were repealed in 1943, and the Luce-Celler Act of 1946 prohibited discrimination against Indian Americans and Filipinos, who were accorded the right to naturalization. The Immigration and Nationality Act of 1952 revised the quotas, basing them on the 1920 census (rather than the 1890 census).

In the meantime, immigration from Mexico began increasing in the 1940s and 1950s, largely as a result of the Bracero Program, which aimed to bring contract laborers temporarily to the United States to fill labor shortages, especially in agriculture. Workers were paid low wages, often endured difficult working conditions, and were expected to return to Mexico after their contract expired. The Bracero Program was extended several times before formally ending in the mid-1960s.[9]

At about this time another momentous piece of immigration legislation was passed—the 1965 amendments to the Immigration and Nationality Act (also known as the Hart-Celler Act). This act did away with the discriminatory national quota system and instead set more uniform annual quotas across countries. While supporters of the bill sought to make immigration policy less discriminatory, they did not think it would drastically affect immigration patterns. Senator Edward Kennedy, chair of the Senate Immigration Subcommittee that was managing the bill, asserted, "First, our cities will not be flooded with a million immigrants annually. Under the proposed bill, the present level of immigration remains substantially the same. … Secondly, the ethnic mix of this country will not be upset."[10] The bill set an overall cap of 170,000 visas per year, later raised to 290,000. A number of people were, and continue to be, exempt from quotas, including spouses, children, and parents of U.S. citizens, as well as refugees and other smaller categories of immigrants. In 2009, for example, about 47 percent of the 1.1 million people who gained legal permanent residential status in the United States were immediate relatives of U.S. citizens who were exempt from the numerical quotas.[11]

Senator Kennedy's assurances notwithstanding, the most significant effect of the Hart-Celler Act was that it spurred immigration from countries that had little recent history of sending immigrants to the United States, especially Asia and later Africa. (Immigration from Latin America had been in increasing in the years before the passage of the law, so it is not clear whether the law was responsible for spurring any further migration from that region.)[12] Figure 12.1 shows the number and changing origins of the immigrant population from 1900 to 2009. While the number of immigrants arriving annually was higher between 1900 and 1909 than in the middle decades of the twentieth century, by the 1990s the number of immigrants arriving surpassed all previous levels. The United States received a historical high of over 1 million legal immigrants annually in the 2000s, with many more undocumented immigrants as well. (About 11 million undocumented immigrants lived in the United States in 2011.)[13] However, because of the

9. Daniels 2002, 310–11.
10. Brimelow 1995, 76–77.
11. Martin and Midgley 2010, 2.
12. Daniels 2002, 311.
13. Passel and Cohn 2012.

smaller population base at that time, the proportion of the population that was foreign born in 1910 (15 percent) was still higher than the proportion foreign born a hundred years later in 2010 (13 percent).[14]

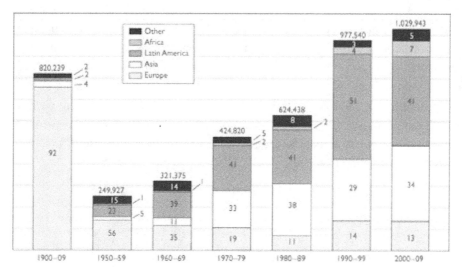

FIGURE 12.1   Annual number of legal U.S. immigrants, by decade, and their percentage distributions, by region of origin, 1900–2009. Note: The Y axis demarcates numbers of immigrants in increments of a hundred thousand. The shadings and numbers within the graph's bars indicate percentages of immigrants from the different regions of origin. The Latin America category includes Mexico, Central America, the Caribbean, and South America. The Other category consists mainly of immigrants from Canada in the 1950–59 and 1960–69 periods, though it also includes immigrants from Oceania and a small proportion of immigrants whose origin was not known in the 1980–89 and 2000–2009 periods.

Source: U.S. Department of Homeland Security 2012.

Whereas 92 percent of all legal immigrants were from Europe in the 1900–1909 period, this dropped to just 19 percent in the 1970s and 13 percent in the first decade of the 2000s. Meanwhile, the proportion of immigrants from Latin America grew from only 2 percent in 1900–1909 to 23 percent in the 1950s to a peak of 51 percent in the 1990s, before dropping back to 41 percent in the 2000s. The proportion of immigrants from Asia grew rapidly in the 1960s through the 1990s; by the 2000s Asians constituted about a third of legal immigrants. Since 2009, the number of immigrants from Asia has surpassed the number from Latin America.[15] Immigration from Africa was negligible over most of the period, though it has increased in the last couple of decades, such that African immigrants made up 7 percent of all immigrants in the 2000s.[16]

Changing immigration patterns and differential fertility rates (higher fertility rates among minority groups than among whites) have had a major effect on the racial and ethnic composition of the U.S. population. Figure 12.2 shows that 63 percent of the population was non-Hispanic white in 2011, down

14. Daniels 2002, tables 6.4 and 16.2; Migration Policy Institute 2012b.
15. Pew Research Center 2013.
16. U.S. Department of Homeland Security 2012.

from 83 percent in 1970. The percentage of the population that is African American held steady, constituting 12 percent of the total population in 2011. Meanwhile, the percentage of the population that is Hispanic has increased rapidly, from 5 percent in 1970 to 17 percent in 2011. The Asian population has likewise increased significantly, from 1 to 5 percent over the period. The U.S. Census Bureau projects that by 2060, just 43 percent of the population will be non-Hispanic white, 13 percent will be African American, 8 percent will be Asian, and 31 percent will be Hispanic.[17] These projections, however, should be viewed with caution, as they incorporate assumptions about immigration trends, fertility rates, and future patterns of racial and ethnic identification. For example, recent research has shown that Latino fertility rates may not be as high as commonly thought, and that how people view their identity over time and across generations often changes.[18] Nevertheless, it is safe to say that racial and ethnic diversity in the United States will continue to increase in the coming decades.

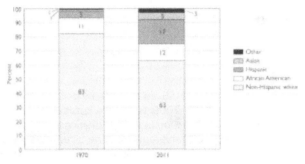

FIGURE 12.2   Racial/ethnic composition of the United States, 1970 and 2011.

Sources: 1970 data from Martin and Midgely 2010, 3; 2011 data from Motel and Patten 2013, table 1.

[...] What Is Assimilation?

Assimilation refers to the reduction of ethnic group distinctions over time. In the past the term has sometimes been used to mean Anglo conformity; that is, assimilation occurs when an immigrant group adopts the mores and practices of old-stock native-born white Americans. More recent assimilation theorists emphasize that assimilation need not be a one-way street on which minority members become more like the majority group members. Rather, assimilation involves a general convergence of social, economic, and cultural patterns that typically also involve the upward mobility of immigrants and their children.[19]

Assimilation is often not a conscious decision in which an immigrant decides to shed his or her cultural practices and heritage in the pursuit of another culture's. Rather, as Richard Alba and Victor Nee note, assimilation is a lengthy process that typically spans generations: "To the extent that assimilation occurs, it proceeds incrementally as an intergenerational process, stemming both from individuals' purposive action and from the unintended consequences of their workaday decisions. In the case of

17. U.S. Census Bureau 2012i.

18. Parrado 2011; Parrado and Flippen 2012; Duncan and Trejo 2011b.

19. Alba and Nee 2003, 11.

immigrants and their descendants who may not intentionally seek to assimilate, the cumulative effect of pragmatic decisions aimed at successful adaptation can give rise to changes in behavior that nevertheless lead to eventual assimilation."[20]

Commentators who believe that immigrants of old were eager to assimilate—unlike contemporary immigrants—are not well acquainted with the historical record. Historian Roger Daniels describes how German immigrants in the nineteenth century came mostly for economic reasons, remained very proud of their homeland, and sought to retain their cultural practices:

> Indispensable for most cultural institutions that were intended to endure beyond the immigrant generation was some way of ensuring that the second and subsequent generations learn and use the ancestral language—what scholars now call language maintenance. ... Beginning with parochial schools, largely but not exclusively Lutheran and Catholic, Germans eventually turned to the public schools and political action in [an] attempt to make German instruction in all subjects available when enough parents wanted it. In such public schools, English might be taught as a special subject as if it were a foreign language, which, of course, it was and is to many young children of immigrants raised in essentially monolingual homes. And in many parochial schools, English was not taught at all.[21]

Daniels notes that German culture remained very strong and proudly expressed until World War I, when the conflict pitting Germany against England, France, and eventually the United States led to strong anti-German feeling in many quarters. Still, even today many communities in the Midwest have strong German roots and cultural heritage.

Ties to the United States were also, at least initially, weak among many immigrants from a number of other sending countries. For example, of the 4.1 million Italians recorded as entering the United States between 1880 and 1920, anywhere from about 30 percent to nearly half returned to Italy.[22] Over the years, many immigrants have been attracted primarily by economic opportunities rather than by the notion of becoming American. Italians, like many other immigrant groups, were also concentrated in particular neighborhoods of particular cities (such as Little Italy in New York City), and they were concentrated in specific occupations as well, such as in low- and semiskilled trades like construction and pushcart vending. Many native-born Americans stereotyped Italians as criminals, pointing to tight-knit criminal organizations such as the Mafia.[23] Here we see that contemporary concerns with crime in immigrant communities (e.g., Hispanic gangs today) and the stereotyping of immigrant groups are nothing new.

Still, just because immigrants of previous waves of immigration from Europe assimilated does not mean that more recent immigrants from Latin America, Asia, and Africa will have the same experience. Commentators have pointed to a number of differences in the conditions under which these different waves have arrived in the United States.[24] Perhaps the most prominent of the arguments is that immigrants today

20. Alba and Nee 2003, 38.
21. Daniels 2002, 159.
22. Daniels 2002, 189.
23. Daniels 2002, 195–98.
24. See Alba and Nee 2003 for a detailed discussion of these issues.

are racially more distinct than those in the past. The counterview is that despite our perception of previous waves of immigrants from Europe as essentially "white," historical accounts indicate that many among those immigrant groups, including the Irish, Jews, and Italians, were perceived to be racially distinct from the majority of native-born Americans. As Daniels writes: "However curious it may seem today, by the late nineteenth century many of the 'best and brightest' minds in America had become convinced that of all the many 'races' (we would say 'ethnic groups') of Europe one alone—variously called Anglo-Saxon, Aryan, Teutonic, or Nordic—had superior innate characteristics. Often using a crude misapplication of Darwinian evolution, which substituted these various 'races' for Darwinian species, historians, political scientists, economists, and, later, eugenicists discovered that democratic political institutions had developed and could thrive only among Anglo-Saxon peoples."[25] The idea that immigrants from different European countries constituted different races diminished only over time as various groups achieved socioeconomic mobility.[26]

Nevertheless, a number of people remain skeptical about the successful integration of many of today's immigrant groups into American society. A competing theoretical perspective—*ethnic disadvantage*—holds that even if new immigrants learn the language and customs of their new country, they may still not be able to achieve significant socioeconomic mobility or acceptance by the white mainstream. Discrimination, for example, may put many educational opportunities or jobs out of reach for newcomers.

One viewpoint somewhere between the two (assimilation and ethnic disadvantage) is *segmented assimilation*. This perspective focuses on divergent patterns of incorporation among contemporary immigrants.[27] It asserts that the host society offers uneven possibilities to different immigrant groups, some of whom might achieve upward mobility and be successfully assimilated into the mainstream, others who will be marginalized and will adopt harmful cultural practices of disadvantaged native-born groups and experience downward mobility, and yet others who will retain strong ethnic ties and still achieve high levels of socioeconomic success. According to this perspective, racial discrimination and the range of economic opportunities available in a particular place at a particular time may shape assimilation trajectories of immigrants and their children. A number of studies have tested these perspectives. [...]

25. Daniels 2002, 276.
26. Alba and Nee 2003, 131–32.
27. Portes and Zhou 1993; Zhou 1999, 196–211.

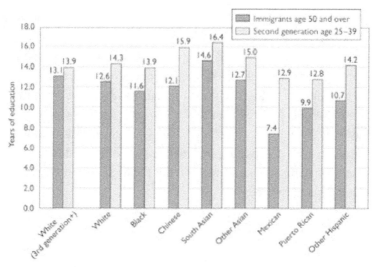

FIGURE 12.3   Years of education, by generation, age, and ethnic origin, among U.S. native born and immigrants, 1995–2007. Note: The first set of bars refers to native-born populace; all others refer to immigrants or their offspring. Following the same key that pertains to the other categories, the first bar in the set for 3rd generation+ whites refers to whites 50 and over, and the second bar refers to 3rd-generation whites ages 25–39.

Source: Reitz, Zhang, and Hawkins 2011, table 1, using Current Population Survey data.

A Final Note on Immigration Policy

Immigration reform has been discussed from time to time in recent years in the United States, mostly focusing on reducing the number of illegal immigrants currently in the country and attracting immigrants that would boost our economy. In some quarters, support for an expanded guest-worker program in the United States is considerable, especially among large businesses that would like to recruit low-wage workers for agricultural work or other labor-intensive work. While there may be good short-term economic reasons to have a guest-worker program, the entry of a large number of temporary, low-skill workers with relatively few rights or prospects for legal incorporation through citizenship may result in the growth of a socially, economically, and politically marginalized constituency. As indicated above, the record of guest-worker programs in western European countries suggests that such immigrants are not usually content to simply go home after they are no longer needed. In fact, approximately 25 to 40 percent of undocumented immigrants in the United States are visa overstayers rather than people who crossed the border illegally.[28] For similar reasons, providing the means for current undocumented immigrants to eventually attain citizenship will likely help them and their children more easily integrate into American society.

On the other hand, policies that favor admitting more immigrants on the basis of education and skills could serve to boost our economy, as such immigrants often engage in highly productive work. They are also more likely to have a positive fiscal impact on national, state, and local budgets through the higher

28. Passel 2005.

taxes that they pay as compared with lower-skill immigrants. As noted above, the children of high-skill immigrants are also more likely to do well in school and in the labor market and are thus less likely to be marginalized and isolated. Of course, it should be said that immigration policy should not be shaped only on the basis of economic cost-benefit analyses. Immigration policy has long had an important humanitarian component that should help inform policy decisions as well. For example, many countries, including the United States and those of Europe, have policies that allow refugees from dangerous, war-torn countries to immigrate, believing that it would be inhumane to allow them to face extreme hardship or death if they remained. Over the years, such groups have included Jewish refugees during World War II, Vietnamese refugees from the Vietnam War, and Somali refugees in the 2000s seeking to escape the anarchy and clan warfare occurring in many parts of the country.

Conclusion

Immigration has contributed to increasing racial and ethnic diversity in communities across the United States. While the United States is a land of immigrants, fears about the impact of immigration and whether new immigrants are capable of assimilating have been frequently expressed over the years and continually crop up in policy debates on the issue. Research on the recent, post-1965 wave of immigration tends to show that immigrants are by and large being integrated into American society. The second generation tends to have higher levels of education and earnings than their immigrant parents, and that generation also achieves greater parity with whites. The native-born second generation also tends to be less residentially segregated than the first generation. Nevertheless, there is significant variation across immigrant groups, with Asians having the highest levels of attainment. Asian immigrants tend to have relatively high levels of education, and this confers advantages to their children in school and in the labor market. Hispanic immigrants come with relatively low levels of education, and while their children tend to do better than their parents, on average they do not achieve parity with whites. The children of black immigrants likewise achieve some measure of mobility but remain disadvantaged relative to the mainstream; racial discrimination may impact their life chances.

Many studies have also examined the economic and fiscal impacts of immigration. They have generally found that immigrants do not have much of an impact on the employment or wages of most of the native born, though there might be a small negative effect on the wages of low-skilled native-born workers. This effect is generally small because immigrants are often complements of rather than substitutes for American workers; also immigrants often create jobs and are consumers too, which can spur economic growth. Indeed, immigrants are more likely to be entrepreneurs than native-born workers, and high-skill immigrants have been crucial in spurring innovative economic activity in science and technology, such as in Silicon Valley.

The fiscal impact of immigration is small in the aggregate. Immigrants consume government services (such as public education), but they also pay taxes. Highly educated immigrants tend to pay more than they consume in public services. The federal government budget may benefit from immigration, because a large majority of immigrants (including many illegal immigrants with fake Social Security cards) pay federal payroll taxes, though some local governments are harder hit because of small tax collections from immigrants and the cost of locally financed services (such as schools).

More diverse areas sometimes experience intergroup conflict and have less social cohesion and social capital than more ethnically homogeneous areas, at least in the short run, but communities that can successfully incorporate immigrants often forge larger, more inclusive identities over the long run. In the United States at least, immigration in recent decades has not been associated with more crime; immigrants themselves often contribute economically to poor communities and are not particularly prone to criminal activity or violence.

International migration is increasing worldwide. Many European countries that used to send migrants elsewhere in the nineteenth century have, in the post–World War II period, received many immigrants from abroad. These countries struggle with many of the same issues that immigration raises in the United States, such as the considerable concern about whether immigrants and their children—particularly those who are "visible minorities"—will integrate into society. While different host countries and different immigrant groups experience considerable variation, there are signs that integration is occurring in many European countries as well. These trends have not silenced debates on immigration in the United States or abroad, as many are still concerned about how immigration will continue to change the character of their country and how immigrants of the future will fare.

References

Alba, Richard, and Victor Nee. 2003. *Remaking the American Mainstream: Assimilation and Contemporary Immigration*. Cambridge, MA: Harvard University Press.

Brimelow, Peter. 1995. *Alien Nation: Common Sense about America's Immigration Disaster*. New York: Random House.

Daniels, Roger. 2002. *Coming to America*. 2nd ed. New York: Perennial.

Duncan, Brian, and Stephen J. Trejo. 2011b. "Tracking Intergenerational Progress for Immigrant Groups: The Problem of Ethnic Attrition." *American Economic Review* 101 (3): 603–8.

Martin, Philip, and Elizabeth Midgley. 2006. "Immigration: Shaping and Reshaping America." Population Reference Bureau, *Population Bulletin* 61 (4) (December).

– – –. 2010. "Immigration in America 2010." Population Reference Bureau, *Population Bulletin Update* (June).

Migration Policy Institute. 2012b. "2010 American Community Survey and Census Data on the Foreign Born by State." Data Hub information. Available at www.migration-information.org/datahub/acscensus.cfm (accessed September 18, 2012).

Parrado, Emilio A. 2011. "How High Is Hispanic/Mexican Fertility in the United States? Immigration and Tempo Considerations." *Demography* 48: 1059–80.

Parrado, Emilio A., and Chenoa A. Flippen. 2012. "Hispanic Fertility, Immigration, and Race in the Twenty-First Century." *Race and Social Problems* 4 (1): 18–30.

Passel, Jeffrey S. 2005. *Unauthorized Migrants: Numbers and Characteristics*. Pew Hispanic Center Research Report, June 14. Available at pewhispanic.org/files/reports/46.pdf (accessed March 13, 2013).

Passel, Jeffrey, and d'Vera Cohn. 2012. *Unauthorized Immigrants: 11.1 Million in 2011*. Pew Research Hispanic Trends Project Brief. Available at www.pewhispanic.org/2012/12/06/unauthorized-immigrants-11-1-million-in-2011/ (accessed August 19, 2013).

Pew Research Center. 2013. *The Rise of Asian Americans*. Pew Research, Social and Demographic Trends Report, June 19, 2012, updated on April 4, 2013. Available at www.pewsocialtrends.org/2012/06/19/the-rise-of-asian-americans/ (accessed August 20, 2013).

Portes, Alejandro, and Min Zhou. 1993. "The New Second Generation: Segmented Assimilation and Its Variants among Post-1965 Immigrant Youth." *Annals of the American Academy of Political and Social Science* 530 (November): 74–96.

U.S. Census Bureau. 2012i. "Table 4. Projections of the Population by Sex, Race, and Hispanic Origin for the United States: 2015 to 2060." Population Division release NP2012-T4. Available at www.census.gov/population/projections/data/national/2012/summarytables.html (accessed February 15, 2013).

U.S. Department of Homeland Security. 2012. "Table 2. Yearbook of Immigration Statistics: 2011." Data on Legal Permanent Residents. Available at www.dhs.gov/yearbook-immigration-statistics-2011-1 (accessed September 18, 2012).

Zhou, Min. 1999. "Segmented Assimilation: Issues, Controversies, and Recent Research on the New Second Generation." In *The Handbook of International Migration: The American Experience,* edited by Charles Hirschman, Philip Kasinitz, and Josh DeWind. New York: Russell Sage Foundation.

Post-Reading Questions

1. What is the Hart–Cellar Act? How did it change immigration policy?
2. What are some of the social debates you have heard about immigration? How are these debates informed by racialized perceptions of immigrants?
3. What are the differences between ethnic disadvantage theory and segmented assimilation theory? Which do you think best helps us understand the experiences of immigrants in society?

Latino Post-Millennials Create America's Future

David Hayes-Bautista

In June 2015, Donald Trump announced his candidacy for the upcoming Republican presidential nomination, and he wasted little time in laying down his nativist platform, announcing in a campaign speech, "When Mexico sends its people ... they're bringing drugs. They're bringing crime. They're rapists."[1] Just before Game Three of the 2013 National Basketball Association finals in San Antonio, eleven-year-old Sebastien de la Cruz sang the US national anthem, dressed in a mariachi suit. As soon as his televised image appeared, nativists exploded in anger on social media. "Who let this illegal alien sing our national anthem?" demanded one such tweet.[2] The blog *Public Shaming,* mentioned by a CNN article on the national anthem flap as an archival source, preserved a number of the tweets, in which Sebastien was described as a "beaner," "foreigner," "wetback," "illegal," "Mexican kid," "illegal alien," "little beaner," "lil Mexican snuck in the country like 4 hours ago," and "9 out of 10 chances that kid ... is illegal."[3] Yet young Sebastien was a native-born US citizen, and his

1. Timothy Egan, "A Refuge for Racists: What Draws Extremist Hate Groups to the G.O.P.?" *New York Times,* 28 June 2015, p. SR11.
2. Cindy Y. Rodriguez, "Mexican-American Boy's National Anthem Sparks Racist Comments," CNN, 16 September 2013, http://www.cnn.com/2013/06/12/us/mexican-american-boy-sings-anthem/ [accessed 13 January 2016].
3. Matt Binder, "Racist Basketball Fans PISSED a[t] Mexican-American Boy [Who] Dared to Sing Their [National] Anthem," *Public Shaming,* Tumblr (blog), 12 June 2013, http://publicshaming.tumblr.com/post/52763976629/racist-basket-ball-fans-pissed-a-mexican-american [accessed 13 January 2016]. Date appears in "View Page Source"; author identified in "About" section of the blog.

father was a US military veteran. In 2012, Angel Rodriguez, a US citizen born in Puerto Rico, playing guard for the Kansas State basketball team against Southern Mississippi, stepped up to the free throw line. In an attempt to distract him, Southern Miss band members chanted, "Where's your green card?" A *USA Today* report on the incident added parenthetically, "A quick geography lesson: Puerto Rico is a part of the United States. If you're born in Puerto Rico, you're an American citizen."[4] That same year, NBC Latino reported on a study showing that, partly as a result of nearly twenty years of nativist complaints about the growing Latino presence in the US, for many Americans "the words 'Latino' and 'illegal immigrant' were one and the same." NBC Latino also quoted the president of the National Hispanic Media Coalition complaining about the disservice the media were doing by presenting "coverage that is misleading the public about Latinos who live in the U.S."[5]

Latino Population Has Been Growing for Five Hundred Years

The idea that "Latino" is synonymous with "illegal immigrant"—and many more such beliefs, broadcast daily—reinforces the widely promulgated nativist perception that Latinos are nearly all fairly recently arrived immigrants, most of whom did not have authorized entry. But this perception is erroneous. Twenty-first-century Latinos are heirs to nearly five hundred years of settled presence within the boundaries of what we now call the United States. [...] After California was acquired by the United States in 1848, Latinos, through a process of ethnogenesis during the Gold Rush and the American Civil War, created a bilingual, bicultural Latino civil society in the state that has continued into the twenty-first century. California's Latino experience is not unique. The same experience of mixed-race, Spanish-speaking settlers bringing Western society into territories now part of the US was repeated widely. The oldest city in US territory has been continuously inhabited for nearly five hundred years, since its founding in 1521: San Juan, in Puerto Rico.[6]

For three hundred years after San Juan was founded, groups of multiracial, Spanish-speaking settlers set out from Mexico, Cuba, Puerto Rico, and the island of Hispaniola, bringing Western society to the landmass to the north. By the time the United States was recognized as an independent country, in 1783, Spanish-speaking populations residing in pueblos, presidios, missions, ranches, and farms were scattered from St. Augustine in Florida to San Francisco in Alta California, their daily activities informed by the Indo-Afro-Oriento-Ibero experiences of Western society. During the nineteenth century, the young US expanded in size, acquiring further territory and people with origins in this Spanish-speaking version of Western society. Its first acquisition, in 1803, was the Louisiana Purchase, which was part of the

4. Nicole Auerbach, "Southern Miss Band Chants 'Where's Your Green Card?'" *USA Today,* 15 March 2012, http://content.usatoday.com/communities/campusrivalry/post/2012/03/southern-miss-band-chants-wheres-your-green-card/1#.Vpbp6xgrLZs [accessed 14 January 2016].

5. Sandra Lilley, "Poll: 1 out of 3 Americans Inaccurately Think Most Hispanics Are Undocumented," *NBC Latino,* 12 September 2012, http://nbclatino.com/2012/09/12/poll-1-out-of-3-americans-think-most-hispanics-are-undocumented/ [accessed 14 January 2016].

6. Felipe Fernández-Armesto, *Our America: A Hispanic History of the United States* (New York: W. W. Norton, 2014), pp. 3–4.

Spanish Empire from 1762 to 1803.[7] This acquisition of Spanish-speaking peoples continued, sporadically, throughout the nineteenth century. The Adams-Onís Treaty in 1819 led to the acquisition of Florida and its people; the Texas Annexation of 1845 brought in the *tejanos;* the Treaty of Guadalupe-Hidalgo, in 1848, acquired California, Nevada, New Mexico, Arizona, Utah, and Colorado, with their respective Spanish-speaking populations. Finally, with the 1898 Treaty of Paris, the US acquired the islands of Puerto Rico and the Philippines, and established a protectorate over Cuba. In each of the acquired territories, the Spanish-speaking population began a process of ethnogenesis, creating local variants of the bilingual, bicultural society of the Latinos of the US. [M]uch the same process took place wherever Spanish-speaking populations found themselves placed by political decisions in a new country without their having to take one step.

But those earlier population movements from Mexico and Latin America did not stop once the US acquired these new territories. Indeed, new waves of immigration occurred after each acquisition. At times these were spurred by events in the US, such as the Gold Rush, the US's need for labor, or changes in immigration law. At other times, they were driven by events in the immigrants' home countries, such as the French Intervention in Mexico in the 1860s, the Mexican Revolution in the early twentieth century, and the Cuban Revolution in the 1950s. Those post-acquisition immigrants generally settled into Latino communities that had taken root prior to their acquisition by the US, and largely learned about American society and identity from their already established neighbors. The newer immigrants tended to live in the same neighborhoods as the established Latino populations, to worship in the same churches, to shop in the same stores, and to attend the same local civic events, such as Puerto Rican Independence Day or the Cinco de Mayo. The children of each wave of Spanish-speaking immigrants tended to marry the children of the earlier, established groups; and as these new families were formed, the bilingual, bicultural society formed generations earlier was renewed, with each new US-born generation giving it new twists and turns.

Most educational curricula in the United States have largely ignored the experiences of these populations acquired by a century of US expansion; as a result, the erroneous general public perception of Latinos is that most of them have only recently arrived in this country. The fact is that from 1980 to the present, the majority of Latinos in the US were born in the US. In 2013, nearly two-thirds (65%) of all Latinos in the US were born in the country; only a little over one-third (35%) were immigrants.[8] Moreover, a 2014 Pew Research Center report announced that the percentage of the population who were Latino was returning, in some western states, to what it had been in the historical past. In 1870, for example, New Mexico was overwhelmingly (89.9%) Latino. By 1910, however, Latinos made up scarcely more than one-third (35.4%) of the state's population; by 1950, the proportion of Latinos had dropped to only about a fourth. Yet by 2012, it had grown again, to almost half the total population (47.0%). In 1870, Arizona likewise was nearly two-thirds (60.9%) Latino. The proportion dropped to about a third (35.4%) by 1910, and fell nearly to 20% by 1970. Since then, however, the Latino population has grown to be nearly a third (30.2%) of the state's total. In 1870, Colorado's population was over a quarter (29.8%) Latino, but by 1910, it was only 3.2% Latino. Yet from that point on, Colorado's Latino population has grown, slowly and steadily,

---

7. In 1803, Spain ceded the territory back to France just weeks before France sold it to the US.
8. Gustavo López and Eileen Patten, "The Impact of Slowing Immigration: Foreign-Born Share Falls among 14 Largest
   U.S. Hispanic Groups" (Washington, DC: Pew Research Center, September 2015), p. 4, figure 1.

and in 2012 was moving toward being one-fourth (21.0%) again. This report attributes these increases to immigration, but the example of California suggests that a good deal of it is due to natural increase as well.[9]

Far from being nearly all recently arrived undocumented immigrants, Latinos have a long-established presence in what is now the US. The wave of immigration from Latin America to the US from 1965 to 2005 was only the latest during nearly five hundred years of population growth. That wave has now receded, and Latino population growth presently comes primarily from births. The US Census Bureau recently estimated that the Latino population of the US will grow over the next forty years, from the 2014 total of 55.4 million to a projected total of 119.0 million by 2060. At that point, nearly one out of every three Americans will be Latino.[10] [...]

Latino Post-Millennials: The US-Born Old Enough to Vote

As repeatedly noted, the vast majority of Latino post-millennials are native-born citizens. The National Center for Health Statistics recently released a report on births in the US, presented in figure 13.1. Although keeping in mind the Pew Millennial Research Project's caution that the years chosen to divide one generation from another are somewhat arbitrary, and may not be identified as such until decades after a generation's birth, we have used the Pew's general rule of thumb that the post-millennial generation consists of those born from 1997 onward. In 1997, about three-quarters of a million (709,767) Latino babies were born in the US. The number of Latino babies increased rapidly, though, and in 2006 a little over 1 million (1,039,077) were born. After staying above the 1 million mark for three years, the number of births then decreased, to a little under 1 million, reaching a low in 2013 of 901,033, then rebounding slightly to 914,065 in 2014. In essence, since 2003, about 1 million Latinos have been born every year.

9. Jens Manuel Krogstad and Mark Hugo Lopez, "For Three States, Share of Hispanic Population Returns to the Past" (Pew Research Center report, 10 June 2014), http://www.pewresearch.org/fact-tank/2014/06/10/for-three-states-share-of-hispanic-population-returns-to-the-past/ [accessed 14 December 2014].
10. Sandra L. Colby and Jennifer M. Ortman, *Projections of the Size and Composition of the U.S. Population: 2014 to 2060*, US Census Bureau Current Population Reports (Washington, DC: US Census Bureau, US Department of Commerce, March 2015), p. 9.

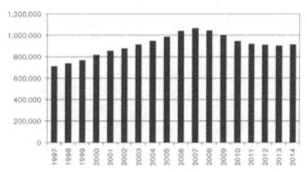

FIGURE 13.1   Latino births in the United States, 1997–2014.

Source: National Vital Statistics Reports, vol. 64, no. 12 (Hyattsville, MD: National Center for Health Statistics, 2015), p. 23, table 5.

The Latino babies born in 1997 turned eighteen in 2015. This means that about three-quarters of a million Latino US citizens became eligible to vote in 2015. A slightly larger number will become old enough to vote in 2016, and the number will increase each year until 2024, by which time nearly 1 million Latinos born in the US will turn eighteen and be of voting age. Every year after that, just under 1 million US-born Latinos will turn eighteen, up to the elections of 2032. The coming-of-age of Latinos born in the US will add nearly 18 million new voters to the US electorate by that year.

In their 1985 book *Habits of the Heart*, Robert N. Bellah and his colleagues pondered the twentieth-century tug-of-war between individual and community stemming from "habits of the heart" that de Tocqueville described in the early nineteenth century as stemming from American daily family life, religious convictions, and civic participation.[11] In trying to understand the tug-of-war between self and society in America, however, de Tocqueville and Bellah pondered only the habits of the white, Protestant, English-speaking heart. Given the large presence of Latinos in the post-millennial generation, particularly in the large metropolitan areas, we would do well to understand the habits of the Latino heart as well. These young people entering adulthood are heirs to traditions forged in nearly five hundred years of the Indo-Afro-Oriento-Ibero version of Western society in what is now the United States. Thanks to their primary socialization as young children with their families, they have absorbed norms and mores that have produced, for seventy-five years, high labor force participation, low welfare use, vigorous family formation, and positive health outcomes. Since beginning their secondary socialization in schools, jobs, sports teams, organizations, and use of English language media, these Latino post-millennials have had to contend with nativist rhetoric that denigrates and rejects their very presence in the United States. Yet since 1849, Latinos in California have proclaimed their adherence to a universalist vision of an America built on equality, freedom, and democracy, even when confronted by the nativist vision that has tried repeatedly to exclude them from the community of Americans. As of 2015, a Latino-post millennial born in the US turns eighteen approximately every thirty seconds, and officially enters adulthood. In those same thirty seconds, approximately two non-Hispanic whites die. The "habits of the Latino heart" are becoming an increasingly larger part of society, and the electorate, every day. The tug-of-war between nativist exclusiveness and

11. Robert N. Bellah, Richard Madsen, William Sullivan, Ann Swindler, and Stephen N. Tipton, *Habits of the Heart: Individualism and Commitment in American Life* (Berkeley and Los Angeles: University of California Press, 1985).

universalist inclusion may well be decided by Latino post-millennials in the struggle for America's soul in the twenty-first century.

Post-Reading Questions

1. According to the author, what are the common stereotypes and negative labels placed upon Latinx individuals in society by the dominant culture?
2. Why are these stereotypes and negative labels misleading? In what ways do they fail to reflect reality?
3. How many Latinx people became eligible to vote in 2015? How many are estimated to reach voting age by 2032? Do you think future generations of Latinx individuals will have a strong influence on our cultural and political landscape? Why or why not?

UNIT V

THE FAMILY

Key Terms and Definitions

Review the key terms and definitions below to strengthen your understanding of the readings in this unit.

Extended Families: Family units that may span multiple generations, consisting of parents, their children, and other relatives who are considered kin.

The Feminization of Poverty: The increasing economic divide between men and women, resulting in higher rates of poverty for females, especially those who are single mothers.

The Gender Binary: The widespread notion that females and males are inherently biologically different and that this difference is set in stone with sex assignment at birth and unchangeable. The gender binary allows for only two gender options and fails to account for over 1 percent of the population who are intersex. It also limits the possibilities for gender identity and expression in society, emphasizing conformity to one's sex assigned at birth.

Nuclear Families: Family units that comprise two generations, consisting of parents and their children.

The Regnerus Paper: A 2012 paper by Mark Regnerus, a sociologist at the University of Texas, that claimed that children raised by parents who have had LGBT relationships face social and emotional setbacks later in life. The study generated enormous social controversy as it was funded by right-wing organizations, had a poor scientific design, and was fraught with biases against LGBT individuals.

Introduction

In the first reading for unit 7, titled "The New Family: Balancing Togetherness and Privacy," Beth Baker highlights the patterns that family groups have followed over the course of human history. For most of human history, **extended families** have been the common model across various nations. These are family units made up of parents, their children, and other kin (such as grandparents, aunts, uncles, and other relatives). Over the course of time, in the United States, **nuclear families** became more common. This became the dominant model from the 1940s through the 1980s. These families usually consist of households where parents and their children live together but without other relatives. In this piece, Baker notes that since 2010, multigenerational households are growing in the United States. This shows a new resurgence in **extended families**. Sometimes, extended family members move in together for economic reasons. For example, adults may move in with extended kin after a mortgage foreclosure or a bout with unemployment. Other times, middle-aged adults make the transition in order to care for elderly parents. Furthermore, older adults may move in with their adult children to help care for grandchildren. Often, the reasons for the merge are multiple and intersecting.

In order to understand this process better, Baker conducts interviews with adults who live in multigenerational households. Through these interviews, she learns that many multigenerational family households find this lifestyle both challenging and rewarding. Many **extended family** members feel close emotional bonds develop after moving in together. At the same time, family members may face boundary issues or struggle to value each other's privacy. Often, family new household rules are established with this transition. With this, some families also renegotiate financial obligations. In the end, regardless of the reason for their household union, extended families are likely to build deep emotional connections. They often learn to share responsibilities and value each other's privacy over time. Although not always an easy route, Baker captures a glimpse into this reemerging lifestyle.

In the second reading, "Marriage Equality in Social Science and the Courts," Philip N. Cohen scrutinizes the **Regnerus paper**, a report written in 2012 by a sociologist named Mark Regnerus. The **Regnerus paper** generated social controversy for suggesting that children raised by parents who have had same-sex relationships face social and emotional setbacks later in life. The study contained many flaws, and the findings are not validated or supported by scientific evidence. In this piece, Cohen points out that the Regnerus paper was an attempt to uphold the **gender binary** in society. The **Regnerus paper** surfaced at the same time as debates amplified over same-sex marriage in US society. Cohen shows that the paper was a last-ditch attempt to promote "traditional" marriage in the wake of struggles for marriage equality. Ultimately, this study undermines the family unit in society by embracing only one socially acceptable model (a nuclear family headed by a man and a woman).

From one angle, the **Regnerus paper** was flawed because it did not actually study same-sex parenting at all. In fact, it looked only at whether one parent in the family had ever had a relationship with someone of the same sex. Furthermore, the study neglected to examine how other variables, such as income, may have impacted children. Sociologists responded to the **Regnerus paper** by signing a response with over 200 signatures calling into question the academic integrity of the study. Gay rights activists also weighed into the conversation, decrying the research findings as false and misleading. Ultimately, the whole debate reveals just how profoundly sociological research can impact the public. In this case, the flawed sociological research study was exposed as an attempt to undermine the fight for marriage equality in a crucial moment of US history. Despite this debacle, same-sex marriage was successfully recognized as a constitutional right in 2015.

In the third reading for this unit, "Single Mothers and Social Support: A Rural Case Study," Margaret K. Nelson conducts interviews with seventy single white mothers in rural Vermont. Her research reveals many of the struggles that these mothers face daily. For various reasons, many of these women cannot rely on the support of their children's father, so they must seek alternative avenues of assistance. For example, many of the mothers in her study have little choice but to borrow money from relatives and friends in order to cover their living expenses.

Nelson highlights the fact that single mothers are among the groups in society most likely to face poverty. This is known as the **femininization of poverty**, or the increasing economic divide between men and women, resulting in higher rates of poverty for females. This trend especially impacts women who are single mothers. In terms of social networks, single mothers may be most connected to other single mothers. Unfortunately, it is difficult for these women to be a source of economic support for one another, because as a group, they collectively lack social resources. They not only struggle with material resources but also lack energy and time. Some single women describe the emotional benefits that they gained when their abusive or neglectful relationships ended. On the flip side, they face enormous economic setbacks. When they are able, family members may step in to help alleviate some of the financial burdens. However, some single women struggle to ask for help. Still, many see that they have little other choice and are forced to accept the harsh reality that they cannot make it on their own.

The readings in this unit capture some of the family relationships and dynamics in the United States. In the first reading, Baker captures the resurgence of extended family households. She shows that families form into multigenerational households for a variety of reasons. In the piece by Philip N. Cohen, we gain a glimpse into some of the social debates about family structure. Unfortunately, even sociological research, without rigorous academic standards and peer review, can be deeply flawed. We see this in the case of the Regnerus paper, which sought to reinforce negative stereotypes about same-sex couples and family units headed by gay and lesbian parents. Thankfully, this research was exposed as biased and was discounted by experts. In the final reading, the author reveals some of the common struggles faced by single mothers in rural America. Faced with enormous economic setbacks, many of these women rely on social support networks within their families to survive. Although it is difficult for these women to ask for help, they often acknowledge that they have little choice but to do so. Each of these readings sheds light on the variety of families that exist in the United States. Furthermore, the authors of each excerpt reveal some of the changes and struggles that families face in modern-day contexts.

The New Family

Balancing Togetherness and Privacy

Beth Baker

Since prehistoric times, humans have banded together in family groups, helping each other through the stages of life. New anthropological research suggests that beginning some thirty thousand years ago, as humanity began to live past thirty years old, the role of grandparents became critical to a family's health and well-being. Elders' wisdom and experience enabled them to teach younger generations how to locate scarce water, forage for food or identify poisonous plants, and pass on tool-making and artistic skills.[1]

For tens of millennia and continuing today in much of the world, extended families live together as the norm. Yet in the United States that all changed, as working people migrated for jobs, family farms went under, or students went off to college and never returned to the fold. Even those who did not leave their hometowns began setting up their own households when they became adults, rather than remaining with their parents and siblings. When baby boomers came of age, multigenerational families living together reached their nadir. The percentage of multigenerational family households plunged from 24.7 in 1940 to 12.1 in 1980. In the United States between 1940 and 2008, 1970 had the fewest people—twenty-six million—living in multigenerational households.[2]

1. Robin McKee, "Wisdom of Grandparents Helped Rise of Prehistoric Man," *The Guardian Observer*, July 23, 2011, *www.guardian.co.uk/science/2011/jul/24/prehistoric-man-helped-as-elderly-survived*.

2. Pew Research Center, *The Return of the Multigenerational Family Household: A Social and Demographic Trends Report* (Washington, DC: Pew Research Center, March 18, 2010), 4, *www.pewsocialtrends.org/files/2010/10/752-multigenerational-families.pdf*.

In recent times, though, there's been a shift in the other direction. In 2010 the portion of multigenerational households rose to 16.1 percent. By 2011, more than fifty-one million Americans—one in six—lived in multigenerational households, a 10 percent increase since the recession began in 2007.[3] (It should be noted that researchers define multigenerational households differently—some count those with three or more generations living together, while others count those with two generations of related adults.)

The living situation of older people has been a rollercoaster since the early twentieth century—going from 57 percent living with their extended families in 1900, to 17 percent in the 1980s and 1990s, and now edging up to 20 percent.[4] As the aging population swells, researchers project this trend will continue.

According to a 2010 Pew report, *The Return of the Multigenerational Family Household*, family members are increasingly moving in together for a variety of reasons, from mortgage foreclosures, to unemployment of young adults, to looking out for elders. Immigrant and African American families have a strong tradition of living in multigenerational households. Nationally, roughly one-quarter of Latinos (22 percent), African Americans (23 percent) and Asians (25 percent) live in multigenerational households, compared to 13 percent of whites.[5]

Although living with extended kin has ancient roots, modern families are changing how they live together. When they can afford a large enough dwelling, today's multigenerational households are more intentional about maintaining boundaries and honoring privacy. They often seek reciprocal relationships, where each has a valued role to play.

Three Units/Four Generations

A poster family for intergenerational living is the Cardozo clan in San Francisco. I met Laurie, of my generation, at the Morning Due coffee shop in the Castro district. It was a bustling café serving Fair Trade organic coffee, with artisan pottery and oil paintings on the walls. After ordering croissants and mugs of coffee, we settled in for conversation. Laurie, a tall, attractive woman with curly brown hair beginning to gray, was full of humor and confidence.

She grew up in Minneapolis and never expected that her extended family would eventually all live under one roof, once she and her siblings were grown. Unlike the familiar pattern of the young adults pulling up roots, her parents were the ones to move, leaving the Twin Cities for San Francisco in 1975 where her father worked in the book-selling trade. Her parents bought a large house that had previously been converted into two full apartments and an in-law suite, thinking that the rental income would help out.

In 1981, when Laurie and her husband decided to move West to work for the family business, her father suggested they rent the apartment above. "My mom said no—that's how she grew up, in an intense

3. Generations United, *Family Matters: Multigenerational Households in a Volatile Economy* (Washington, DC: Generations United, 2011), 1, *www.gu.org*.

4. Ibid., 6.

5. Pew Research Center, *The Return of the Multigenerational Family Household*, 7.

and large Jewish family that she ran away from," Laurie recalled. But she and her husband and children did move in, and "Thirty-one years later, I haven't left."

Today, the house is comprised of Laurie and her husband on the top floor, her parents in the middle, and her daughter, son-in-law, and their baby in the in-law suite on the lower level, making it four generations. "I hope this arrangement will continue on into the future, for many generations," said Laurie.

To her, the privacy and boundaries that come with each having their own unit makes it all work. "I couldn't do it otherwise," she said. On Friday nights they all gather to have dinner, but otherwise they do not share meals.

Like every group of people I interviewed, the family hits rough patches now and then. Laurie recalled the time when her father was in his early sixties and went to Findhorn, a spiritual community in Scotland. He returned insistent that he had found "the spiritual answers to life," and that the entire family should follow suit. After a few sessions of family therapy, they were able to move on. "We all have our quirks," she said. "We process it, and leave my parents alone. In true Midwestern fashion, no one likes to confront each other."

She acknowledged how fortunate her family is. For one, her daughter is a social worker who is used to dealing with difficult issues when they arise. Moreover Laurie's son-in-law is a home health aide who not only has a flexible schedule but is entirely comfortable and skilled in dealing with the age-related problems of her parents, who are now in their eighties. He and Laurie's husband, now retired, provide much of the childcare, while she and her daughter work outside the home as a high school teacher and social worker, respectively.

"My son-in-law takes the baby up to see my parents daily," she said. "And I've gotten to watch my daughter be a new mom. When I was a new mom, I was alone in a city in Minnesota." The nuclear family living alone, she concluded, makes no sense and reflects poorly on the US culture of individualism. In contrast, she said, "In our counter-culture stuff a lot of us are trying to stay more connected to our children and our parents. The sense of community is really important."

That she views this deep sense of family connection as counter-cultural is somewhat ironic, since so often baby boomers were labeled the "me generation," portrayed as a bunch of selfish ingrates thumbing their nose at authority in adolescence and now acting as "greedy geezers" defending their Social Security and Medicare.

Laurie's own grandparents all wound up in nursing homes. The places weren't "horrific," she said, "but if we can take care of [our elders], I think we should."

That view represents the majority opinion, according to a 2012 survey of how different generations (baby boomers and younger) view family responsibility. Among baby boomers, 55 percent thought adult children had a strong or absolute responsibility to ask their parents to live with them if they needed caregiving help, with another 26 percent believing this was a moderate responsibility. They were somewhat less charitable about taking their parents in if they were having financial difficulty—47 percent thought it was a strong responsibility and 28 percent thought moderate.[6]

---

6. MetLife Mature Market Institute, *Multigenerational Views on Family Financial Obligations* (New York: MetLife Mature Market Institute, January 2012), 15, *www.metlife.com*.

It would be a mistake, though, to view intergenerational living, as a one-way "take care of the old folks" street. Modern grandparents, among them a growing number of baby boomers, are exceedingly generous to their grandchildren, according to a 2012 MetLife Mature Market Institute study. Some 62 percent helped out their grandchildren financially, for clothing and education for example. The average gift was more than $8,000 total for their grandchildren, and more than half the grandparents gave more than $5,000.[7]

The study also found that many grandparents were generous with their time and attention. Nearly one-third of grandparents babysat for their grandchildren five days a week, and one in ten provide full-time care for a grandchild. Twenty percent lived in multigenerational households.[8] Happily, the most frequently cited reason why people took care of their grandchildren was that they enjoyed doing so, followed by "so their parents can work."

The traditional role of grandparents as wise counselors, givers of unconditional love, and transmitters of strong values can be strengthened when families live together or in close proximity. In the MetLife study, a majority of grandparents saw themselves as the ones to pass on such values as honesty, good behavior, self-sufficiency, higher education, and good health habits. Twenty-two percent said they provided care to their grandchildren *in order* to pass on family values.

In Laurie's family, her parents have always been close to their grandchildren, as a result of living under one roof. Laurie remembers her daughter as a picky eater who, if Laurie's dinner didn't sound appetizing, would run upstairs to grandma and grandpa's to check out their menu, and if she gave that a thumbs down she knew her aunt in the basement apartment would make her what she wanted.

"For me, as a mother and now as a grandmother, it's so much easier and so much better for the kids to have more loving adults around them," Laurie said. "When my daughter was frightened by my son's health [her son had a seizure disorder], she'd run and climb in my parents' bed. That's the best thing—seeing what it does for children. As a high school teacher I see that the youth want adults to care for them and help them. My kids would do crazy things as teenagers. They would know there would always be at least one adult who would be there for them."

The In-Law Suite

Families choose to live together in all sorts of configurations and for all sorts of reasons. Unlike Laurie's family, whose younger members moved into the elders' home, in many cases the elder moves into the adult child's home. That was the case for Cheri and her wife, Ann, who live in a large house outside Grove City, Ohio, with an in-law suite for Cheri's eighty-four-year-old mother, Della. "I live alone, but they're there if something would happen to me," said Della. "It works out really well for us."

---

7. MetLife Mature Market Institute, *Grandparents Investing in Grandchildren: A MetLife Study on how Grandparents Share their Time, Values, and Money* (New York: MetLife Mature Market Institute, September 2012), 5, *www.metlife.com*.

8. MetLife Mature Market Institute, *Grandparents Investing*, 4.

Della grew up in a large farm family in South Dakota, with seven sisters and four brothers and attended a one-room school. She never dreamed she would live to old age. Most of her family died in their early seventies, and she had always assumed she would too.

She first moved to Columbus and rented a house with another woman, but there were problems. "Cheri thought it would be best to get out of that situation," she said. She had worked as a registered nurse all her life, but her retirement prospects were dim. Divorced and with substance abuse problems, she had very little money to live on. Cheri and Ann offered to share their home with her. Twenty years and two homes later, the two generations still lived together. Della contributed $8,000 to the down-payment on their first house, and later helped out with utilities.

As an extended family, they knew from the beginning they wanted to set clear boundaries. Early on, Della often cooked dinner for Cheri and Ann, who were free to take their plates to their own part of the house if they wished. As Della grew older, cooking became more of a challenge, but she still helped out as best she could. She took care of Cheri and Ann's cat and dog, for example, when the couple went out of town.

Their friends often included Della in dinner invitations, and a few would come by to visit her. Della, who had no friends left of her own, was grateful for the companionship of family. "There was a little church close by, and I met several ladies there and was in a craft club," she said. "At that time, these ladies were all older. They died one by one." She also used to meet former nursing colleagues once a month for lunch, but physical ailments—her own and her friends'—made it impossible to keep up.

"I like having my own space," she said of the separate apartment. "I really feel like this is my place." She decorated however she wished, and had her own deck to be outside. I asked her if Ann and Cheri would approve of her having a "gentleman friend." "That would be nice!" she laughed. "I'm sure they would let me know if they approved."

I later spoke individually to Cheri and Ann. Ann recalled that when Cheri first proposed the idea of her mother moving in with them, Ann had no problem with it. "I was clear about specific boundaries," she said. "I knew this was not a trial—this was going to be it."

She knew that Della's living situation was not good and neither were her finances. So Ann appreciated that Della helped with their first down payment. "We all benefited, and it's still working," she said. In the beginning, Della was in her sixties and still "vital," said Ann. "She cooked for us, she did our laundry."

But the house design was not ideal. Della had a humble basement bedroom and bath. When Cheri found their current home with an in-law suite, they decide to move, even though it meant a longer commute.

"It's important from a family perspective," Ann said. "We get to see extended family more than we would normally. Having Della with us draws the family together."

When I asked what would happen if Della needed more care, Ann responded, "We're winging it."

One issue that caused friction was Della's smoking. Ann and Cheri insisted that she smoke by her sink or on the deck. "We caught her a couple times," Ann said. "We had very strong words. My concern is fire. This is our life, and she's part of the household."

Still, Ann added, "Della's a peach. I don't know if you'd get that every time. My grandmother lived with my family when I was a child. My mom and grandmother didn't get along all the time—she was my dad's mom."

She and Cheri tried to encourage Della to get out and meet friends and offered to take her to the senior center. But, they concluded, "She's a homebody. She wouldn't ever go," Ann said.

For Cheri, the idea of housesharing came after several occasions when they had to help her mother with problems stemming from her alcoholism and addiction. "I thought maybe it made sense to think ahead," she said.

Cheri felt good about their current living situation. Her mother "loves the birds. She has a big bedroom, a nice bathroom, a kitchen/dining room, and a nice big living room, with her own fireplace. On her deck the grandkids help her with flowers, and she waters the plants and fills the birdfeeders."

Della also got a lot of pleasure from Toby, a deaf cat whom she adopted after finding the teeny white ball of fur up in a tree. The cat, said Cheri, had gone from needing Della's care to being Della's caretaker, giving her companionship and plenty of lap time.

As Della grew somewhat frailer, they began to cook for her. During the week, she ate in her apartment, and on the weekends they dined together.

Cheri's niece and nephew chose to go to college nearby to be closer to Della, who enjoys cooking for her grandchildren. "My mom's life in the last few years is better than ever," Cheri said. Her mother has always been open to Cheri being a lesbian, and was happy when she and Ann got married. "Ann has helped support her," Cheri said. "They have a great relationship." Ann helped Della through recovery from substance abuse.

"In twenty years, there's never been a period of time that we thought this isn't working," Cheri said. "Still today, she watches the dog for us. She lets repair people in. And we're emotional support for her. If she lived somewhere else, it would be much harder to deal with if she needed help. It's been beneficial for me—my mother is my friend too."

The main advice she and Ann give to families considering living together is to talk about rules and boundaries. Early on, for example, Della would go through their mail or open their packages. They were able to work through that.

At the end of our conversation, I had the chance to talk to Liz, Della's granddaughter. "My mom [Cheri's sister] appreciated this when Cheri and Ann opened their doors to my grandmother," she said. "We don't have to worry or think about putting her in assisted living."

Liz laughed that there may come a day when she would be helping out her own parents, Della, and Cheri and Ann. "The running joke is I'll get all of them," she said. "I'll have a commune or a farm. This has been really nice for me. Before I only saw Grandma once a year, when I was in Montana. When I come to visit, I'm not pressured to see all of them. We try to take Grandma out on her own. She still makes the best cookies in the world. All the grandkids come and help her with Christmas cookies."

Recently, I checked in with Cheri to find out how Della was doing. She had died a few months earlier, from an aneurysm. "She lived with us until the day she died," Cheri wrote, "and frankly I still miss her every day."

The GRAMS

As Cheri and Ann described, having boundaries and discussing them up front is important for families making the decision to live in the same household.

Social psychologist Susan Newman, author of *Under One Roof Again: All Grown Up and (Re)learning to Live Together Happily*, agrees. "There are a lot of questions they should ask as they're thinking about moving in together," she said in an interview, assuming there is a choice and that the move is not prompted by truly dire circumstances. "What they should ask themselves first is why are we doing this? How am I going to feel about this move? Am I going to feel I'm at the mercy of my children? How can we make this equitable?"

If the older person or couple is moving in with their adult children, she said, they should make a financial contribution as Della did, such as helping pay to fix up an in-law suite. "The older generation wants to contribute," she said. "Even if you don't really need their money, take it anyway. It makes them feel they are part of the building process, and they have some ownership in this move."

That was the case for another family. Anne, at sixty-five, pulled up stakes in San Diego and moved north to the Bay Area to be near her two children. She had been in San Diego for thirty years and had a successful psychotherapy practice.

"One day my son called and said, 'Mom you always wanted to live in the Bay Area.' They were getting ready to have their first baby," she explained. "He said, 'We need you here, and you don't want to miss your first grandchild.'"

With that, she decided to move, gradually scaling back her therapy practice as she slowly made the transition. She invited me over to the lovely house she purchased with her son and daughter-in-law. Together they had planned an addition that included a family room on the main floor and a small apartment below for Anne, a hip-looking grandmother wearing blue jeans, who was heading out to canvass for President Obama's reelection after our interview.

"I had a lot of trepidation, as you can imagine," she said of the move. "I had never lived in one room before. I had piles and piles of junk from not only my life, but my mother's and grandmother's. I didn't know what it would be like to live so near my kids and grandkids."

She knew that she wanted a separate entrance to her space, but was conflicted over whether to have her own kitchen. She's glad now that she doesn't. She goes out a lot, and when she's at home she enjoys eating with the family. "My daughter-in-law and I love and respect each other, luckily," she said. "She wants to be in charge of cooking, and I don't like to cook. I do the dishes, and she doesn't mind that." That gives her daughter-in-law and son the opportunity to be with the children after supper.

"One thing that's awkward is that if I want to have people for dinner, I wait until they're gone for the weekend," she said.

Initially, she did a lot of childcare. Her grandchildren, ages three and five, are now in school until three o'clock each afternoon, then she takes care of them for two hours during the week and some on the weekends. During the day, Anne found she had too much time on her hands, so she volunteered on the political campaign and joined the Berkeley Community Chorus, which is open to all ages and abilities. At the time of our conversation, the chorus was preparing to tour in Europe and take a master class with the head of the Vienna Boys' Choir.

She showed me her space, a snug apartment with a desk, bed, and bathroom. The apartment opens on to the backyard full of fruit trees and tomato plants.

"I've made a few compromises," she said. She had longed to live in Berkeley, her alma mater, and be able to walk to the campus, but the other two wanted to live in Oakland, which was more affordable and had lots of young families. She also acknowledged that every bump in the road makes her heart clutch—"When there's tension in the house, I can't just go home," she laughs.

But, she said, the arrangement works beautifully and she hopes to stay there indefinitely. The neighbors include her as part of the family at get-togethers. I ask if she's thought about what would happen if she grew frail or unable to care for herself. "We didn't really discuss this in depth," she said. "If it turns out it would be better for me to be someplace else, I'll move. My son has said, 'If you're sick I'd much rather take care of you here than drive across town.'"

The bottom line, she said, is, "We like each other. That makes a big difference. And I don't need to be in charge."

Anne is part of a close-knit group of women who chose to move in order to live near their children and grandchildren in the greater San Francisco area. They've dubbed themselves the GRAMS, for Grandmothers Relocating After Midlife Successfully.

At a gathering they'd organized on my behalf, they shared their stories about what this huge transition has meant in their lives. Each had taken a somewhat different path.

My friend Karen, an artist, and her husband had moved from my hometown and bought a parcel of land outside Santa Cruz together with their son and daughter-in-law. The latter moved into a modest home on the property, and Karen and Frank built a small, energy-efficient home just steps away. Their other son and daughter-in-law live a few miles away. Each son has one little boy.

Mary Helen had retired from a scientific career with the pharmaceutical industry in Salt Lake City to become a weaver, moving to Berkeley where she lives in an apartment one mile from her daughter, son-in-law, and grandchildren.

Judith moved from Seattle in order to be near her two daughters, their husbands, and her six grandchildren, aged nine months to eighteen years. She lives on the first floor of a beautiful old house on a corner lot in Berkeley, where we were meeting.

Mary, a long-time public school administrator, and her husband also moved from Maryland and now live next door to their daughter.

Sitting on comfortable chairs in Judith's living room, the women shared heart-felt thoughts on their new lives. The group formed after initially meeting each other at a neighborhood park as they were taking care of their grandchildren. As they chatted at the park, they realized how much they had in common and eventually formed the GRAMS. They had been meeting monthly for four years.

"The GRAMS have been lifesavers for my sanity," said Mary. Her daughter had urged them to move, saying she'd like to be a support for them as they grew old. "So I took it that's what we're going to do. My husband came here reluctantly, and he remembers our conversations differently." While Mary loves being so close to their daughter, her husband has strict boundaries. He did not grow up in a close family, and it doesn't come naturally to him, she said. It was a difficult family transition, and for a time Mary suffered from depression. But they have gotten through it.

Mary Helen and Judith also had been urged by their children to move to the area. Five years earlier, Mary Helen's daughter said, "'We are going to have children, and I always pictured you in the picture,'" Mary Helen recalls. "We left it very open. But something inside me shifted then. I didn't know this was what I wanted until it was offered. I retired early and moved out here."

Judith's son-in-law told her, "You'll move down." At first she rented an apartment and came for frequent visits while still working in Seattle. After a time, she came for good. She has an especially close relationship with her oldest grandson, who has learning disabilities. He has always been her pal, and she helps tutor him. Both daughters live within a mile or so of her. Judith sees the younger one a couple of times a week, for childcare and dinner; the older she sees five times a week. "I'm very integrated with their lives," she said. Despite their close relationship, she has no desire to live with either of her daughters. But she has thought about getting a housemate.

Karen does a considerable amount of childcare for both her grandsons. One daughter-in-law has a demanding career as a chef and owner of three businesses. Karen's husband also helps with the kids and is a master gardener who tends the vegetables and fruit trees on the property. Karen feels they play a central and important role of support and stability in the family. But it has also been wrenching, as they left a strong network of close friends and other family members back East.

I asked the GRAMS about the challenges of moving to a new place at this time of life. "When you uproot your life you leave behind a lot of who you were as a person—the support, the friends," said Mary Helen.

"Your identity," Karen added.

"A lot of people aren't willing to do that," Mary Helen said. "It's uncomfortable to be a newcomer. You have to be prepared for that and realize half your neighbors may have their own dance cards full. You have to be confident or relentless enough to say, 'I'm going to make a place here.'"

"Is it worth it or not?" Karen said. "You did it, and there's no going back. The gifts are—I will die with no regrets. If I hadn't done it, I would have had regrets. I have found meaning in my new life. That's worth it."

I asked them if the grandchildren were the magnet, or if they would have moved anyway to be near their adult children. While the grandchildren were the immediate draw, they felt that being near their adult children was also compelling.

"I think it's essential to life," said Judith. "I have no regrets."

"I feel like I'm more alive now," said Karen. "I'd known for years I wanted to be near my kids, but fear held me back. Being near my kids is the center of my life. I believe this is about my spiritual development. We must say yes. And this whole move was what my body and soul wanted."

***

Not everyone articulates such lofty reasons for moving in with family. Often it's something as mundane as needing to share the electric bill and rent or offering shelter when a family member suddenly loses his spouse or job or has a medical crisis. Or it simply feels like the way life should be.

The Murphy family, who recently moved to Maryland from Washington, DC, has always had one or more of their adult children living with them. They moved to a roomy house with a basement apartment a block from their two daughters' small business, a bakery and café.

"The café took over all of our lives," said Caitlin, the baker and co-owner of the business. Because of a vision problem, Caitlin is unable to drive, so her parents' new home allows her to walk to work and for them to pitch in at the café on the spur of the moment.

Caitlin's mother, Sharon, said her husband had grown up in the model of the 1950s, with a nuclear family and grandparents who moved to nursing homes when they grew old. She, on the other hand, grew up "dirt poor" in Detroit. For her, "It's a way of being, that grandparents live with you," she said, "or adult kids who lost their job or their partner."

She recalls her own grandmother who in her eighties was still working in the family pub. She would rise at four a.m. and walk through East Detroit in order to make the meat pies. "It was endearing," she said. "It didn't matter if she were slow or even if someone else could make the meat pies better. She was part of the family and people appreciated her."

Sharon and her husband founded a nonprofit to provide transitional housing for families in crisis, especially for new immigrants and refugees. They raised their children in a large house where some of the families lived, so life was always full of people and hubbub.

Sharon grows impatient with our generation who she believes spends too much time "processing" ad nauseam such decisions as allowing your adult children to move home for a while. "I think it's the greatest gig in the world to have kids and to have them want to live with you when they're adults," she said. "Our generation feels they need to understand everything. It's so much more fun not to invest energy in that."

As she's building up her business, Caitlin said she could not afford to live on her own. "I put on fifteen pounds when I went home," she laughed. "My mom cooks every night. My dad replaces my light bulbs. It's great." But she admits that at first she struggled with being thirty years old and moving back home.

"It's a legitimate question, but then you have to let it go," her mother said. "That's more about [other people's] perceptions."

Caitlin is realizing that more and more of her friends and customers are making a similar choice. "I enjoy the fact that I can hang out with my parents when they're strong and healthy," she said. "We hang out every day I'm off. We're best friends."

Sharon nods, but she said she knows she has to keep clear about when she needs to separate emotionally from her "mom" role. When she gave Caitlin a ride for a medical consultation, for example, Sharon had to leave the doctor's office to keep from putting in her two cents. "She would have decked me if I'd spoken out," she said, as Caitlin nodded.

They both stress that living together is not a bed of roses. They bicker and fight and drive each other crazy. Then they let it go. Sharon recalls one of the arguments that Caitlin and her sister had over their shared business. "It was horrible," she said. "I was worried it would ruin our family. I was driving to work praying to God, praying to the grandmothers. I was a wreck. Then I come back home at the end of the day and they're laughing and everything's fine."

Post-Reading Questions

1. According to the author, how have family units evolved over time?
2. What is the difference between a nuclear family household and an extended family household?
3. What are some of the reasons for the reemergence of extended family and multigenerational households? What are the rewards and challenges of this living arrangement?
4. Have you ever lived in an extended family household? If so, what was your experience like?

Marriage Equality in Social Science and the Courts

Philip N. Cohen

Philip N. Cohen, Selection from "Marriage Equality in Social Science and the Courts," *Enduring Bonds: Inequality, Marriage, Parenting, and Everything Else That Makes Families Great and Terrible*, pp. 88–96, 216–217, 227–248. Copyright © 2018 by University of California Press. Reprinted with permission.

A press release from the publisher circulated on June 7, 2012. The tone was dramatic, promising to "challenge established views about the development of children raised by gay or lesbian parents." The journal, *Social Science Research,* would offer "compelling new evidence that numerous differences in social and emotional well-being do exist between young adults raised by women who have had a lesbian relationship and those who have grown up in a nuclear family."

Within a day, as journalists worked on their stories to meet the journal's embargo deadline, sociologists were circulating copies of the paper, by University of Texas sociologist Mark Regnerus. And the initial round of articles featured a dose of skepticism from researchers. The *New York Times* opened with reference to "bitter debate among partisans on gay marriage," as "gay-rights groups attacked the study, financed by conservative foundations, as biased and poorly done even before its publication."[1]

The story in *Time,* by Belinda Luscombe (quoting me and others), captured most of the red flags in the study that we would debate over the next few years: the right-wing funding, the dated nature of the accounts provided by young adults (describing their childhoods decades earlier), the histories of family disruption inherent in the cases of children whose parents were described as lesbian or gay, and the virtual absence of children in the study who

---

1. Carey (2012). The paper itself is Regnerus (2012a).

were actually *raised by* lesbian or gay couples (as opposed to having parents who simply had a same-sex affair or briefly lived with a same-sex partner).

The study compares "any parent who ever 'had a relationship' with someone of the same sex to those who lived with both married biological parents from birth to age 18," I told Luscombe. "It is not about people who were 'raised by' lesbians or gay men."[2]

I didn't recognize it at first, but as the controversy unfolded I began to see this as a new front in the same war in which marriage promotion was just one battle: the struggle to preserve the gender binary itself—perhaps the final, core pillar of patriarchy.

The battle over same-sex marriage—which was not yet popularly known as *marriage equality*—was already raging in 2012.[3] But it intensified as activists on both sides raced to seize upon the broader implications of the issue, and a Supreme Court showdown seemed inevitable. On one side was the bitter and oddly mean-spirited attempt to preserve the "traditional" family—the married man-woman family, in which the two spouses play different yet complementary roles tied to the essential nature of their gender identities, and in which boys and girls are properly raised to replicate these inherent gender differences. On the other side—in a coalition demanding much more than simply marriage rights for gays and lesbians (as important as that issue was)—were the arrayed forces for tolerance, diversity, and equality in all things related to gender and sexuality and for the possibility of forming new families (or no families) without sacrificing the social support and community esteem that comes from conformity to accepted norms of family life.

By the end of what we might call the Regnerus Affair, we would know that his paper was the outcome of a concerted political campaign, waged by a coalition of activists and funded by right-wing foundations dedicated to preventing marriage equality, in which Mark Regnerus (and his collaborator, University of Virginia sociologist W. Bradford Wilcox) were essentially moles who easily penetrated the weak defenses of liberal academic social science and planted the research under a false facade of peer review in order to sway public opinion and the courts. But I didn't know all that in June of 2012; it came out in dribs and drabs on sociology blogs and activist websites, at once generating and testing our ability to respond in the face of political conflict and threats to our disciplinary integrity.

The first thing I noticed that put the Regnerus paper in a different category—not just conservative-leaning research but potentially the sharp end of something larger—was the conservative funders, the Witherspoon Institute and the Bradley Foundation. These were acknowledged in the paper and featured in the early news reports, with the *New York Times* story quoting Regnerus saying he had to turn to conservative foundations because "government agencies 'don't want to touch this stuff.' " In fact, the government was already touching "this stuff" in a very large way. At that time the National Institutes of Health was already $1 billion into the National Children's Study, a massive federal study of one hundred thousand children from birth to age twenty-one that aimed to include complete data on family structure, health, and behavioral outcomes (although it was later canceled because of poor planning and

---

2. Luscombe (2012).

3. In 2010 I had referred to the implications of same-sex parenting for social science as a "demographic revolution" (Cohen 2010b). Research at the time found no evidence of systematic disadvantage for children whose parents were lesbian or gay. See Biblarz and Stacey (2010).

management).[4] Further, government agencies from the Centers for Disease Control to the Census Bureau were engaged in major studies on how to improve measurement and collection of data about sexual orientation and same-sex couples—all of which would make studying gay and lesbian families a routine part of social science.[5]

In his media promotion of the study, Regnerus contrasted his conservative funders with the Ford Foundation, remarking that "every academic study is paid for by someone. I've seen excellent studies funded by all sorts of interest groups."[6] But the Witherspoon Institute and especially the Bradley Foundation are not just any special interest groups. Bradley, one of the largest foundations in the country, sees itself as a "righteous combatant in an ideological war," directing its millions with "single-minded focus" toward conservative causes, according to Jane Meyer, the *New Yorker* writer and author of *Dark Money: The Hidden History of the Billionaires behind the Rise of the Radical Right*.[7]

Beyond the funding, the time line of the paper, as reported by the journal, also set off early alarm bells. The article was submitted to the journal twenty days before the data collection was even complete, and it was revised and accepted within six weeks of the submission. Swift acceptance is not inherently unethical, but it is highly unusual for that journal (or any traditional peer-reviewed journal), enough so to draw attention. And submitting a paper before the data are complete without disclosing that fact is simply unethical.

Finally, there was the immediate promotion of the article by antiequality advocates. In fact, the paper was cited (and not in a cursory way) in an activist brief against same-sex marriage the *day after* the study was published online.[8] The brief was for the *Golinski* case, which challenged the federal Defense of Marriage Act (DOMA), then being heard by a federal appeals court.[9] Despite Regnerus's denials, he was obviously coordinating with the opponents of marriage equality.

What Regnerus Did Wrong

With these obvious red flags, the paper attracted heightened scrutiny—which it deserved. And then Regnerus and his supporters overplayed their hand, misrepresenting the study and its implications. The press release had quoted Regnerus saying that "children appear most apt to succeed well as adults when they spend their entire childhood with their married mother and father." And the release described the

4. Kaiser (2014).

5. For a CDC study, see Ward et al. (2014); for a Census Bureau study, see US Census Bureau (2011). Although studies on same-sex couples are obviously not a top research priority, the National Science Foundation has funded them going back at least to the early 1980s. See Brody (1983).

6. Regnerus (2012c).

7. A fact indicative of both the liberal bent of mainstream sociology and the extreme nature of Bradley support: my search of two hundred academic journals in the field of sociology (in the JSTOR database) reveals only eight papers that have acknowledged receipt of funding from the Bradley Foundation; none of these were in a major sociology journal, and none were written by sociology faculty.

8. American College of Pediatricians (2012).

9. Golinski v. United States Office of Personnel Management, 2012, 824 F. Supp. 2d 968. Dist. Court.

respondents as "children raised in eight different family structures," although the study had virtually no children actually raised by gay or lesbian couples, instead grouping together all those whose parents (by the child's report) had ever had a same-sex romance. The court brief submitted by the conservative pediatricians group also falsely described the study as focusing on children "raised by same-sex couples."

In a piece at *Slate,* Regnerus used the results to argue that "the household instability that the [study] reveals is just too common among same-sex couples to take the social gamble of spending significant political and economic capital to esteem and support this new (but tiny) family form while Americans continue to flee the stable, two-parent biological married model, the far more common and accomplished workhorse of the American household, and still—according to the data, at least—the safest place for a kid."[10]

To look in more detail at the study design, Regnerus collected survey responses from young adults who described their family structure growing up, and then he divided them into different groups (see figure 15.1). In one group were all those who said either of their parents had ever had a same-sex romantic relationship. The other group—who said neither parent had ever had such a relationship—he divided again, setting aside all those who were adopted, or whose parents had ever divorced, separated, or been widowed. Then he compared what he called the "gay father/lesbian mother" group to the always-married parent group. The finding: those in the former category were more likely to report having a variety of economic, behavioral, and emotional problems. Two design problems rendered the study unfit for drawing meaningful conclusions. First, the parents who had ever had a same-sex relationship were a widely diverse group that shared not only sexual orientation but, more importantly, a history of family instability. Although a tiny number of them had raised their children as long-term, committed partners, the vast majority were single or divorced parents. Any difference that might be the result of parents' sexual orientation was confounded with the differences between those in long-term stable marriages versus those in disrupted families.

10. Regnerus (2012d).

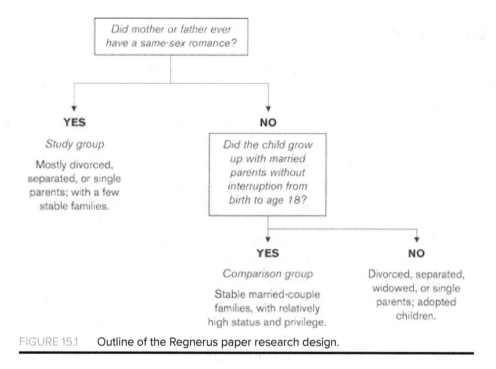

FIGURE 15.1   Outline of the Regnerus paper research design.

Second, the study did not take into account many background factors known to have dramatic effects on child well-being. For example, it is a sad fact that those from wealthy backgrounds are (on average) more likely to get and stay married (to each other) and more likely to have children who grow up to be rich and successful. Totally apart from sexual orientation, any study of how family background affects adult outcomes needs to take such material factors into account. The Regnerus study could not do that adequately. The research was derailed by its obsessive focus on sexual orientation—over more tangible factors that do affect children's well-being. That is why Regnerus lumped all gay and lesbian parents together, rather than differentiating families on the basis of parenting practices, family stability, or access to resources such as wealth and social status. (There were also other serious flaws with study, which I return to below.)

For children to grow up happy and successful, loved and secure, parenting does matter—a parent or parents who love, care for, and develop a positive relationship with their children. Also vitally important are access to financial resources, community support, good schooling, housing, health care, and basic security. When families have these assets, they are very likely to have positive outcomes regardless of the gender of their parents. This is what researchers and child welfare organizations mean when they say the sexual orientation of parents should not be a determining factor in children's adoption, placement, or support. In fact, the major American medical academies and associations—pediatricians, psychiatrists, psychologists, social workers—all support the adoption and parenting rights of gay and lesbian couples.

Sociology Responds

By June 29, Gary Gates, a longtime demographer of the lesbian, gay, bisexual, and transgender population, had assembled two hundred signatories for a "researchers respond" letter, which I published on my blog (it was later published by *Social Science Research*).[11] In addition to the substantive critique, the letter called out "the academic integrity of the peer review process"—which was to become a central issue later, when more details emerged.

Momentum built over the summer of 2012 for an effort to head off the study before it might sway the impending court decisions on same-sex marriage. Sociologists spoke out against it in the *Huffington Post* and on sociology blogs like *Scatterplot*, *OrgTheory*, and *Social (In)Queery*.[12] On the other side, one group of conservative scholars spoke out in Regnerus's defense on a Baylor University website, and in an impassioned defense, Regnerus's dissertation chair, Christian Smith, writing in the *Chronicle of Higher Education*, referred to Regnerus's treatment as an auto-da-fé.[13]

The time to intervene legally seemed short, as lower courts began citing the Regnerus study in marriage equality cases. In the *Golinski* case, the American Psychological Association led a group including the American Medical Association and the American Academy of Pediatrics that criticized the study and its misrepresentation in the courts.[14] But the American Sociological Association (ASA), with its lack of organization infrastructure for political intervention, was slower to respond. To push the association, I and a number of other sociologists brought the issue to our sections (subgroups within the association focused on particular research topics) in preparation for the August meeting of the ASA. At the time I was in the leadership of the Family Section, to which I brought a proposal asking ASA to intervene in the pending court cases to counter the Regnerus study.

The chair of the Family Section at the time was Paul Amato, a professor at Penn State University and a consultant on the Regnerus study—but he nevertheless supported the resolution. (Amato also had a secret: he had been one of the anonymous peer reviewers who approved the paper for *Social Science Research*.) The ASA campaign was successful in leading to an amicus brief from the association, under the research direction of Wendy Manning, which was finally published in February 2013.[15] Manning, a top-notch sociologist with a nonideologue reputation, struck the right balance in evaluating the evidence and drawing justifiable conclusions. On the issue of same-sex parenting and children's well-being, she wrote, we have the closest thing possible to a scholarly consensus: "When the social science evidence is exhaustively examined—which the ASA has done—the facts demonstrate that children fare just as well when raised by same-sex parents ... Unsubstantiated fears regarding same-sex child rearing do not overcome these facts and do not justify upholding DOMA and Proposition 8 [which banned same-sex marriage in California]."

---

11. Gates (2012).
12. See Pascoe (2012); Rojas (2012); Perrin (2012); Umberson (2012).
13. Johnson et al. (2012); C. Smith (2012).
14. American Psychological Association et al. (2012).
15. American Sociological Association (2012).

In response to the firestorm, *SSR* editor James Wright commissioned an internal audit of the publication process, written by Darren Sherkat, a fervent critic of right-wing religious sociologists who was also on the editorial board of the journal. Sherkat's report said the Regnerus paper should not have been published, as "scholars who should have known better failed to recuse themselves from the review process." In an interview Sherkat called the study "bullshit."[16] With the controversy spreading beyond academia, and the apparent unification of mainstream sociology against someone deemed heretic, conservatives rallied. Regnerus was lionized in a *Weekly Standard* cover story titled "Revenge of the Sociologists: The Perils of Politically Incorrect Academic Research"—with a cover cartoon showing him in a medieval torture chamber.[17]

The knives were indeed out for Regnerus. And it wasn't just scholarly debate over the technicalities of the research. Leftwardly inclined sociologists like me were naturally motivated to intervene because we thought the research was bad *and* we didn't like the effects it might have on civil rights, social equality, and the hoped-for demise of the traditional social order.

The tension was elevated by the interaction between the more staid academic critics and the less decorous social activists, who worked in closer contact—and at higher velocity—than either group was accustomed to. Any sociologist remotely connected to the issue was deluged with e-mails from gay rights activists, who relied on the academic criticism to validate their attacks on the research, in the same way that Regnerus and his coconspirators used their academic credentials to lend legitimacy to their cause. Thus, when a sociologist criticized the Regnerus paper, Scott Rose—a gay rights activist who was everywhere during this incident—wrote at the New Civil Rights Movement website, "Prominent Sociologist Delivers Devastating Professional Evaluation." Some of Rose's sensational accounts also viciously singled out the various actors for personal attacks, with headlines such as "Regnerus Editor James Wright a Worse Scumbag than Imagined." For low-profile professors immersed in the slow process of academic research and publication, the harsh spotlight and fast pace were disorienting. Worse, for some, was that Rose filed a charge of scientific misconduct against Regnerus at the University of Texas, which prompted a formal inquiry (the university decided the ethics charges weren't worth pursuing).[18] Academics of all persuasions shuddered.

Besides raising the profile of the scandal and its volume, the activists dug up vital information. While Rose was pressing his case, investigative journalist Sofia Resnick, working with the *American Independent,* filed public records requests with the University of Texas (where Regnerus was a state employee). It took months to overcome the university's legal objections, but by February 2013 Resnick started to publish Regnerus's e-mails and other documents.[19] Academics were shocked to see a peer's personal paper trail

16. Bartlett (2012).

17. A. Ferguson (2012).

18. See UT News (2012). As much as most concerned sociologists disliked the work Regnerus had done—and how he had done it—many still breathed a sigh of relief as public university administrators dismissed a complaint from a nonacademic activist directed at a professor that demanded sanctions for politically unpopular research.

19. See Resnick (2013). The e-mails that I draw from in this account are available on reporter Sofia Resnick's Scribd site, here: https://www.scribd.com/user/65082544/Sofia-Resnick. Resnick described the e-mails in Resnick (2012). My write-up appeared the next day in Cohen (2013h).

publicly dumped online (and gmail addresses started proliferating among professors at public universities), but the revelations were riveting and ultimately justified.

What had at first looked like a bad piece of research by a political hack was eventually revealed to be an actual conspiracy involving the biggest conservative think tank in the country (the Heritage Foundation), the giant Bradley Foundation, and a network of influential right-wing culture-war activists. The public records and the later disclosures demanded in high-profile court cases ended up exposing the conspiracy.

References

American College of Pediatricians. 2012. Brief of *Amicus Curiae,* Nos. 12–15388 and 12–15409. US Court of Appeals for the Ninth Circuit.

American Psychological Association et al. 2012. Brief of *Amici Curiae.* Nos. 12–15388 and 12–15409 US Court of Appeals for the Ninth Circuit.

American Sociological Association. 2012. Brief of Amicus Curiae. Nos. 12–144, 12–307. Supreme Court of the United States.

Bartlett, Tom. 2012. "Controversial Gay-Parenting Study Is Severely Flawed, Journal's Audit Finds." *Chronicle of Higher Education,* July 26.

Biblarz, Timothy J., and Judith Stacey. 2010. "How Does the Gender of Parents Matter?" *Journal of Marriage and Family* 72 (1): 3–22.

Brody, Jane E. 1983. "Sex in America: Conservative Attitudes Prevail." *New York Times,* October 4.

Carey, Benedict. 2012. "Study Examines Effect of Having a Gay Parent." *New York Times,* June 11.

Cohen, Philip N. 2010b. "Demographic Science and Gay Civil Rights." *Huffington Post,* March 18. www.huffingtonpost.com/philip-n-cohen/demographic-science-and-g_b_316760.html.

———. 2013h. "'More Managerial Than Intellectual': How Right-Wing Christian Money Brought Us the Regnerus Study." *Family Inequality,* March 11. https://familyinequality.wordpress.com/2013/03/11/more-managerial-than-intellectual/.

Ferguson, Andrew. 2012. "Revenge of the Sociologists." *Weekly Standard,* July 30.

Gates, Gary J. 2012. "Letter to the Editors and Advisory Editors of Social Science Research." *Social Science Research* 41 (6): 1350–51.

Johnson, Bryon, et al. 2012. "A Social Scientific Response to the Regnerus Controversy." June 20. www.baylorisr.org/2012/06/20/a-social-scientific-response-to-the-regnerus-controversy/.

Kaiser, Jocelyn. 2014. "NIH Cancels Massive U.S. Children's Study." *Science Insider,* December 12. www.sciencemag.org/news/2014/12/nih-cancels-massive-us-children-s-study.

Luscombe, Belinda. 2012. "Do Children of Same-Sex Parents Really Fare Worse?" *Time,* June 11.

Pascoe, C. J. 2012. "How Not to Study Families." *Social (In)Queery,* June 20. https://socialinqueery.com/2012/06/19/how-not-to-study-families/.

Perrin, Andrew J. 2012. "Bad Science Not about Same-Sex Parenting." *Scatterplot,* June 23. https://scatter.wordpress.com/2012/06/23/bad-science-not-about-same-sex-parenting/.

Regnerus, Mark. 2012a. "How Different Are the Adult Children of Parents Who Have Same-Sex Relationships? Findings from the New Family Structures Study." *Social Science Research* 41 (4): 752–70.

———. 2012c. "Q & A with Mark Regnerus about the Background of His New Study." *Patheos,* June 10. www.patheos.com/blogs/blackwhiteandgray/2012/06/q-a-with-mark-regnerus-about-the-background-of-his-new-study/.

———. 2012d. "Queers as Folk." *Slate,* June 11.

Resnick, Sofia. 2012. "Conservative-Backed Study Intended to Sway Court on Gay Marriage." *Huffington Post,* March 10. www.huffingtonpost.com/2013/03/10/supreme-court-gay-marriage_n_2850302.html.

———. 2013. "Journalists Win Release of Documents Tracing Right-Wing Funding for Texas Gay Marriage Study." *AlterNet,* February 3. www.alternet.org/investigations/journalists-win-release-documents-tracing-right-wing-funding-texas-gay-marriage-study.

Rojas, Fabio. 2012. "Comments on Regnerus." *Orgtheory,* July 29. https://orgtheory.wordpress.com/2012/07/29/comments-on-regnerus/.

Smith, Christian. 2012. "An Academic Auto-Da-Fé." *Chronicle of Higher Education,* July 23.

Umberson, Debra. 2012. "Texas Professors Respond to New Research on Gay Parenting." *Huffington Post,* August 26. http://www.huffingtonpost.com/debra-umberson/texas-professors-gay-research_b_1628988.html.

US Census Bureau. 2011. "Census Bureau Releases Estimates of Same-Sex Married Couples." September 27. www.census.gov/newsroom/releases/archives/2010_census/cb11-cn181.html.

UT News. 2012. "University of Texas at Austin Completes Inquiry into Allegations of Scientific Misconduct." University of Texas at Austin, August 29. http://news.utexas.edu/2012/08/29/regnerus_scientific_misconduct_inquiry_completed.

Ward, Brian W., James M. Dahlhamer, Adina M. Galinsky, and Sarah S. Joestl. 2014. "Sexual Orientation and Health among U.S. Adults: National Health Interview Survey, 2013." *National Health Statistics Reports,* no. 77 (July).

Post-Reading Questions

1. What was the major claim of the Regnerus paper? According to the author, what are the problems and inaccuracies of this claim?
2. What is the gender binary? How did the Regnerus paper attempt to uphold the gender binary in society?
3. What vision of family did the Regnerus paper convey? How does this vision of family differ from the diverse models of family that we see in society?

Single Mothers and Social Support

A Rural Case Study

Margaret K. Nelson

When Sheila Davis, a relatively well-off-woman who has been divorced for two years, does not have enough money in her savings account to cover the year's property taxes, she borrows from her parents and friends. Because she cannot (or does not want to) mow her own lawn or shovel her own driveway, she relies on the assistance of a neighbor. When she faces a scheduling conflict and cannot be there for her children at the end of the school day, Sheila asks one of her friends to drive them to their after-school activities.

Anne Davenport has been divorced from her husband for only a year, and she has an income that, as a combination of welfare, employment, and child support, is less than a quarter of Sheila's income from waged work ($9,300 versus $42,000). Like Sheila, Anne draws extensively on others. She relies regularly on her parents (in whose backyard her own trailer home sits) for babysitting, grocery money, and the loan of a working car. In addition, she counts on assistance from her single-mother friends for help with child care, transportation, and emotional support.

If both Sheila and Anne turn to other people for a broad range of assistance, they do so with different frequency and different sentiments. Perhaps it is because she expects more of herself at age forty-one that Sheila Davis is humbled by this new experience of not being able to make the necessary adjustments to her diminished income and manage on her own. Her financial management skills actually compound this feeling of inadequacy: "I feel sort of embarrassed that I don't have it together. I make my living as an accountant so I should know how to do it. And I *do* know how to do it. It's just about lifestyle changes [since the divorce]."

Anne shares Sheila's desire to be self-sufficient, but at age twenty-nine asking for help seems to come a little more easily to her: "If I run out of money for the week, I ask my mom."

Age (and personality) differences aside, the two women have different resources. Not only can Sheila purchase more help to respond to her needs, but outside of her work hours she has more time and energy to focus on meeting those needs, both because her children are no longer toddlers and because they spend almost half of their time with their father. Sheila also has many friends in the community in which she lives. And, although she lives some distance from them, members of her family are wealthy, and she remains in close contact. Anne, by contrast, has more "free" time outside of employment because she only works part-time. But both of her children are young and Anne cannot rely at all on *their* father, whose alcoholism prevents him from being a reliable caregiver to his sons. Without his help, Anne has both accepted and nurtured other significant assets. Not only does she live near her family, but she has also built up a large network of friends in the community. While neither her family members nor her friends are as affluent as Sheila's, both still serve as important resources.

Clearly, the different conditions under which these two women live significantly affect their experiences of single motherhood. This reading is not focused on the impact of these differences, however, or even on the amount of support these two women receive. Instead my interest is on the question of how single mothers who rely heavily on others make sense of, justify, and enact that reliance in a world both where independence and self-sufficiency are enshrined as social values and where asking for help exposes them to the judgment that the single-parent family must be inadequate.

Sample Population

To answer this question I draw on interviews I conducted in the rural state of Vermont with approximately seventy single mothers. All of these single mothers, like Anne and Sheila, are white custodial parents of a child under age eighteen, but they differ considerably from the common stereotype of single mothers as members of a minority group who live in an urban ghetto and are extremely poor. The single mothers in this study are all white, and in this they are *not* so atypical, despite the racist stereotype: In 2000, 64 percent of the nation's single mothers with a child under eighteen were white.[1] The women in this study live in rural areas and small towns and in this they are less typical: In 2000, less than one fifth of all single-mother households were found in non-metropolitan areas.

Since 1978 when Diana Pearce coined the phrase "the feminization of poverty," it has become an acknowledged truism that children and adults in families headed by single women live less well than do those in families headed by married couples.[2] The situation for single mothers in the rural state of Vermont is little different from that of single mothers in the rest of the country, even though the former are predominantly white and the latter are more diverse in their race/ethnicity. A significant proportion of single parent families—almost one-third of those with related children under eighteen and almost half of those with related children under five years of age—live below the poverty level in Vermont. By way

1. U.S. Census Bureau 2001.
2. Pearce 1978.

of comparison, for married-couple families with related children under eighteen the poverty level is just below ten percent (9.7 percent) and for those with related children under five it is slightly above that (13 percent). The situation in Vermont is not anomalous: In the United States as a whole comparable figures show that slightly over one third of all female headed families with related children under eighteen live in poverty as do 46 percent of those with related children under five in comparison with all families where poverty rates for those with related children under eighteen is 14 percent and for those with related children under five 17 percent.[3] Among the women in this study incomes extended from a low of $5,980 to an outlier high of $66,000; the median was $21,782 (almost precisely the state median of $21,175). Sheila is representative of those at the top of the income scale; Anne is representative of those towards the bottom.

Reciprocity in Theory and Practice

Social exchange theory focuses our attention on a rational actor's attempts to benefit from social interaction. However, unlike social theory alone would predict, reciprocity does not operate only to ensure benefits or even only to secure balance. Rather, reciprocity is also a *norm,* something that "holds that people should help those who help them."[4] And the normative imperative attached to reciprocity differs from the obligations attached to kin: The status duties of kinship "may require an almost unconditional compliance in the sense that they are incumbent on all those in a given status simply by virtue of its occupancy. In contrast, the generalized norm of reciprocity evokes obligations towards others on the basis of their *past* behavior."[5] Hence the norm of reciprocity requires not just assessments of future gain, but also the fulfillment of prior "debts."

With respect to their moral and practical commitment to these normative obligations, Sheila and Anne converge. When asked about those times when she drew on her friends, Sheila claimed that she fulfilled her obligation to give back as much as she received: "I make them dinner or I take care of their kids. ... And that feels like it equals out." Later in the interview, she mused about the exchanges in which she was involved, and she insisted that valuing reciprocity carried considerable material costs of time and energy: "I lean on the side of doing too much for people, at my expense—like not sleeping or something. ... Nobody is saying you should even it up, but I do that." Anne Davenport said that she, too, believed in the obligation of reciprocity, and that she also made efforts that enabled her to make returns for assistance received. Her explanation combined family ties and friendships in a way that showed that a similar broad norm applies to both sets of relationships: "I try really hard to reciprocate with friends. Same with my family. I always feel obligated to give back."

Anne and Sheila thus find themselves in a bind. They have to ask for help but they neither want to jeopardize a stance of self-sufficiency nor expose their need or their failures to meet that need within the single-parent family structure. They also have limited time and energy with which to enact reciprocity. The

3. U.S. Census Bureau 2000 (Vermont and United states).
4. Gouldner 1960, 170.
5. Hansen 2004.

solution to this dilemma is found in the way they divide their world of social support into three central groupings—others in the same boat, family and friends deemed to have superior resources, and those who are part of a broader community—and apply a different form of reciprocity to each set of relationships.

Reciprocity with Those "In the Same Boat"

Most of the single mothers in this study spoke about their involvement in rich relationships of exchange with other single mothers. As was true of the women interviewed by Carol Stack in *All Our Kin*, a classic study that looked at exchange within a poor Black community within a Midwestern city in 1974, the women I interviewed shared a variety of resources, including transportation, child care, and small sums of money; they also shared emotional support, advice, and conversation.[6]

As was also true of the women Stack studied, the women in this study used kinship terminology to represent the nature of the bonds they shared with other single mothers. In so doing, the women demonstrated that they differentiated between biological kin (i.e., individuals with a similar background but possibly different current circumstances) and individuals who acted as kin (i.e., those with similar circumstances who shared resources).

For example, when asked to talk about the people with whom she exchanged goods and services, Sheila Davis explained, "My immediate family is not in Vermont and what I realized is that all of these people [in my network] are my family; I mean not in that intimate kind of way, but they're definitely my support system." Anne Davenport similarly reversed causality to make explicit how "gifts make friends" and to explain how gift-making friends become "family":

> It's always been clear to me that my friends [who are single mothers] are my family here, because I can count on them more than I can count on my own family often. I mean, I can call up and say, "Look, I need this or I need that," and they're available.

Anne also insisted that this form of mutual obligation trumps biology:

> I have a group of friends that are absolutely amazing as far as the sacrifices that we make for one another are huge. Easter was a really good example. I had lunch with my parents, which was the traditional lunch with my parents and our minister ... and then I had dinner with my friends. Somebody asked me what I was doing for Easter and I said, "I'm having lunch with my parents and I'm having dinner with my real family."

If kinship terminology helps to bind individuals in trusting relationships, trust does not rely on the assertion of kinship alone. Perhaps even more important to the creation of trust (and the claiming of others as kin) is the assurance that those who live in similar circumstances will understand, and be sympathetic about, one's circumstances. In drawing on this support from this group, single mothers can avoid the stigmas associated with both poverty and a "deviant" family structure. Forty-year-old Kara Lattrell, the mother of one daughter, described a variety of people on whom she depended. She subsequently spoke with particular warmth about her relationship with two of her friends. In accounting for why they helped one another, she referred to their common situation:

6. Stack 1974.

You know, we're really kind of in the same boat. I mean all three of us are single parents and we all have one child. We were all older parents when we had our children. ... So I think there's a lot of that common bond ... you know, sort of a shared life situation. It kind of makes it easy to think about helping each other out.

Other respondents also referred to a "shared life situation" as the reason why other single mothers would understand the strains in their lives and be sympathetic about the *need* for support. Using precisely the same image as did Kara, Anne Davenport said of her friendship with Joan Meyer: "We talk four times a day. ... She's a single mom and I think we're both in the same boat. ... I can trust her that she's not going to judge me or look at me in any different way and [that she] respects me for me." And Megan Paige listed a variety of reasons for wanting to shift her friendship circles when she became divorced. She put first the practical needs that motivated her creation of new friendships:

When I became single, I went out and I sought other single women friends. ... I realized that I particularly needed to be friends with other single parents because they were going to be the people that would be most receptive to having a network of helping each other out.

These networks do not arise by chance: They are not naturally existing communities to which the women gain entrance simply by virtue of being single mothers, but rather they represent careful creations comprised of those with shared demographic characteristics. Single mothers put considerable effort into establishing a social network that includes within it like-minded individuals in similar circumstances. This effort encompasses the work of evaluating potential network members and choosing from among them, of traveling to be with those selected for inclusion in a network, and of creating opportunities for congeniality even in the midst of the pressing demands of daily life. Indeed, in the rural community in which this research was conducted, access to other single mothers requires this effort; rural dispersion means that neighborhoods do not necessarily supply a ready-made set of individuals for a network. As Megan Paige said, she actively "sought" other single mothers to become her friends. Another single mother, Sarah Stanley, noted that her friends were located "all over the place," that she might have to "drive half an hour out of [her] way and drop [the children] at someone's house," and that she "worked really hard to make these friends." Sarah insisted as well that even though she found it hard to find the time to be with her friends, she considered doing so a priority because otherwise she would miss out on both the congeniality and the vital material support offered through friendship:

It's hard to take the time to even be with friends sometimes, but I always make time—I always make a lot of time for friends. I have friends over; I do a lot of entertaining. Because friends are like our mainstay. We have a great time together and also we know that we're going to be there for one another. So there you go.

All of these efforts constitute significant costs for single mothers, even as they lay the groundwork for significant benefits.

If Sarah focused on the efforts that went into creating and making use of her network, other women made it clear that as participants in intimate relationships of support they had to learn to abide by implicit rules. The members of these networks might make exceptions for extraordinary needs, but by and large they operate on the basis of a fairly balanced exchange of equivalencies within a limited time span, even though the language of more generalized reciprocity—"what goes 'round comes 'round"—prevails. When asked whether she had needed help with child care during the past six months, Kara Lattrell, one of the few women who lived in close proximity to other single mothers, described a constant flow of goods and services:

> We're sort of like the old, across-the-fence kind of neighbors. We trade back and forth, you know? The odd roll of toilet paper goes back and forth from house to house … and the cup of sugar, that kind of thing. We've traded child care a little bit, and [Mary] gives me rides sometimes now because she has a car.

Kara explained that it was "easy to think about helping" out Mary because she could assume that what went 'round would, indeed, come 'round. She approached her relationship with Claudia, another single mother, in the same way. Indeed, she described a support "triangle" among the three women: "If it's me, it means that sooner or later I'll help her and sooner or later Claudia will help me and then I'll help Mary and then Claudia will help Mary, and you know …"

As the women are questioned more fully about the details of these relationships, it becomes clear that notwithstanding the loose language of sharing, a balanced exchange of equivalencies *is* expected. On the one hand, Cathy Earl, like Kara, said she did not operate on a strict basis of immediate tit for tat. When asked by the interviewer, "Do you try and keep track, for example, with your friends? If you've asked one at one point do you try and ask someone else another time?" Cathy responded, "No, not with my friends, I don't." On the other hand, she also suggested that she kept a mental balance sheet of who had loaned, and of who was owed, as well as of their awareness of her reliability in paying back her debts. Furthermore, she reiterated that the sharing was acceptable because—as "true" kin—they would understand both how her need emerged and how it felt to experience that need.

Interviewer: If you needed money, for example, what do you think you would do?

Cathy Earl: Actually, Sarah has loaned me money before, so I could probably ask her, and Dorothy, for small amounts. … I feel okay about that. I always pay them back and I've done the same for them. Like I say, they know what it's like so it feels okay.

Anne Davenport indicated that the requirement of reciprocity was motivated by her awareness of the distinctive pattern of needs among women living close to the margin. Indeed, she believed she had special obligations to the single mothers in her network:

> Because my group of support involves single women, single parents, moms … I want to make sure that it's reciprocal. [All that] comes into the decision: When have I last called them? Are they able to handle this right now? What can I do for them in exchange? Is there something I could do this week to help them out? I mean, you're always thinking about that.

Reciprocity with Family and Friends in a More Fortunate World

While single mothers appear to find comfort in, and rely heavily on, equitable and balanced exchanges in their relationships with other single mothers, these close networks cannot fulfill all their needs because others are likely to be as poor as themselves. Single mothers thus also reach out to other members of their social worlds as they strive to meet the demands that caregiving, employment, and the everyday activities of housework make on their time and energy.

Family members can become especially important as sources to draw on for assistance; this is especially likely when they are perceived as being more fortunate than the single mothers themselves. Friends who are not single mothers can also be drawn into relationships of support. Like the single-mother friends, these others, both family and friends, offer a wide range of goods and services to the respondents, including emotional support, limited financial support, and help with the tasks of daily survival (e.g., transportation and babysitting). However, these "other" individuals are more likely than are single-mother friends to offer substantial financial support, which is a form of assistance unavailable from those who have little extra themselves. If the elements of what the single mothers receive from these other individuals are otherwise the same, the understanding of the relationships is quite different. Indeed, the women are far more likely to acknowledge imbalance in the material content of these relationships than they are in their relationships with those considered to be in "the same boat," even as they proclaim their commitment to reciprocity.

The failure to be able to reciprocate in kind is not surprising. Single mothers *do* have acute and unpredictable needs, and for the most part, limited material resources, time, and energy with which to make exchanges. This is not to imply that the women readily accepted unmitigated dependence. In order to accept substantial assistance without admitting to dependence, the single mothers I interviewed developed strategic explanations for how their behavior could be conceived of as fitting within the norm of reciprocity. They also made whatever concrete gestures they could to enable them to accept help without incurring debt.

Much theoretical writing about reciprocity would suggest that exchange relationships can be balanced by repaying material goods with gratitude, emotion work, and loyalty. What is striking, however, is that it is only with respect to those identified as being more fortunate than themselves, that single mothers define gratitude, emotion work, and loyalty not merely as vital elements of repayment for goods and services received, but sometimes as the sole repayment. In asserting that these are sufficient items of exchange in some, but not all, of their relationships, the single mothers distinguish among sets of relationships; they also accept the costly burden of engaging in actions that can undermine their position as social equals, even as they claim reciprocity as a way to fulfill the obligations incumbent on an adult in our society.

A straightforward "economy of gratitude" operates in some cases.[7] Phoebe Stark, a forty-one-year-old mother of twin sons, first asserted that her relationships with others were "all pretty reciprocal" and she noted that she preferred it that way because she didn't want to "be obligated to people." Yet she also acknowledged that she was the recipient of gifts for which she incurred debts fulfilled by simply offering thanks: "People are always giving [Christmas presents] to my kids and ... I don't give gifts anymore, except for my immediate family. ... We make sure that [people who give presents are] thanked and we are grateful." Phoebe Stark added as well that in relationships with those more fortunate she viewed "emotion work" as a valuable item of exchange: "I might give in other ways. I have a tendency to give in other ways to people, not in material ways—by being there or calling and, you know, checking on people and friends and talking."[8]

7. This term comes from Hochschild 1989, 2003.
8. This term comes from Hochschild 1983.

In addition to gratitude, emotion work, and loyalty, single mothers view affiliation with their children, and in some cases affiliation with themselves, as resources that meet the demands of reciprocity. If the quid pro quo is so attenuated here as to seem to vanish, in context the women make it clear that they embed affiliation within their notion of the obligations of reciprocal exchange.

Indeed, children frequently become "pawns" in the strategy of giving and receiving.

Betsy Black, a thirty-eight-year-old mother of two sons, simultaneously asserted her rights as a single mother with ongoing needs to have care provided by her own mother *and* suggested that she was not left in debt because her mother derived pleasure simply from being with the grandchildren: "Because I'm a single mom I ask [my mother] to spend time with the kids. ... And it's a really good experience for the kids and she loves it of course." She also said that she rarely repaid her friends in kind because their children so loved having her children visit, it made their parenting easier: "And then my kids go for sleepovers because their kids like having them there." When Kara Lattrell was asked "what's given and received" in her relationship with her brother and sister-in-law, she responded, "Well, let's see. I probably get more from them than I give, but I give them my kid! That's a lot!"

A different, but closely related, gesture of reciprocity involves drawing on evidence that a mother has satisfied the giver's expectations and desires. Most simply, the women point to their own survival and the survival of their children, as meeting the perceived desire of friends and relatives to ensure the livelihood of those they love. In doing so, single mothers often highlight the positive outcomes of divorce or separation. Respondents suggest, for example, that relatives and friends who have watched them suffer emotional pain and even physical violence in their prior relationships are "reimbursed" when they see the women escape. As one woman said, "It was very clear that it was no strings attached and [my father and brothers] didn't want [the money] paid back at all. They were really proud that I had gotten out of a bad situation and they wanted to help me out and make sure it worked."

And sometimes single mothers describe simply how the giver derives pleasure from an act of generosity and argues that this pleasure is sufficient to expunge any further obligation. One mother said that she was not sure what she offered in her relationship with a downstairs neighbor ("I guess to some extent some emotional support"), but that in a sense, returning something of equivalent value didn't matter because that convenient neighbor was "an incredibly giving person." Alexis Smith similarly could accept presents from her brother because he was "sweet, very sweet" to think of buying her sheets for her new household, and she could accept clothing from her mother because her "mom tends to like to buy my daughter a dress or something."

Single mothers strive to find ways to reconcile dependence with independence and the need to expose insufficiency with the possibility of scorn for that insufficiency. When they fail to reconcile the competing needs—when they believe they have become too dependent or too exposed to contempt—the single mothers sometimes break off relationships with individuals from whom they may very well need support. Cathy Earl preferred to borrow small sums of money from her friends rather than from her brothers because she could not stand being seen as "as somebody who just can't make it." Cathy indicated that this calculated decision to privilege her pride over their disdain meant forgoing vital support, and that sometimes she had to make the opposite choice. Even then, however, she chose carefully from within her network:

If it's something financial, something I just can't swing, I would call my brother Kenneth. He would be first on the list. My brother Michael, he's second because he's not quite as understanding. For small things, a ride somewhere, or could you help me pick up the kids or something like that, I have Dorothy, I have my friend Sarah, I have a couple of other friends that are nearby here that I would rely on.

Cathy also suggested that she tried to avoid a man who had previously been her boyfriend, because he humiliated her with his constant reminders that she might have been better off staying with him:

He's the type who would pitch in and help, but there's a price there. You know, the price is, you have to listen to him say, "See, you couldn't make it on your own, could you, Cathy." And so he rubs it in, so even though he's willing to do a lot for me … but he'd go, "Hey Kid, you really need me, don't you, after all. You couldn't make it on your own." And so, as much as I need him, or it would be nice [to have his help], you have to put up with that attitude, and so I really try not to [ask him].

Ultimately, women who cannot accept the price of "gifts" may withdraw from and even terminate relationships with those to whom they perceive themselves as being in debt:

I haven't called [my friend Peter] for a long time because … I really want to pay [back the money I owe him] and I hate not being able. And he says, I mean, he says over and over and over again, "I know you'll pay it when you can." It's very hard for me. And so I have withdrawn. … I haven't talked to him in almost six months.

Generalized Reciprocity in an Idealized Community

As the women we interviewed discuss their relationships with the broader community in which they live, reciprocity emerges in a new guise. At one level, the women sound as if they believe the world should operate on the basis of an easy flow of generalized reciprocity over time. When asked what it is appropriate to ask of the community in which she lived, twenty-year-old Polly King responded, "I feel it's appropriate to ask as little as you can get away with, give as much as you can, and somewhere along the line everybody gets what they need." Liz Miles, who is considerably older than Polly, also described a world of generalized reciprocity:

I believe if there are balances other places, that it doesn't necessarily have to be between two people, in the sense of somebody may give me something and I may give someone else something. But when it doesn't feel balanced to me is when I feel like I can't give to anyone else, when people are giving to me and I can't give to anyone else.

At another level, if these two women do accept the requirement to make returns for gifts received, they acknowledge that the constraints are much looser than those that apply in their more intimate relationships: Liz may give to one person today and assume that person will pass on the favor, and Polly needs only to give what she can.

As Polly and Liz shift their attention to the flow of goods and services throughout a community, they rely on an idealized vision of human nature in which individuals readily hold themselves responsible for, and eagerly respond to, the needs of others. The language women employ when they describe that ideal rests, at least in part, on the imagery of a traditional, rural community in which everyone knows everyone else, where needs and wants are public concerns. Addressing this issue more directly, Sarah Stanley said, "I would like to see communities where neighbors are there for one another, to help out in the middle of the night if there's like a crisis or a flood. I believe in giving and receiving and helping, helping one another. That makes sense."

If Polly, Liz, and Sarah believe in generalized reciprocity, they also resist the notion that the obligation to give falls equally on everyone's shoulders at any given point in time. Although Sarah said she believed "in giving and receiving and helping," she rejected the notion that there was a "should" attached to this ideal: "Some people have more time, more money. They're not overwhelmed in their daily lives and they have the time and the energy to devote to the communities." Sarah thus excluded herself—and others in similar circumstances—from the obligation to give during periods of acute distress. Similarly, when Rose Bishop says that she believes "people are pretty understanding right now [that] I can't offer a whole lot," she acknowledges that she is not now in a position to engage in reciprocal behavior (though she anticipates that there may be a time when she will be able to play a different kind of role in the chain of generalized reciprocity). Mary Farmer, now owes ninety hours to her babysitting pool. When asked to discuss her feelings about this, she said, "I don't feel like I reciprocate as much as I'd like to, but a lot of times it's because [the others] don't really have the same needs that I do in terms of child care." Grace Jordan, a fifty-one-year-old, never-married mother of one adopted daughter, provided yet another, subtle variation on this theme. While she originally accepted the obligation to reciprocate to a friend who had done much for her over the years, ultimately she rejected that obligation because she deemed her friend's needs excessive and even trivial when compared to her own:

> I never figured out how to reciprocate with her except this one time. I said, "Let me! Tell me what I can do." And so when she asks me, she says, "I'm flying to California and David can't take me to the airport, could you take me?" She's finally asking me for a very concrete way I can help her. And I said, "I can't do it on that day, I'm really sorry!" And she said, "Well, David can't either and I don't know what I'm supposed to do." And I said, "I've got to tell you something. No one ever drives me to the airport. I drive myself and leave my car in the long-term parking lot." It's not a big deal; that was my subtext.

Learning to Ask for Help

When single mothers rely on others for assistance to get by, they do so through practices that enable them to believe in their own independence, avoid scorn and humiliation, and sustain commitment to the ideal of an idealized community. Thus they simultaneously solve practical problems of daily life and the moral problem of conceiving of themselves as *worthy* citizens. In doing so, they not only have to work to develop appropriate networks, but they also must overcome their own resistance to asking for help, and develop the fine art of asking.

Many women said that it had been difficult for them to ask for help because doing so changed their own self-image; some even described the act as leading to feelings of resentment about having to ask at all. Kara Lattrell believed that sometimes she should simply be the recipient of "pure" generosity and that she should not have to ask for needed assistance. In explaining how she arrived at this position, she told a story about having yelled at her child in public, which led to her being the object of a neighbor's gossip. She examined her anger with her neighbor and found its roots in the neighbor's failure to make extra efforts to meet the needs of single parents:

It kind of sunk in that the reason why I was angry at her was not because she was talking about it, or not because she noticed it, or not because she was concerned about it, but because what the hell had she ever done to prevent it? ... And [I want to tell her] that the thing to really look at is not how awful I was that I yelled at my kid, but how, if she doesn't want to be part of the problem, she needs to be part of the solution. And part of the solution means that ... she has a responsibility to the kids, and having a responsibility [means] really going to a parent and saying, "Hey, you know, I noticed you're a single parent. I'll bet that's pretty stressful." And it's like, "Gee, I guess I could have your little Billy or little Susie come over to my house and play with my kid, like, you know, once a week for a couple of hours." And how would that be? That would really help you out. God! If somebody did that to me I'd feel like I was in seventh heaven.

Amy Phelps, the divorced mother of two daughters, expressed the same sentiment in a less ferocious way:

I just did [my own snow shoveling and plowing] and then eventually [a neighbor offered] to plow and that was nice. I think there's still some people out there that will see that it's just her and her two kids and maybe I can help out. There still are a few nice people like that. And that's happened to me a couple of times so that's been great. ... Sometimes I feel kind of weird—like you think I can't do this—and then sometimes, I guess it depends on the day, it's like, "Oh, thank you." Most of the time I don't refuse them. I say, "Thanks so much."

In short, while the single mothers want to see themselves as equal participants in a world where generous giving prevails, they also believe that their current situation of need entitles them, at least temporarily, to be on the receiving end of that generosity; they thus introduce a notion of noblesse oblige (even as they reject its associated costs of deference). In so doing they retain their social status as citizens who have (eventual) obligations to a community and they locate the help they receive within the moral framework of what decent people do for others. By insisting that decent people respond to need without being asked, they shift the burden of responsibility from their shoulders to the shoulders of others.

If they resent having to ask for help, the women know that they often have no choice; they have to accept the fact that they cannot manage on their own. As this acceptance seeps in, they come to regard their acquisition of the skill of seeking out assistance, as a concrete achievement emerging from their changed circumstances. As one woman described it, she had never had to ask for help before, but she believed that in learning to do so she had acquired an important new set of skills:

Well, I really think that [asking for help is] something I never did before and I just, as a single parent, I've realized that I have to ask for the support I need. So I've learned to do that. And it may have been hard at first, but I really, at this point, I feel like okay, they can say no, you know. And the financial part—that's just a small, small piece of the whole picture. Mostly what I need is support with the kids. And I do ask for help. ... I've just gotten a lot better at [asking for help] than I was before. ... It's easier because I've been practicing.

Moreover, those who have mastered the fine art of asking suggest that they have also acquired the challenging skill of judging who is available, competent, and appropriate for a given need. Janet Linden explained, "It's really hard to trace my thought processes because there's just an image that comes up and when I feel like I need someone to talk to, a face appears, and that's who I call, and I would be real hesitant myself to try to trace what has happened." Alexis Smith spoke similarly about an elaborate process of determining whom she could ask for assistance with each of the different tasks of daily survival:

> So I decide by—I try to decide by checking in and seeing what I need. And if it's a financial thing I call my dad—or my mom. And if it's an issue of like an immediate thing or an immediate crisis or decision, I would call a friend; but also, if it's something I feel like my mom just wouldn't get it, I just wouldn't call her. ... I guess it's pretty intricate. ... Because then you're thinking about what is this person's relationship to you? And I guess different parts of me are out there with different people.

Kate Harrington, the woman whose network was dissolving, spoke eloquently about not yet having acquired the necessary skills during this unsettled period in her life. While her focus in the quote below is on learning how to be a single mother—what she calls this "24-7, just me"—her comments also made clear that she had not yet learned about how being a single mother had changed her needs, and with them her relationships with those in her circle of friends. The comments also suggest that she is still learning how to balance her own needs with what she can offer to others in return for their assistance. As she considered this issue, she both assessed her own gifts and acknowledged the limits of her energy and understanding:

> Well, you know, this is kind of new. You know, before [my daughter was born], friendships were friendships and I didn't have as many needs. Since then, you know, it's just kind of like trial and error. There's a lot I can do. I'm really good at giving emotional support. You know, I'm good at that. But there're a lot of other things I can do too that people—like my one friend didn't accept my offers to help her move. ... I have to be careful because I don't have a lot to give right now. So I have to be careful about how much I ask for because I don't have a lot. I mean everything is pretty much going into learning how to be a single mother and handling this like 24-7, just me. So I don't have a whole lot to give out.

Conclusion

This reading has shown that when single mothers rely on others they distinguish among different groups of people in their social worlds, and they operate within the constraints of a broadly defined reciprocity even as the enactment of that norm shifts with the perceived situation of the giver. The analysis has also shown that maintaining relationships of support, balanced or not, is challenging work. In some ways the dispersed rural setting of Vermont intensifies the work of community: Because they live in relative geographical isolation from others in similar situations, single mothers have to work especially hard to make exchanges with, or to do favors for, others who share their circumstances of need.

At the same time, the dispersion means that these women are not segregated into tightly bounded or segregated ghettos of poverty where no one has much to give. Single mothers living in very poor neighborhoods receive less cash assistance from family and friends than do those who live in somewhat better or more varied surroundings.[9] The latter women, like those in this study, are more likely to be in contact with individuals who possess greater resources, even as they are more likely to be exposed to direct scorn from those whose lives differ from their own.

Discussion Questions

1. Do you agree that self-sufficiency is an important value in U.S. society? What evidence can you give to show that people place a value on self-sufficiency? How has this value manifested itself in your life?
2. Why are the single mothers Nelson interviewed so committed to reciprocity? Are you equally committed to reciprocity?
3. Do you think reciprocity would be easier for single mothers in an urban area? Why or why not?
4. Do you think that those on the receiving end view "gratitude, emotion work, and loyalty" as adequate returns for the assistance they provide single mothers?

References

Edin, Kathryn, and Laura Lein. *Making Ends Meet: How Single Mothers Survive Welfare and Low Wage Work.* New York: Russell Sage Foundation, 1997.
Gouldner, Alvin W. "The Norm of Reciprocity: A Preliminary Statement." *American Sociological Review* 25, no. 2 (April 1960): 161–78.
Hansen, Karen V. *Not-So-Nuclear Families: Class, Gender and Networks of Care.* New Brunswick, NJ: Rutgers University Press, 2004.
Hochschild, Arlie Russell. *The Managed Heart: The Commercialization of Human Feeling.* Berkeley: University of California Press, 1983.
–––. *The Second Shift.* New York: Penguin Books, 1989, 2003.
Pearce, Diana. "The Feminization of Poverty: Women, Work and Welfare." *Urban and Social Change Review* 11 (February 1978): 28–36.
Stack, Carol. *All Our Kin: Strategies for Survival in a Black Community.* New York: Harper and Row, 1974.
U.S. Census Bureau. "Profile of Selected Economic Characteristics: 2000: United States." In *American Fact Finder.* 2000. http://factfinder.census.gov/servlet. Accessed October 22, 2004.
–––. "Profile of Selected Economic Characteristics: 2000: Vermont." In *American Fact Finder.* 2000. http://factfinder.census.gov/servlet. Accessed October 22, 2004.
U.S. Census Bureau, Department of Commerce. By Jason Fields, and Lynne M. Casper. *America's Families and Living Arrangements*, 2001.

9. Edin and Lein, 1997.

Post-Reading Questions

1. What did Margaret K. Nelson learn by interviewing single mothers in rural Vermont? What are some of the common struggles that these women face?
2. What is the feminization of poverty? How does this contribute to gender inequalities and society and lead to difficult circumstances for single mothers?
3. What struggles does poverty pose for single mothers? What kinds of social policies might help to alleviate some of these struggles?

UNIT VI

Key Terms and Definitions

Review the key terms and definitions below to strengthen your understanding of the readings in this unit.

Education: A societal institution that aims to provide knowledge, skills, and information to the population, conveying a series of beliefs, values, and social norms.

Institutional Prejudice and Discrimination: Prejudice and discrimination that is embedded in societal institutions including the economy, mass media, the education system, the criminal justice system, and other arenas. These patterns can put marginalized racial and ethnic groups including Black people, Latinx people, and others at a severe disadvantage in society.

No Child Left Behind Act (NCLB): A federal education policy that passed in 2001 with bipartisan support and was replaced by the Every Student Succeeds Act in 2015. The original act held the federal government accountable for student performance through standardized testing. The goal was to help close the achievement gap faced by poor and minoritized student populations.

Prison Industrial Complex (PIC): The convergence of government, the surveillance industry, and the prison system into a system that maintains social control of the population through extreme measures.

Schooling: The formal lessons that students receive from trained instructors in the education system.

The School-to-Prison Pipeline: The criminalization of people of color from a young age, leading to encounters with law enforcement and the criminal justice system and interrupting the schooling process. This phenomenon contributes to the disproportionate number of marginalized racial and ethnic groups in the prison system.

Zero-Tolerance Policies: Strict school policies that emphasize harsh punishment, such as suspension or expulsion, for violating certain campus rules.

Introduction

In the first reading for unit 8, "On Education and Democracy," Richard A. Quantz contemplates whether education is a privilege or a right. He ponders the meaning of education and what it entails. Quantz cites a quote by the American philosopher John Dewey, who believed **education** begins at birth and does not require formal **schooling**. Education is also a means to become part of a community. Over time, the primary ways in which we receive an education have evolved. In the past, we primarily received knowledge, skills, and information through informal encounters in the family. Over time, other institutions like schools and mass media have taken on the role of educating the public as well. In an ideal world, schooling would contribute greatly to our education. However, since schools are flawed, we may not always receive the skills, knowledge, and information we truly need from these institutions. Although schools may provide some level of technical training, they do not always successfully teach us how to analyze, interpret, and think critically about the world. Furthermore, even though schools are designed to be democratic institutions, in reality, they are unequal.

In the second reading for this unit, titled "The State of Our Education," Terence Fitzgerald describes the barriers that Black males face in the education system. He notes that out of all racial groups, Black people have the largest achievement gap compared to white people. Socioeconomic factors such as poverty do not account for these differences. Unfortunately, **institutional prejudice and discrimination** in our education system are to blame. Black males face the most setbacks out of any group in the US school system. Fitzgerald notes that Black males are more likely than other racial groups to be suspended, expelled, and disciplined by school authorities. Latino males also face higher rates of suspension, expulsion, and discipline. Some studies show that Black and Latinx students who are suffering academically are the ones who face the most risk of punishment. Unfortunately, this can have life-altering impacts, leading to negative financial, social, and political consequences. For example, researchers have identified a trend called the **school-to-prison pipeline**, whereby Black students are routinely criminalized from a young age and face discipline at the hands of school administrators and law enforcement, interrupting their education. For example, if a Black student breaks a campus rule, it is very common for police to be called. On the other hand, if a white student breaks the same rule, parents are called instead. **Zero-tolerance policies** in schools contribute to this pattern. Zero-tolerance policies rely upon harsh forms of punishment, such as suspension and expulsion, to discipline students. These policies lead to major disruptions in students' education and can coincide with increased encounters with law enforcement and the criminal justice system. Rather than funding schools and providing them with necessary educational resources, our nation instead allocates enormous sums of money to private prisons. This funding contributes to the formation of a **prison industrial complex (PIC)**, where the government, the surveillance industry, and prison systems work together to subject the population to social control. Fitzgerald points out the tragic irony in this picture, showing how the school-to-prison pipeline, zero-tolerance policies, and the prison industrial complex (PIC) contribute to solidifying already-existing racial inequalities in society.

In the last reading for this unit, "The Zip Code Effect: Educational Inequality in the United States," Wayne Au analyzes how a student's zip code can help to predict their retention and success in the education system. As he notes, a zip code alone cannot predict or determine a student's performance, of course. However, as geographical markers, zip codes do in fact define the social divide between the rich and poor. The author describes his own experience as an educator in Berkeley, California, noting that social class and racial inequalities can be seen prominently in Berkeley High School, which consists of rich, predominately white students as well as Black and Latinx students who are mostly from economically disadvantaged, working-class communities. The author shows that these demographics reflect a trend elsewhere in the United States as well. The author identifies some of the problems with the **No Child Left Behind Act**, or (NCLB), which was legislation passed in 2001. The act proposed to help close the achievement gap for poor and minoritized students. However, with its emphasis on standardized testing, many critics believe it instead reinforced some existing inequalities. Many educators point out that standardized tests tend to contain biases and do not accurately measure student abilities. White students from privileged backgrounds tend to score the highest on these measures. On the other hand, students from poor communities, Black and Latinx students, and English language learners often struggle with these types of assessments. Furthermore, some students showed that drop-out rates increased when rigorous standardized testing became the norm. The author takes a Marxist perspective to show that schools can perpetuate social inequalities by using high-stakes standardized testing and maintaining the economic status quo.

On Education and Democracy

Richard A. Quantz

Everyone seems to have an opinion about education: whether it is worth having; whether it is necessary; whether they've had enough of it, not enough of it, or too much of it; how bad it is; how to make it better or less expensive; or how to make a profit from it. But even though everyone seems to have an opinion about it, few stop to reflect about what education might actually be.

Is education a privilege or a right? If it is a privilege, how do we decide who is to have it and who is not? If it is a right, why is it that some people have so much more access to it than others? When does education begin? At birth, or at age five or six when a child starts school? When does it end? At age sixteen; eighteen; twenty-two, when a young adult leaves school; or when a person simply decides to stop pursuing it regardless of age? Perhaps it never ends until we die? Is education something to "have" (that is, a thing) or is it something that is "done" (that is, a process)? What does it mean to be educated? Does it mean a person now has the skills necessary to get a good job? Does it mean that a person knows how to learn through reading and reasoning? Does it mean that a person knows the primary knowledge that it takes to be a well-functioning, adult member of a particular community? How do we know when a person is making progress toward being educated? How do we know when a person has made sufficient progress that she or he can stop?

The Latin root, *ēducātiō*, refers merely to the process of bringing up children. And, of course, the upbringing of children begins when they are born and ends when they are recognized as adults. This idea that education is the process of raising children into adulthood remains one of the major uses of the term in English today, but it is hardly the only way the term *education* is used in contemporary English. At least since the sixteenth century,

English speakers have used the term to refer to the cultural development of knowledge, understanding, and character.[1]

John Dewey began his 1887 educational manifesto, "My Pedagogic Creed," by stating,

> I believe that all education proceeds by the participation of the individual in the social consciousness of the [human] race. This process begins unconsciously almost at birth, and is continually shaping the individual's powers, saturating his consciousness, forming his habits, training his ideas, and arousing his feelings and emotions. Through this unconscious education the individual gradually comes to share in the intellectual and moral resources which humanity has succeeded in getting together. He becomes an inheritor of the funded capital of civilization.[2]

Dewey's understanding of education adds some specificity and clarity to the traditional understandings mentioned above. He understands education to be something that begins at birth and does not require schools. He also understands education as a process by which individuals become members of a larger community. Typically, of course, this refers to children who wish to become members of good standing in the adult community within which they are raised, but a careful reading of the above quotation suggests that Dewey's community includes all humanity, which, it would seem, requires all of us to pursue education throughout our lives as our circle of humanity widens as we grow, age, and learn. To "share in the intellectual and moral resources which humanity has succeeded in getting together" is surely a lifelong project.

Dewey's conception of education also clearly refers to the process through which individuals become integrated into human society. It is a process that seeks the development of the whole person in a multitude of knowledge, skills, habits, and attitudes. It is primarily, though not exclusively, intellectual and moral. It is the preparation of the individual to accept their responsibility and perform their part in continuing the ever-evolving improvement and growth of our communities. It is the process by which human civilization itself grows and progresses.

Education versus Training

In today's world, many people equate education with training, but education is much more. We can train a dog, but we cannot educate a dog. We can train a person, but we can also educate a person. Mere training may be sufficient for dogs, but people deserve more: they deserve education. *Training* is the process through which we learn a technique or a skill or a job. It is the process of learning to reason technically—to solve given problems by applying set rules. It comprises specialized knowledge and technical learning. In training, we typically learn how to do very specific things, such as operate a computer or balance a budget. Learning about computers becomes *educational* when it moves beyond the mere techniques of using the computer to a broader understanding through a critical inquiry into computers; their uses; their

1. *Oxford English Dictionary* (online), s.v. "education," March 5, 2013, www.oed.com.proxy.lib.muohio.edu/view/Entry/59584?redirectedFrom=education.
2. John Dewey, "My Pedagogic Creed," *School Journal* 54 (1897): 77–80, http://dewey.pragmatism.org/creed.htm.

problems and possibilities; and their multiple social, ethical, and other meanings. In a similar way, although balancing a budget may be important training, it only becomes educational when budgeting comes to be understood as a way of thinking and approaching the world.

Certainly, teachers need some training, but they need much more than training if they are to be successful teachers—they need education. Teacher training only becomes teacher education when the techniques taught in methods courses are understood within broader philosophical, ethical, political, historical, and sociocultural contexts. Part of the purpose of this book is to help students gain a better understanding of the broader contexts of education. Its purpose, then, includes helping students, whether in a teaching major or not, move beyond mere training to gain part of what is necessary to become educated about education.

Education versus Schooling

All societies educate their young even if they don't have schools. They teach their young the customs, language, traditions, myths, and knowledge that their society upholds as true, good, or normal. Similarly, these societies teach their young what they believe to be false, bad, or abnormal. Traditional societies use educational practices that are mostly integrated into everyday life, controlled closely by the members of the local community, and only sometimes situated outside of daily life. An example of this would be coming-of-age rituals when an age group of boys or girls is often removed from the community for a period of time where, under the tutelage of an adult, they are introduced to the special knowledge of the community.

On the other hand, even though modern societies certainly have many educational practices in the everyday family and community life of the child (such as dietary and moral education), modern societies rely heavily on institutions that are removed from the practices of family and community life, such as schools and the media. In traditional societies, the customs, language, traditions, and knowledge considered true or false, good or bad, and normal or abnormal arise in the daily practices of interacting with one's parents and other adults integrated into a common culture. In these societies, education is assumed to be an integral part of daily life. But in modern societies, much of what is learned takes place outside of the family in a public space controlled by public institutions, such as schools and the media, leading many people to equate education with formal institutions, as something separate from ordinary daily living. Equating education with schooling, however, is inappropriate; traditional societies may not have schools, but they have education. Also, much of the education in the contemporary, modern world still occurs in the ordinary daily life of families and communities.

If we follow Dewey's reasoning as explained above, to be educated involves a lifelong process of learning and growth; to be schooled is a formal process of instruction organized by a particular institution (typically the state, but sometimes religious or other private organizations) and usually lasting for a limited time in a person's life span. In the contemporary world, schooling is typically compulsory, sequential, and ends in young adulthood. To become an educated person, however, requires learning after schooling ends. It is a long-term, lifelong goal. If a person has received good schooling, he or she will have developed the knowledge, skills, reasoning, creativity, and dispositions necessary to continue the process throughout life.

If all a person received through schooling is a set of acquired knowledge and skills, that schooling will not have prepared her or him well for a life in pursuit of education.

Even though many people in today's modern societies equate education and schooling, education is a larger concept. Education encompasses both informal and formal learning. It involves our everyday lived experiences as well as what we learn in such formalized institutions as schools. *Schooling* is an institutionalized system that we hope leads to education. Unfortunately, too often schools focus on training, on mere knowledge and skill acquisition, and not on a full education.

Even worse, much schooling is *mis*educative. That is to say, rather than coming "to share in the intellectual and moral resources which humanity has succeeded in getting together" (to use Dewey's phrase above), too often schooling leads students to confuse their training with education, to embrace their ignorance and reject the intellectual qualities that are inherent in education, or to denigrate themselves as someone unable to become educated. In other words, schools have the potential to educate, but education does not always occur in schools.

Colleges and universities are schools. Whether or not students gain mere training while being schooled in college, or whether they gain some education, depends partly on their instructors, but largely it depends on them. Do they want an education, or do they just want to be trained for a job? Do they even know what one needs to do to gain an education?

Many educational scholars, myself included, believe that most American students have spent at least twelve years in schools dedicated to training them to be good technical readers, technical writers, and technical thinkers, but not interpretive readers, analytical writers, and critical thinkers. Having spent twelve years gaining "knowledge and skills," most American students are well prepared for continuing their training. But having had little in the way of education beyond training, many American college students may be at a loss as to how to move beyond the technical requirements of knowledge and skill acquisition to the intellectual and moral prerequisites required to gain an education. Too often these well-trained students treat education as if it were a consumer product—something to pay for, ingest, and master. They wait eagerly, perhaps, but futilely, for their instructors to train them to be educated. Unfortunately for them, education is not a consumer good, and it is not something that one can gain through training. It is something that students have to do for themselves.

Nonetheless, that doesn't mean they have to do it alone. In fact, there is good reason to think that trying to gain an education alone is futile. Students must have the help of other students and their instructors; otherwise, how can they possibly become integrated into the larger community? Part of being a member of a community is the ability and inclination to engage others in the pursuit of education. To gain an education in college requires that students move beyond mastery of knowledge and skills and learn to read the world, to reason critically, and to engage others in a joint pursuit of wisdom. These are the purposes of this book: to help students learn to read the world in order to read the word,[3] to learn to reason critically in order to critique the world of education, and to stimulate engagement with others in the sociocultural process that leads to wisdom.

3. See Paulo Freire and Donaldo P. Macedo, *Literacy: Reading the Word and the World,* Critical Studies in Education Series (South Hadley, MA: Bergin & Garvey Publishers, 1987).

Liberal Education

Many colleges and universities in the United States require that students not only engage in a specialized course of study (i.e., a major) but take courses in liberal education as well. When asked why they are required to do this, most college students respond that a liberal education broadens students' knowledge so that they know about more than just their own major area of study. But when asked why this is desirable, few can give a good reason. And why a broad education is considered "liberal" is equally unclear.

One of the primary reasons for this confusion is that in ordinary usage, the term *liberal* tends to describe a particular political orientation that is primarily understood as the opposite of conservative. Later in this book, that usage will be explored and complicated, but here I wish to explore an earlier, more fundamental, and original meaning for the term *liberal*. If we think about it for a moment, we should notice that the word "liberal" appears to have the same root as some other English words such as *liberty, liberalize,* and *liberate,* all words that in one way or another have something to do with freedom. We shouldn't be surprised at this because the root for all of these words is the Latin word *liber,* which means "free."

We should suspect from this that a liberal education has something to do with freedom. But what is that connection? To understand it, we need to know that the idea that we refer to as liberal education is inspired by the education provided to free citizens of ancient Athens. Whether true or not, in American mythology,[4] the American democracy was inspired by the democracy of ancient Athens, where all free, adult males were members of the governing Athenian senate. From this sense, a "liberal" education should be understood as the education needed by a free citizen who must accept and carry out his or her responsibilities in the governing of the city-state.

Mortimer Adler, one of America's best known classical philosophers, argues that a liberal education, in the classic sense, is the education one needs to pursue a fully human life in one's leisure time, that is, outside of one's vocation. According to Adler, education for work is the kind of education one provides slaves who have no right or responsibility to the governing of public space. In contemporary America, where slavery is no longer legal, nearly all of us must have some sort of occupation, so, Adler concedes, we all need some sort of vocational training. However, he also vigorously argues, we are all also citizens and share both the right and the responsibility to actively participate in the governance of public life. This is the purpose of liberal education—to provide the kind of education needed by everyone in a democratic society in order to provide the knowledge, skills, values, and dispositions necessary to fulfill their roles as citizens in a democratic society.[5]

---

4. Many scholars point out that the Hau de no sau nee (also known as the Six Nations or the Iroquois Confederacy) may actually be the oldest democracy. Certainly the founding fathers of the American experiment drew inspiration from ancient Athens, but they also drew inspiration from the Hau de no sau nee nations who occupied the New England territory when the Europeans arrived. The reality of an actual democracy among a confederacy of nations on the North American continent was influential in their own commitment to develop a democratic confederacy from the thirteen English colonies. For a good and accessible discussion of the Hau de no sau nee democracy and its contribution to the American conception of democracy, see David T. Ratcliffe, *The Six Nations: Oldest Living Participatory Democracy on Earth* (Roslindale, MA: Rat Hous Reality Press, 1995–2013), www.ratical.org/many_worlds/ 6Nations/.

5. Mortimer Adler, "Labor, Leisure, and Liberal Education," *Journal of General Education* 6 (1951): 35–45.

Education and Democracy

Earlier in this [reading], I pointed out that Dewey understands education to be a lifelong pursuit "to share in the intellectual and moral resources which humanity has succeeded in getting together." But Dewey's emphasis on "humanity" should not be taken to mean that he was unaware of social and cultural differences among different communities and nations. Clearly, a child needs to be integrated into a successive series of different communities, starting with the family, then the local community and the nation. For Dewey, one of the key differences among nations is their different political systems, and of all political systems, according to Dewey, democracies are the most dependent on education. In fact, for Dewey, democracies not only require education, true education requires democracy—not just at the national level, but also at the school and classroom levels.

To understand why democracy and education are so intertwined, we must gain a better understanding of what Dewey meant by "democracy." Put simply, "A democracy is more than a form of government; it is primarily a mode of associated living, of conjoint communicated experience."[6] Dewey argued that there were two aspects of democracy that people often confused. One aspect he referred to as "the idea of democracy," or the wide commitment to a way of living together as expressed in the definition above. One might think of the democratic idea as a commitment to a process where everyone is respected and included as we all figure out ways for all of us to live and work together.

The idea of democracy should not be confused with the political mechanisms of democracy found in such institutions as government, secret ballots, majority rules, constitutions, courts, and any mechanism used to try to institutionalize democracy. These mechanisms are just tools that we agree upon in the hopes of achieving democracy. When these mechanisms fall short and fail to help us achieve a form of association marked by "conjoint communicative experience," they must be rejected, and the democratic community must continue its search for ways to move forward democratically.[7]

For Dewey, democracy is a way in which people come together to deliberate in order to adjust to the ever-changing world that we inhabit. It should be clear that a community that depends on conjoint deliberation needs to ensure that its citizens are competent and capable in this process. A society that wishes to be democratic but fails to ensure its children are brought into adulthood with the necessary intellectual, moral, and dispositional elements of democratic engagement will soon lose any chance of true democracy. In other words, for democracy to succeed, its citizens must be educated to democracy.

But, also consider that for people to come together to deliberate about adjusting to an ever-changing world requires that those people and that society must commit to their own continuous education. After all, what is the end result of honest deliberation if not the shared learning of all involved? When public discussion is merely my side beating down your side and pushing our thinking onto you, we do not have democracy. For that matter, when all we do is let everyone "do their own thing" and each "go our own way" and in doing so fail to learn or teach each other, we also do not have democracy. For a society to survive, it must learn. And for it to learn, it requires that as many of its citizens as possible be willing to learn, to teach, to reason, and to commit. Democracy is not easy. It is not sitting around a campfire and holding

6. John Dewey, chapter 7 in *Democracy and Education* (New York: Teachers College, Columbia University, 1994).
7. John Dewey, *The Public and Its Problems: An Essay in Political Inquiry* (Chicago: Gateway Books, 1946).

hands. It is often quite combative. But, ultimately, at least according to Dewey, democracy is a commitment to the idea that by working, thinking, speaking, and learning together, we can continually grow as a society and meet whatever challenges the future might bring.

The Public and the Private

Dewey also makes a distinction between public events and private events. Private events refer to all of those interactions among people in which the effects of their actions affect no one beyond themselves. When a committee of people makes a decision and acts on it, if only the members of that committee are affected, it is, according to Dewey, a private act. Public events refer to all of those interactions among people in which their action affects people beyond those participating in the decisions and actions. When a committee of people makes a decision and acts on it, and people who are not a part of that committee are affected, we have a public event. In a democratic society, public events must be held in the spirit of democracy.[8]

Private events, because they are private, can be democratic or not. If a nuclear family wishes to organize its family democratically, it may. If, however, the family chooses to be an oligarchy of adults, that is permitted as well. In a society such as the United States, certain institutions are generally understood to be private, including families and churches. Some churches organize themselves in a manner committed to democratic association, whereas others are quite hierarchical. In the same way, private schools, because they are private, may or may not organize themselves in a manner congruent with democracy.

Public schools, however, because they are public, must always operate with the idea of democracy at their center. Here is a good example to clarify the distinction between the idea of democracy and the mechanisms of democracy. Public schools are a mechanism that hopefully fulfills the need of democratic societies to educate their citizens into democratic public life. That is their purpose; they are not public schools just because the government runs them. They are not public schools because they are tuition free. They are public because they serve the interests of the public to have an educated populace in order for a democratic society to continue to grow and develop democratically. Their purpose is to serve as a mechanism for a democratic society to create and maintain its democracy.

Conclusion

The national debate about education in the United States seems to address a very narrow set of questions. First of all, it equates "education" with "schooling." Second, it equates "public schools" with "free schools paid out of taxes." Third, it focuses on job training. Fourth, it zeroes in on schools' effectiveness at promoting student knowledge acquisition. In other words, despite the wide variety of questions and answers about what education should be in a democracy, the debate around education in this country acts as if these are all settled questions and no longer up for debate. But such an assumption is premature, at best, and downright wrong, at worst. This [reading] opens up these questions so that anyone interested

8. Ibid.

in public education (including teachers, parents, and citizens) or their own education (i.e., students) might gain a better understanding of what the fundamental debates are actually about, in the hope that by learning to recognize the fundamental issues and a variety of positions possible around these issues, we can begin to have an honest and vigorous debate about the purposes and practices of public education in a democratic society.

Bibliography

Adler, Mortimer. "Labor, Leisure, & Liberal Education." *Journal of General Education* 6 (1951): 35–45.

Dewey, John. *Democracy and Education.* New York: Macmillan, 1916.

———. "My Pedagogic Creed." *School Journal* 54 (1897): 77–80.

———. *The Public and Its Problems: An Essay in Political Inquiry.* Chicago: Gateway Books, 1946 [1927].

Freire, Paulo, and Donaldo P. Macedo. *Literacy: Reading the Word & the World.* Critical Studies in Education Series. South Hadley, MA: Bergin & Garvey Publishers, 1987.

Ratcliffe, David T. *The Six Nations: Oldest Living Participatory Democracy on Earth.* Roslindale, MA: Rat Hous Reality Press, 1995–2013. www.ratical.org/many_worlds/6Nations/.

Post-Reading Questions

1. According to the American philosopher John Dewey, what does an education entail? Do you agree with this definition?
2. What is the difference between education and schooling? In your experience, did you receive an adequate education through your own schooling? Why or why not?
3. How do schools succeed in promoting democracy? How do they fail?

The State of Our Education

Terence Fitzgerald

> To Whom It May Concern ... Keep This Nigger-Boy Running.
>
> —Ralph Ellison

The Coalition of Schools Educating Boys of Color (COSEBOC) in 2007 stated that Black men suffer from the largest achievement gap of any racial or ethnic group in the United States.[1] Twice as many Black women receive college and university degrees than Black men.[2] The COSEBOC in 2009 went on to state that Black young men were twice as likely as their White counterparts to drop out of high school.[3] And the achievements of Black males while in school are far below those of other demographics.

There has been a lot of speculation about the causes of these achievement disparities. Some have speculated that the academic gap between students of color and White students

---

1. The Coalition of Schools Educating Boys of Color, "Standards and Promising Practices for Schools Educating Boys of Color: Executive Summary," available at http://coseboc.org/pdfs/Executive_Summary_Standards.pdf.
2. The National Center for Education Statistics, *Status and Trends in Education of Racial and Ethnic Minorities 2008*, available at http://nces.ed.gov/pubs2010/2010015/chapter6.asp.
3. Sharon Lewis, Candace Simon, Renata Uzzell, Amanda Horwitz, and Michael Casserly, *A Call for Change: The Social and Educational Factors Contributing to the Outcomes of Black Males in Urban Schools 2010*, available at http://dl.dropbox.com/u/3273936/A%20Call%20For%20Change-%20Revised.pdf, 22.

is primarily due to socioeconomic factors, not racial disparities.[4] But studies show that this is not the case. A case study in 2009 looked at the performance of both White and Black male students who were eligible for free and reduced lunches at school because of their low socioeconomic status (SES). Among these SES-matched students, Black male students academically performed twenty points lower than their White counterparts. The study also compared White and Black males who did not receive free and reduced lunches; in this cohort, Black students performed eleven points lower than their White counterparts. Other studies show these same discrepancies in middle-class and affluent populations. Blacks from affluent suburban areas suffer from the same concerns as poor urban students. And Black and Latino students from middle-class homes ranked last in comparison with White and Asian students of equivalent SES backgrounds.[5]

Clearly there is more than SES at work here. All of these studies indicate that low Black and Latino achievement is linked to something more than just the financial status of individual families. Something corrosive is occurring within public education and affecting the development and achievement of people of color, particularly Black males, regardless of social class, resources, funding, and educational opportunities within their immediate environment.

Black Male Underachievement: The Quiet Crisis

Education has been the subject of intense scrutiny in the last decade or so. Government efforts such as the No Child Left Behind Act of 2001 (NCLB) and the Race to the Top program have been followed by extensive media coverage and debate. But while education in general has received great attention, the greatest crisis in education—the underachievement of young Black men—has been almost entirely absent from the debate. A review of the major publishing outlets in the US in the last thirty years—such as *Time* magazine, *Newsweek,* and the *New York Times*—showed only a handful of articles specifically dealing with the plight of Black males in education. One such article was "Native Son" in *Time* magazine, which drew on a comparison between Richard Wright's fictional character Bigger Thomas and the generations of Black males in the 1980s. But such articles are rare and are often written by the same handful of authors.

One of the few outlets to touch on the subject has been Black-oriented and -produced art. In 1993, the film *Menace II Society* was a revelation to young Black men like me who felt a powerful identification with the movie's depiction of a racially insensitive and intolerant White American education system, Black-male-on-Black-male violence, and the consequences of urban poverty. The theme was repeated in hip-hop songs, Black TV shows, and films throughout the 1990s. Although this attention faded as the new century went on, these artistic expressions of a society-wide problem left a profound mark on me and other young Black men of the time.

---

4. In general, all non-Whites would be considered people of color. But for the purpose of this book, Blacks, Latinos, and specific Southeast Asian groups are referred to as people of color.
5. John U. Ogbu, *Black American Students in an Affluent Suburb: A Study of Academic Disengagement* (Sociocultural, Political, and Historical Studies in Education) (Mahwah, NJ: Lawrence Erlbaum, 2008). See also Christopher Jencks and Meredith Phillips, *The Black-White Test Score Gap* (Washington, DC: Brookings Institute, 1998).

The Role of School Discipline in Black Underachievement

The difficulties of Black young men in school are based on more than simply test grades or attendance, however. Central to the Black male experience in school is the issue of discipline. During their middle and high school years, Black males are disciplined, suspended, and expelled more frequently than all other demographic groups. This trend is amplified when the student is not only a young man of color but also poor.[6] Most of these suspensions are due to non-violent acts such as abusive language, not attending assigned classes, truancy, and tardiness.[7]

This trend is consistent across the country. In Palm Beach in 2006, Black males were suspended at a 53 percent rate while White males were suspended at a 6 percent rate.[8] During the same year, in places like Milwaukee, San Antonio, and Miami-Dade, Florida, Black males were suspended at rates of 52 percent, 42 percent, and 41 percent, respectively, rates far above the rates of their White peers. In Washington, DC, administrators blame the dismal 41 percent graduation rate of Black males on the extremely high rate of suspensions.[9]

It's important to remember that suspensions and expulsions are not awarded on objective criteria. It's easy to think that such disciplinary measures are earned, but this is often not the case. While writing this [reading], I was confronted with the truth of this when my quiet twelve-year-old nephew was suspended from middle school. My nephew and a fellow student, a White girl, had been involved in horse play that started when she first hit him. In normal, childlike retaliation, he hit her back and she reported him to the teacher. Soon after he was called to the assistant principal's office and told that he was being suspended. But the White girl who initiated the hitting received no such discipline.

When I heard of my nephew's suspension I drove to his house and asked him to get in the car. We were both quiet until I pulled into the local police station. "They are waiting on you," I said. "Go in and make yourself at home." He was visibly shaken, but I wanted to convey to him the seriousness of even minor physical altercations. He then let the whole story spill out, admitting his own fault but emphasizing that the girl had started it and had not been punished at all. "She got away with hitting me. The rules are not fair."

"There is no such thing as fair," I told him. "The public school system, like so much of the world, is not fair and wasn't built to be. The quicker you learn this fact, the easier it will be for you to navigate the potholes waiting for you. If you continue to be blind to the ways of the world, this [pointing to the police station] is where this country will send you. And the effects will follow you all the days of your little life."

6. Daniel J. Losen and Russell Skiba, "Suspended Education: Urban Middle Schools in Crisis," available at http://www.splcenter.org/sites/default/files/downloads/publication/Suspended_Education.pdf, 4.

7. Linda M. Raffaele Mendez, "Predictors of Suspension and Negative School Outcomes: A Longitudinal Investigation," in *Deconstructing the School to Prison Pipeline,* ed. Johanna Wald and Daniel J. Losen (San Francisco: Jossey-Bass, 2003), 27.

8. Mendez, "Predictors of Suspension," 6.

9. Kavitha Cardoza, "Report: D.C. Schools Still Struggling to Produce Black Male H.S. Grads," available at http://www.nbcwashington.com/news/local/Report_D_C_Schools_Still_Struggling_to_Produce_Black_Male_H_S_Grads-100965584.html.

It pained me to talk to him this way. As one of the few male role models in his life, I had tried to protect him as long as possible from the racial realities of American life. But a pre-teen ready to become a young man sat before me now. I no longer could afford such indulgences. I tried to let him know that the world was his to conquer, but also that he had to understand and navigate the pitfalls of oppression in order to thrive as I knew he could.

Underachievement, Discipline, and the Prison Pipeline

The academic underachievement of young Black males and the systematic over-discipline in the school system has lifelong consequences for many young men. Educational attainment obviously has a direct effect on the financial, social, and political livelihood of individuals. But for young Black men, their educational experience has an additional consequence: entanglement with the prison system.

Researchers have shown how the chronically guided pathway traveled by incarcerated Black males can be predicted as early as their middle school years.[10] A 2003 study tracked 400 Black males who were incarcerated during their freshman year in high school in a major northwest US city. The author concluded that the young men most likely to end up in the prison system were those who were struggling academically in middle school. These young men attended class only about 58 percent of the school year. They were categorized as reading at a sixth-grade level at the beginning of their ninth grade of school. And they were suspended at least once within their eighth-grade year of school. This study showed more clearly than ever the strong correlation between educational underachievement and eventual imprisonment. And it raised the question: If one could be addressed, could not the other be avoided?

School-sanctioned punishment is an area that harshly affects the state of Black males in education. This area of punishment has ominous effects on the condition of Black males within the criminal justice system. Instead of simply viewing the plight of them in the classroom, one could trace the same area of concern inside local, state, and federal prisons across the country.

"Where does discipline end?" asked Francois Mauriac (1885–1970). "Where does cruelty begin? Somewhere between these, thousands of children inhabit a voiceless hell." Scholars such as Daniel Losen, senior education law and policy associate of the esteemed Civil Rights Project at UCLA, and Russell Skiba, director of the Equity Project, Center for Evaluation and Education Policy at Indiana University, in conjunction with the Southern Poverty Law Center, answered just that question in their report "Suspended Education: Urban Middle Schools in Crisis."[11] The report focused on the racial and socioeconomic inequities in middle school discipline in the US. Overall, the report states, Blacks and Latinos are disproportionately suspended in comparison with their White peers. Zero-tolerance policies have been shown to do more harm than good in relation to these populations. In fact, the implementation of the zero-tolerance policies since the 1970s has been ineffective and racially unfair.[12] The American Civil Liberties Union (ACLU) has gone

---

10. Losen and Skiba, "Suspended Education," 3.

11. Losen and Skiba, "Suspended Education."

12. Losen and Skiba, "Suspended Education." Zero tolerance relates to school discipline policies that impose removal from school for violent to truancy school violations. This can also be applied to dress code violations.

as far to state that within the US, there exists "a disturbing national trend wherein children are funneled out of public schools and into the juvenile and criminal justice systems."[13] They argue that the creation and increasing use of zero-tolerance discipline policies has created a growing rate of school-based arrests and that placing students in disciplinary alternative schools has impacted students with a history of poverty, neglect, and disabilities.[14]

In the end, policies such as these have marginalized those most at risk while denying them access to education. Even though zero-tolerance policies have had consequential effects on all races, those males who are poor, Black, and Latino are the populations affected the most.[15] The Black male population has been shown to have an increased rate for involvement with the criminal justice system.

Education, Prison, and the New Jim Crow

In 2011, the NAACP reported on six US cities in state and federal prison jurisdictions in a publication titled *Misplaced Priorities: Over Incarcerate, Under Educate.*[16] The report indicated that, over the past thirty years, these six cities had invested more in the incarceration of Blacks and Latinos than in the system that was supposed to educate them. The report simply confirms what researchers and scholars have time and time again shown: the ludicrous and dangerous manner in which the country responds to the social, academic, and mental issues of people of color (specifically males). But this report in particular highlights that the plummeting resources dedicated to public education are matched by the skyrocketing resources dedicated to prisons.[17] In addition, there exists a connection between monies spent and low-performing schools that are located in neighborhoods with high incarceration trends.

For large numbers of Black and Latino males who fall short in surviving the warring confines of public and higher education, the prison system is placed within our society to catch and utilize their attributes. In 1994, 678,300 Black males were locked up in federal, state, and local prisons, for which our country spent $10 billion,[18] whereas 549,600 Black males were enrolled in college during the same year, costing $2.8 billion.[19]

In 2011, 1,598,780 prisoners were incarcerated under state and federal jurisdictions.[20] Of these, 93 percent were male, and 555,300, 331,500, and 465,100 were Black, Latino, and White males, respectively.[21]

13. American Civil Liberties Union, *School-to-Prison Pipeline*, available at http://www.aclu.org/racial-justice/school-prison-pipeline.
14. American Civil Liberties Union, *School to Prison Pipeline: Talking Points*, available at http://www.aclu.org/racial-justice/school-prison-pipeline-talking-points.
15. American Civil Liberties Union, *School to Prison Pipeline*, 2–3.
16. National Association for the Advancement of Colored People, "Misplaced Priorities: Over Incarcerate, Under Educate," April 2011, available at http://naacp.3cdn.net/01d6f368edbe135234_bq0m68x5h.pdf.
17. National Association for the Advancement of Colored People, "Misplaced Priorities," 2–3.
18. Tom Mortenson, "Black Males in College or Behind Bars in the US, 1980 to 1994," *Post Secondary Opportunity* 45 (1996): 212.
19. Mortenson, "Black Males in College or Behind Bars."
20. E. Ann Carson and William J. Sabol, *Prisoners in 2011*, available at http://bjs.gov/index.cfm?ty=pbdetail&iid=4559, 2.
21. Carson and Sabol, *Prisoners in 2011*, 26.

Some 63 percent of the Black and 69 percent of the Latino incarcerated population are below the age of 39 and thus are imprisoned at a significantly higher rate than White males.[22]

This commitment by the US to imprison Black males is nothing new. Scholars in fields ranging from sociology to education have discussed this topic for decades.[23] Many contend that the US prison system is a modern-day example of a once-thought-dead system in which people of color were permanently forced into a minority caste. From birth on within this designated social placement, individuals guilty of no crime other than being the delegated "other" are seen as inferior.[24] In fact, being a part of a Black minority caste comes with a foundation set in a negative ideology that dictates a set of behaviors, actions, procedures, and policies directed by non-Blacks toward people of color. Operations are increasingly explicit toward Blacks within major institutions such as the judicial system and public and higher education settings. For instance, Black males are used for cheap labor in the context of the prison industrial complex. From the end of the Civil War until World War II, they were subject to involuntary slavery in states such as Alabama, Florida, Mississippi, Louisiana, and Georgia through human labor trafficking for companies involved in pine tar production, coal mines, road construction, timber mills, farm labor, and ditch digging.[25]

The racial caste system many thought was destroyed at the end of the Jim Crow era was in actuality cleaned, redesigned, and made to fit a new time in US history. In order to control those within the Black caste, the criminal justice system came to serve the function of control previously exerted through the operation of Jim Crow. I would propose that this redesign is also seen within public schools since the end of legal segregation. [...]

In terms of education attained by those incarcerated, 41 percent did not receive a high school diploma before entering a correctional facility (68 percent in state prisons).[26] Allen J. Beck and Thomas P. Bonczar in 1997 produced a report called *Lifetime Likelihood of Going to State or Federal Prison* that noted that, within their lifetime, they statistically had a one in four (25 percent) chance of having some personal connection within the prison system.[27] In contrast, Whites and Hispanics/Latinos, respectively, had a one in twenty-three (5.9 percent) and one in six (17.2 percent) likelihood of some involvement with the prison system. In 2001 Bonczar estimated that more than 5.6 million US adults had served a varying amount of time in either state or federal prison systems.

22. Carson and Sabol, *Prisoners in 2011*, 27.
23. Thomas P. Bonczar, *Prevalence of Imprisonment in the U.S. Population, 1974–2001*, U.S. Bureau of Justice Statistics, 2003, available at bjs.ojp.usdoj.gov/content/pub/pdf/piusp01.pdf.
24. Michelle Alexander, *The New Jim Crow: Mass Incarceration in the Age of Colorblindness* (New York: New Press, 2010); John U. Ogbu, *Minority Education and Caste: The American System in Cross-Cultural Perspective* (New York: Academic Press, 1978).
25. Alan Whyte and Jamie Baker, "Prison Labor on the Rise in US," available at http://www.wsws.org/articles/2000/may2000/pris-m08.shtml.
26. Caroline Wolf Harlow, *Education and Correctional Populations*, U.S. Bureau of Justice Statistics, 2003, available at bjs.ojp.usdoj.gov/content/pub/pdf/ecp.pdf.
27. Allen J. Beck and Thomas P. Bonczar, *Lifetime Likelihood of Going to State or Federal Prison*, U.S. Bureau of Justice Statistics, 1997, available at http://bjs.ojp.usdoj.gov/index.cfm?ty=pbdetail&iid=1042.

A variance between White and Black males has also been observed from 1974 to 2001.[28] For example, the number of White males incarcerated in state and federal facilities increased from 1.4 percent to 1.9 percent to 2.6 percent in 1974, 1991, and 2001, respectively. In contrast, Black males increased their rate of incarceration from 8.7 percent to 12.0 percent to 16.6 percent in those same years. This amplification would be expected when taking into account that one in every four Black children born in the year 1990 had a parent in prison.[29] Black children born in 1978 had a one in seven chance of having a father "doing time" in prison by their fourteenth year of life.[30] In 1990, the likelihood increased to one in four. Over a twelve-year period from 1978 to 1990, these numbers represented a growth rate of 80 percent. This speaks to a 50 percent rate of growth in comparison with the rates for Black males born in 1945–1949 to 1965–1969.[31] White children, during the same periods of 1978 and 1990, were estimated at one in forty and one in twenty-five, respectively.

Angela Davis argued, "Imprisonment has become the response of first resort to far too many of the social problems that burden people who are ensconced in poverty. These problems often are veiled by being conveniently grouped together under the category of 'crime' and by the automatic attribution of criminal behavior to people of color. Homelessness, unemployment, drug addiction, mental illness, and illiteracy are only a few of the problems that disappear from public view when the human beings contending with them are relegated to cages."[32] I would add that the plight of Black and Brown males in the many correctional facilities across the country is not only a sign of an unwillingness to address social problems but the betrayal of a trusted institutional entity; public education has a dynamic that creates barriers for people of color, specifically Black males, and this dynamic continues for those who later walk upon the college and university campuses.

28. Bonczar, *Prevalence of Imprisonment.*
29. Christopher Wildeman, "Parental Imprisonment, the Prison Boom, and the Concentration of Childhood Disadvantage," *Demography* 46 (2009): 265.
30. Wildeman, "Parental Imprisonment," 270–71.
31. Wildeman, "Parental Imprisonment," 271.
32. Angela Davis, *Masked Racism: Reflections on the Prison Industrial Complex,* available at http://colorlines.com/archives/ 1998/09/masked_racism_reflections_on_the_prison_industrial_complex.htm.

Post-Reading Questions

1. What is the school-to-prison pipeline? Which students are at highest risk of incarceration at an early age?
2. How do zero-tolerance policies contribute to racial inequalities in society? What are some examples from the reading?
3. What is the prison industrial complex (PIC)? How do institutions in society work together to create inequalities?

The Zip Code Effect

Educational Inequality in the United States

Wayne Au

> And your education! Is not that also social, and determined by the social conditions under which you educate, by the intervention, direct or indirect, of society, by means of schools, etc.?
>
> Karl Marx & Frederick Engels (1848/1977, p. 55)

When I taught at Berkeley High School in California, administrators and teachers there, myself included, often referred to a phenomenon called the zip code effect. This effect was a crude approximation for relative levels of academic achievement at Berkeley High. Graduation rates, grade point averages, discipline rates, dropout rates, and standardized test scores could be relatively accurately predicted by a simple analysis of where in the city of Berkeley a particular child lived.

To be sure, this zip code effect was an unsophisticated and perhaps unfair analysis of the phenomenon of educational inequality at Berkeley High, and the vast majority of teachers there recognized this fact. Most of us used it with a tone of despair and as a critique of the educational conditions that existed there. In reality, we teachers felt that none of our students' academic achievement was totally predetermined or completely pre-ordained no matter from which neighborhood they hailed. We saw evidence to the contrary on most days, where individual students from anywhere in Berkeley worked hard, sometimes against

201

overwhelming odds, and performed well in school. However, at the end of the day, at the end of the school year, after all of the test scores had been tallied, and after all of the statistics were processed and reported, students from some zip codes seemed to do well while students from other zip codes did not.

Zip codes, of course, are just numbers used to organize our mail delivery. However, because zip codes are geographical markers, in the case of Berkeley, California, they also serve to delineate between neighborhoods with distinctly different racial and economic class demographics, because in essence, Berkeley High School serves two largely disparate communities. The Berkeley "hills" are very rich and predominantly White; The Berkeley "flats" are mostly poor/working class and are predominantly African American and Latino. Even though the recent surge in gentrification in the Bay Area has changed the demographics of the flats to varying degrees, when I taught there during the 2001–2003 school years, the patterns were unmistakable. Kids from the hills generally did well in school, and kids from the flats generally did not—making the race and class disparities of the education of Berkeley High School students only that much more pronounced (Au, 2005a; Maran, 2000; Noguera, 2001, 2003a). In the end, the zip code effect was simply another name for the existence of deeply entrenched race and class inequality in the city of Berkeley generally.[1]

Unfortunately, Berkeley High's race and class based educational inequality cannot be relegated to Berkeley alone: It represents a trend that appears in public education in the United States generally, where, according to any number of markers, poor students and students of color[2] are simply less "successful" than their wealthy and/or White counterparts (see, e.g., Coleman et al., 1966; Hunter & Bartee, 2003; Sirin, 2005; The Education Trust, 2004). The debate over this inequality in the United States is similarly widespread historically, politically, and geographically. For instance, educational inequality has been a subject for research, discussion, debate, and action in the African American community for well over 100 years (see, e.g., DuBois, 1903; Washing-ton, 1903; Woodson, 1990/1933). Educational and social inequality was the stated impetus behind the passing of the Elementary and Secondary Education Act (ESEA) of 1965 and remains the central theme for federal education reform in the United States since then (Jennings, 2000). However, despite various reform efforts, race and class based inequalities in public education persist

1. Please note that this is not to be overly critical of the faculty, staff, and students at Berkeley High. I have many friends and colleague there whom I love and respect greatly, and whom I know are working very hard to help all of their students succeed. Further, I believe that some of the best education possible can and does take place there. Finally, Berkeley High's students are a politically conscious, intellectual, intelligent, and lively bunch whom I enjoyed working with.

2. I recognize that the term "students of color" is problematic for several reasons, one of which is that it normalizes Whiteness. However, other racial signifiers, such as the commonly used "non-White," are also problematic. "Non-White," for instance, does now allow for "mixed-race" individuals who are "half-White," such as myself (my father is Chinese American and my mother is European American), and therefore upholds notions of racial purity (in addition normalizing Whiteness as well). Further, to use such phrases as "racialized as White" or "racialized as not White" seems too cumbersome and overly academic, particularly when most community and education activists I know who are not academics use the term "students of color." Therefore, given that we are somewhat shackled by the imperfection and power relations in language, I use the term "students of color" to refer to students who have been racialized as not White.

today (Hunter & Bartee, 2003; Noguera, 2003a), with researchers noting that these inequalities seem to reflect similar inequalities that exist in society at large (Anyon, 2005; Barton, 2003).

In its most recent iteration, U.S. federal education policy—now referred to as the No Child Left Behind Act, or NCLB (U.S. Department of Education, 2002)—has taken the issue of educational inequality and stitched it together with standardized testing. Systems of standardized testing are now used to hold teachers, schools, districts, and states "accountable" if their students do not perform well on the tests (Apple, 2006a; Darling-Hammond, 2004; Kim & Sunderman, 2005; McNeil, 2000; Moe, 2003; Nichols & Berliner, 2007). Over the last 25 years, these "high-stakes," standardized tests have become the central tool for public education reform in this country (Kornhaber & Orfield, 2001), as politicians from both political parties, the business community [...], and some segments of poor communities and communities of color have lent their support (Apple, 2006a; Apple & Pedroni, 2005; Karp, 2006b; Pedroni, 2007) to this purportedly neutral, fair, accurate, and meritocratic measure of educational performance (Berlak, 2000; Hoffman, 1962; Lemann, 1999; Popham, 2001). But is this final assumption, that high-stakes, standardized testing is neutral, fair, accurate, and meritocratic, actually true? Can high-stakes tests not only mark educational inequality but also prove to be the tool to fix such inequality as well?

Research on the outcomes of high-stakes testing would appear to answer, "No," to the above questions. The race and class based inequalities associated with the zip code effect at Berkeley High School seem to reproduce themselves nationally on high-stakes, standardized tests. A central finding of the research is that, while all students are feeling some effects, the weight of the high-stakes testing environment falls heaviest on the shoulders of low income students and students of color who are consistently found to be negatively and disproportionately affected by high-stakes, standardized testing (Amrein & Berliner, 2002b; Groves, 2002; Haney, 2000; Lomax, West, Harmon, Viator, & Madaus, 1995; Madaus & Clarke, 2001; Marchant & Paulson, 2005; McNeil, 2005; McNeil & Valenzuela, 2001; Nichols, Glass, & Berliner, 2005). This finding has caused some researchers to conclude that high-stakes standardized testing connected to grade promotion increases drop-out rates, produces no lasting educational benefits, and impacts Latino and African American children disproportionately in schools (Orfield & Wald, 2000).

The educational consequences of high-stakes testing have been particularly tangible for low income students and students of color. For instance, in Texas, whose state-level educational policy became the blueprint for the federal level No Child Left Behind Act, Black and Latino students have been feeling the brunt of the statewide testing program there (Hampton, 2005; Haney, 2000; McNeil, 2000, 2005; McNeil & Valenzuela, 2001; Sloan, 2005; Valenzuela, 2005b). The high-stakes testing and accountability movement in public education in Texas witnessed conservatively estimated school drop-out rates of 40% in 2001. This translates into Texas public schools losing between 90,000 and 95,000 students a year, the vast majority of which are African American and Latino (McNeil, 2005). The irony of Texas' drop-out rates is that the state claims to have made strong gains in test scores.

Darling-Hammond (2004) tells the story of the "Texas Miracle," where highly publicized gains in test scores were discovered to be the product of disappearing students, most of whom were students of color. For instance, Darling-Hammond explains how at Sharpstown High School in Houston, "a freshman class of 1,000 dwindled to fewer than 300 students by senior year—a pattern seen in most high-minority high schools in Houston, including those rewarded for getting their test scores 'up'" (p. 21). The miracle is that in Houston, not a single drop out was reported. This impossibly low drop-out rate came through the designation of missing students as incarcerated, transferred (with no follow up address), returned to Mexico, or having received a General Educational Development certificate, any of which would keep these disappeared students from officially counting as drop outs while simultaneously keeping these students, often low test scorers, from counting on the tests (McNeil, 2005). Ironically, despite these and other extremely disproportionate numbers associated with the education system in the State of Texas, some researchers still maintain that the Texas system of educational accountability is a success (see, e.g., Evers & Walberg, 2004; Winick & Kress, 2004).

Unfortunately, the Lone Star State of Texas is not alone in terms of high-stakes testing, inequality, drop-out rates and test-related scandal. Scores on the 2005 National Assessment of Educational Progress show White students outscoring African American and Latino students by 26 points in scaled reading scores, by 20 points in fourth-grade mathematics scores, by 23 points in eighth-grade reading scores, and by more than 26 points in eighth-grade reading scores. Further, these disparities are persistent over time (Ladson-Billings, 2006). High school exit exams produce similar gaps in performance (Darling-Hammond, McClosky, & Pecheone, 2006; Zabala, 2007), and while Beatty and colleagues (Beatty, Neisser, Trent, & Heubert, 2001) are reluctant in positing a causal relationship between high-stakes tests and high school drop outs, they do concede that:

> ... [T]here is reason to believe that high-stakes testing at any level may sometimes be used in ways that have unintended harmful effects on students at particular risk for academic failure because of poverty, lack of proficiency in English, disability, and membership in population subgroups that have been educationally disadvantaged. (p. 7)

Other research analyzing data across eighteen states finds that 62% of states with high school exit exams saw an increase in drop-out rates when they implemented their exams (Amrein & Berliner, 2002a). Given that, according to the National Center for Educational Statistics, African American and Latino students are twice as likely as White students to drop out of school, and students from low-income families are five times more likely to drop out than students from high-income families (Laird, Lew, DeBell, & Chapman, 2006), these findings would seem to support a relationship between high-stakes testing, dropout rates, and a disproportionate impact on low income students and students of color (see also Nichols & Berliner, 2007; Roderick & Nagaoka, 2005).

For all of the high-minded rhetoric surrounding high-stakes, standardized testing and issues of equality in educational achievement, the empirical reality appears to be just the opposite. Systems of high-stakes testing damage the education of low income and students of color (Amrein & Berliner, 2002b; Darder & Torres, 2004; Darling-Hammond, 2007; Groves, 2002; Haney, 2000; Kane & Staiger, 2002; Madaus & Clarke, 2001; McNeil, 2005; McNeil & Valenzuela, 2001; Roderick & Nagaoka, 2005). Such findings raise serious, fundamental questions about high-stakes, standardized testing. Is it possible that systems of high-stakes, standardized testing only help (re)produce the very same inequalities they purport to measure?

In this [reading] I explore the relationship between high-stakes testing, as part of broader school structure and education policy, and the (re) production of socioeducational inequalities. Specifically, my research hinges on the possibility that high-stakes testing produces classroom level changes in the educational experiences of students and teachers that increase inequality. Thus, in this [reading] I focus on the question: *What is the relationship between high-stakes, standardized testing and the (re)production of educational inequality?* The essential reason why this question is important is that social and economic inequality has only increased in the United States (and the world) in recent years (Brown & Lauder, 2006; McLaren & Farahmandpur, 2005). Such increased inequality bodes poorly because there have been corollary increases in educational disparity (Anyon, 2005). Thus, an analysis of the relationship between high-stakes testing and the (re)production of inequitable educational-social relations, as this [reading] hopes to achieve, can only help critical educators work toward a more just society within their educational contexts.

My central question, however, requires unpacking before proceeding. The rest of this [reading] is devoted to this task. First, I explain the definition of "high-stakes testing"[...]. Second, I explain the conceptual ideas that guide and shape my analysis [...].

High-Stakes Testing

In very specific terms, high-stakes tests are a part of a *policy design* (Schneider & Ingram, 1997) that "links the score on one set of standardized tests to grade promotion, high school graduation and, in some cases, teacher and principal salaries and tenure decisions" (Orfield & Wald, 2000, p. 38). As part of the accountability movement, stakes are also deemed high because the results of tests, as well as the ranking and categorization of schools, teachers, and children that extend from those results, are reported to the public (McNeil, 2000), in turn shaping the reputations of states, districts, schools, principals, teachers and students. As part of a policy design, high-stakes tests represent one "*instrument* the State uses to implement the policy and to allocate its values" (M. L. Smith, 2004, p. 6) of "good" and "bad" schools, teachers, and students. Thus, the term "high-stakes testing" simultaneously implies two things: 1) Standardized testing as the technology and tool/instrument used for measurement, and 2) Educational policy erected around the standardized test results that usually attaches consequences to those results thereby making such tests "high-stakes." Any discussion of high-stakes testing therefore requires that we discuss policy and testing itself, as well as the curricular implications of the testing.[3]

Social Reproduction in Critical Educational Theory

The overarching arguments in this [reading] regarding the relationship between high-stakes testing, educational inequality, and socioeconomic relations, recalls a broader argument amongst critical educational theorists regarding the role of schools in the reproduction of socioeconomic inequality associated with capitalism, one that can be traced back to Marx. In the *Preface to a Contribution to the Critique of Political Economy*, Marx (1968a) writes:

> In the social production of their life, [humans] enter into definite relations that are
> indispensable and independent of their will, relations of production which correspond to

---

3. I must note that, for the purposes of this [reading], I will use "high-stakes, standardized tests," "High-stakes tests," "testing," "testing policies," and their grammatical derivatives fairly interchangeably. Specifically, within the context of this [reading], these terms all refer to "high-stakes, standardized testing."

a definite stage of development of their material productive forces. The sum total of these relations of production constitutes the economic structure of society, the real foundation, on which rises a legal and political superstructure and to which correspond definite forms of social consciousness. The mode of production of material life conditions the social, political and intellectual life process in general. It is not the consciousness of [humans] that determines their being, but, one the contrary, their social being that determines their consciousness. (p. 183)

These four sentences outline what is commonly referred to as the base/superstructure model in Marxism, where the "legal and political superstructure" rises out of the "relations of production" that make up the base "economic structure of society." Marx's formulation, having been interpreted in a variety of ways, has proved useful (if not controversial) for activists and scholars interested in understanding how social, cultural, and institutional inequalities relate to capitalist economic relations. Consequently, critical educational theorists have made use of Marx's conceptualization, or some related derivative, to analyze educational inequality in terms of economic inequality (Au, 2006a).

The modern contours of this theorizing were sparked by Bowles and Gintis (1976) and the publication of their book, *Schooling in Capitalist America: Education Reform and the Contradictions of Economic Life*. Bowles and Gintis generated a debate amongst critical educational scholars about the relationship between schools, society and the economy, one that generally revolved around the central question: Are schools completely determined by the structure of our economy, or do they have some amount of autonomy from economic forces? Bowles and Gintis answer this question with the "correspondence principle" of educational relations. According to this principle, in capitalist societies,

> ... the division of labor in education, as well as its structure of authority and reward, mirror those of the economy... [and] in any stable society in which a formal educational system has a major role in the personal development of working people, there will tend to emerge a correspondence between the social relations of education and those of the economic system. (Bowles & Gintis, 1988, p. 237)

Bowles and Gintis' formulation asserts that schools mainly function to serve the needs of capitalist production in nearly a one-to-one correspondence, and thus provide one explanation of how and why schools reproduce inequality.

Critical education theorists sharply criticized Bowles and Gintis' correspondence principle (also commonly referred to as "correspondence theory"), arguing that the correspondence principle ignores the role of teachers, culture, and ideology in schools, is too mechanical and overly economistic, and neglects students' and others' resistance to dominant social relations (see, e.g., Apple, 1979/2004, 1980–81, 1988a; Cole, 1988; Edwards, 1980; Giroux, 1980, 1983a; Moore, 1988). Arnot and Whitty (1982) provide a clear summary of these critiques when they state:

> [T]he political economy of schooling as presented by Bowles & Gintis ... failed to describe and explain classroom life, the conflicts and contradictions *within* the school and the distance and conflict *between* the school and the economy. Further, it could not account for the variety of responses of teachers and pupils to the structures of the school—some of which were liable to threaten the successful socialisation of the new generation. (p. 98, original emphasis)

Instead of schools reproducing an exact reflection of norms of behavior, attitude, and ideological dispositions required for capitalist production, critics argue, individuals within those schools possess *agency* and *consciousness* which allows them to *mediate* and *resist* the dominant social relations reproduced through institutions. This critique, while suggesting that the transmission of inequitable social relations is not a mechanical one, still maintains that individuals do feel the effects of, succumb to, or are products of an unequal socioeconomic system. Put differently; that a message is communicated through an institution such as school does not mean that this message is heard and universally embodied by its intended recipients. Transmission is one process, acquisition is another process altogether, and the mechanisms of mediation between the two are critical (Bernstein, 1996).

The above critiques withstanding, I do not want to downplay either the importance of understanding the transmission of social relations via education or the importance of Bowles and Gintis' contribution to this debate. As Lankshear (1997) recalls:

> ... [H]indsight reveals that *Schooling in Capitalist America* and the debate it stimulated made an enduring contribution to our understanding of the extent to which, and ways in which, social relations, practices, and outcomes of formal education are enmeshed with the (re)production of economic life under capitalism. (p. 309)

Given the vast disparities in educational achievement along lines of race and class, it is fairly clear that schools do play a role in (re)producing social inequality through the (re)production of educational inequality (Apple, 1995; Bourdieu & Passeron, 1977; Carnoy & Levin, 1985). For most critical education scholars, the question is not, "*Do* schools reproduce inequality?" Based on the empirical evidence, discussed earlier, it is inarguable that schools generally maintain and reinforce the hierarchies associated with the social and economic status quo. But this is a general position that in some ways does not stray too far from Bowles and Gintis' original formulation. Rather, the more nuanced question has been: *How* do schools reproduce social inequality in a way that still accounts for the complexity of human agency, intervention, and resistance in this overall process? Indeed, students, teachers, and communities have resisted schooling's tendency toward social reproduction in very counter-hegemonic, and at times even revolutionary, ways (see, e.g., Apple & Beane, 2007; Gibson, Queen, Ross, & Vinson, 2007; Rethinking Schools, 2008).

In response to the mechanistic and deterministic analysis offered by Bowles and Gintis (1976) and others, critical educational theorists, particularly neo-Marxists, applied the concepts of "hegemony" (Gramsci, 1971) and "relative autonomy" (Althusser, 1971) to their analyses of schools and socioeconomic reproduction. These two concepts provide utility for critical educational theorists because they account for some level of control of education by the socioeconomic relations associated with capitalism, while simultaneously providing for forces within education to resist such control. Gramsci (1971), the Italian communist credited with the most elaborated formulation and application of hegemony, posits that power was maintained less often by direct, physical force and more often through the maintenance of consciousness that allows the masses to grant "spontaneous consent" to control by dominant elites. This consent, however, often relies upon offering compromises to the subordinate in order to maintain the legitimacy of the dominant (Apple & Buras, 2006b), even if these compromises act as "an umbrella under which many groups can stand but which basically still is under the guiding principles of dominant groups" (Apple, 2000, p. 64).

Applied to education, the concept of hegemony creates the space for an analysis of schools and social reproduction that allows for the contradictory role that public education in the United States has often played, thus challenging the economic determinism of Bowles and Gintis while still recognizing that capitalist production plays a significant part in the shaping of our common sense understandings of education and social relations (Apple, 1995). As Apple (1995) explains:

> On the one hand, the school must assist in accumulation by producing both agents for a hierarchical labor market and the cultural capital of technical/administrative knowledge. On the other hand, our educational institutions must legitimate ideologies of equality and class mobility, and make themselves be seen as positively by as many classes and class segments as possible. ... The need for *economic* and ideological efficiency and stable production tends to be in conflict with the other *political* needs. What we see is the school attempting to resolve what may be the inherently contradictory roles it must play. (pp. 52–53, original emphasis)

While schools play a key role in reproducing social inequality, their contradictory role in legitimating ideologies of equality also allows some room for resistance to this reproduction (Carnoy & Levin, 1985).

Similarly, Althusser (1971), a French communist and philosopher, is often credited with the concept of "relative autonomy." In his discussion of the relationship between the economic base and the superstructure, Althusser arrives at two conclusions: "(1) there is a 'relative autonomy' of the superstructure with respect to the base; (2) there is a 'reciprocal action' of the superstructure on the base" (p. 136). It is Althusser's conception of relative autonomy that has been taken up by critical education theorists. For instance, Apple (1995) explains that:

> ... [T]here was a dynamic interplay between the political and economic spheres which was found in education. While the former was not reducible to the latter—and, like culture, it had a significant degree of relative autonomy—the role the school plays *as a state apparatus* is strongly related to the core problems of accumulation and legitimation faced by the state and a mode of production ... (p. 26, original emphasis)

Strands of Althusser's formulation can also be found running through the work of theorists such as Bourdieu and Passeron (1977) and Bernstein (Apple, 2002; Bernstein, 1990). The concept of relative autonomy holds a utilitarian value for resolving the problems posed by economic determinism and aids critical education theorists in developing theories of resistance (Dance, 2002; Giroux, 1983b; Willis, 1977), because it attempts to both acknowledge human intervention through cultural practices and to establish schools as relatively autonomous from the economic base, and thus as spaces where the possibility of social transformation might be created.

Arguably it is the intent of all Marxist, functionalist, and/or neo-Marxist formulations to analyze the relationship between schools and society—the empirical evidence connecting schools and inequality is too overwhelming to deny such a relationship. The devil, however, is in the details, in *how* we conceive of the interconnections between things within an organic, interrelated totality. Sayers (1990) provides a glimpse of such a conception in his summation of Marxist dialectical relations:

> Social processes have their own internal dynamic, their own inner contradictions. The different aspects of society—forces and relations of production, base and superstructure—are aspects of a single whole, internally and organically interrelated,

in dialectical interaction and conflict. It is these interactions, these conflicts, these contradictions—which are internal to society—that lead to historical change. In the process, none of these aspects is inert or passive: the forces and relations of production and also the superstructure are all transformed and developed. (p. 164)

The importance of understanding social and economic processes as having their own internal dynamics cannot be overstated, for it recognizes that there are logics of development at play within these relationships, that there are social and economic systems in a sense have their own life *and* are made up of the lives of individual humans. As Creaven (2000) observes,

The existence of such relationships of structural dependence (of polity, law, major cultural institutions, etc.,) upon economic production and exploitation is what justifies the Marxist view that societies are systems, or totalities, following their own logics of development, rather than a heterogeneous ensemble of "autonomous" structures or practices, moving in no particular direction. (p. 67)

The conception of these relationships as systematic, as processes that develop in particular directions and that exhibit particular characteristics, means they function in ways that can be interrogated, understood, and ultimately, changed.

Elsewhere I have argued that the neo-Marxist turn away from what was labeled as traditional or orthodox Marxism toward analytical tools such as hegemony and relative autonomy was fundamentally misguided because it was based upon a deep misunderstanding of Marxist dialectical materialism, and that Marx and Engels' original, dialectical materialist conception of the base/superstructure relationship was not only adequate, but provided the basis for both Gramsci's and Althusser's own conceptions (Au, 2006a).[4] The important piece of the neo-Marxist impetus, however, is to recognize that within a Marxist, dialectical analysis, human beings are not totally determined beings. As Marx (1968b) himself asserted, humans "make their own history, but they do not make it as they please; they do not make it under self-selected circumstances, but under circumstances existing already, given and transmitted from the past" (p. 97). Or, in Engels' (1968c) words, "In the history of society...the actors are all endowed with consciousness, are [humans] acting with deliberation or passion, working towards definite goals; nothing happens without a conscious purpose, without an intended aim" (p. 622). Indeed, within a Marxist conception, humans do have agency, they can be and are subjects of history. This was the goal of both Lenin's (1975) and Vygotsky's (1978; 1987) conceptions of consciousness (Au, 2007c) and is the backbone of Freire's (1974) conception of "liberatory pedagogy" (Au, 2007a; Au & Apple, 2007): That humans, as subjects, as agents, as individuals, and as individual classes, develop consciousness of the imposition of structures on their lives and, based on that consciousness, take action to change it.

However, as Anderson (1980) explains, the terms "agent" and "subject" both are internally contradictory: "agent" signifies both "active initiator" and "passive instrument" (e.g., the agent of a foreign power), and "subject" signifies both "sovereignty" and "subordination." Such internal contradiction perhaps points to the appropriateness of both terms, for it provides analytic space, in a Marxist conception, for

---

4. Despite such criticism, I do want to acknowledge that critical education theorists have used these concepts fruitfully to analyze the relationship between schools and socioeconomic inequalities in nondeterministic ways (see, e.g., Apple, 1992; Apple, 1995; Bernstein, 1990, 1996).

both individual consciousness and schools to be "relatively autonomous" from the relations of production associated with the economic base. Thus, while schools play a key role in reproducing social inequality, their contradictory role in legitimating ideologies of equality also allows room for resistance to this reproduction (Apple, 1979/2004, 1995; Carnoy & Levin, 1985). It is absolutely critical for us to recognize this room for resistance because students *do* resist the inculcations of schooling on many levels (Au, 2005a; Dance, 2002; McNeil, 1986; Shor, 1992; Willis, 1977), and teachers, as laborers within the political economy of education (Apple, 1986, 1995), also resist the reproduction of inequitable capitalist socialist relations in their classrooms and schools (Allman, 1999; Allman, McLaren, & Rikowski, 2000; Carlson, 1988a, b; Shor, 1987). In this way, a dialectical conception of the relationship between schools and capitalism, in a Marxist, dialectical materialist sense, poses a significant challenge to the economic determinism of Bowles and Gintis, one that still recognizes that the superstructure is emergent from, but not reducible to, the economic base (Apple, 2000; Creaven, 2000).

In a Marxist conception, schools, as part of the superstructure, have a contradictory relationship with the relations of capitalist production. Fritzell's (1987) explanation of the contradictory nature of the State's relationship with the economic base is apt for the present discussion about education, when he observes that:

> [It] could be argued that in a functional context the autonomy of the State refers essentially to a *potentiality*, insofar as it is granted that even under empirical conditions of advanced capitalism the State cannot in the long run enforce policies and interventions that are basically destructive to the commodity form of economic production. (p. 27, original emphasis)

Fritzell roots the essential contradiction of the position of the State in the fact that it is fundamentally outside of the process of producing commodities—"autonomous from the commodity form," yet it still is required under capitalism to support the production of those commodities and thus "cannot ... enforce policies ... that are basically destructive to the commodity form." In relation to capitalist production and social reproduction, the State is required to work out this internal contradiction. Schools, on behalf of the State-superstructure, have to simultaneously accomplish the fundamentally contradictory goals of reproducing the social and material relations of capitalist production while hegemonically working to win the "spontaneous consent" of the students/workers through appeals to individual equality within the educational and social meritocracy (Apple, 1995). This contradiction presents a dialectical relationship between production of capitalist social relations and the maintenance of bourgeois hegemony vis-à-vis education.

Bibliography

Allman, P. (1999). *Revolutionary social transformation: Democratic hopes, political possibilities and critical education.* Westport, CT: Bergin & Garvey.

Allman, P., McLaren, P., & Rikowski, G. (2000). After the box people: The labour-capital relation as class constitution—and its consequences for Marxist educational theory and human resistance. Retrieved May 1, 2004, from http://www.ieps.org.uk.cwc.net/afterthebox.pdf

Althusser, L. (1971). *Lenin and philosophy and other essays* (B. Brewster, Trans.). New York: Monthly Review Books.

Amrein, A. L., & Berliner, D. C. (2002a). *An analysis of some unintended and negative consequences of high-stakes testing.* Tempe: Arizona State University, College of Education, Language Policy Research Unit, Educational Policy Studies Laboratory.

Amrein, A. L., & Berliner, D. C. (2002b). High-stakes testing, uncertainty, and student learning. *Education Policy Analysis Archives, 10*(18). Retrieved September 27, 2005, from http://epaa.asu.edu/epaa/v10n18

Anderson, P. (1980). *Arguments within English Marxism.* London: Verso.

Anyon, J. (2005). *Radical possibilities: Public policy, urban education, and a new social movement.* New York: Routledge.

Apple, M. W. (1979/2004). *Ideology and curriculum* (3rd ed.). New York: RoutledgeFalmer.

Apple, M. W. (1980–81). The other side of the hidden curriculum: Correspondence theories and the labor process. *Interchange, 11*(3), 5–22.

Apple, M. W. (1986). *Teachers and texts: A political economy of class and gender relations in education.* New York: Routledge & Kegan Paul.

Apple, M. W. (1988a). Facing the complexity of power: For a parallelist position in critical educational studies. In M. Cole (Ed.), *Bowles and Gintis revisited: Correspondence and contradiction in educational theory* (pp. 112–130). New York: The Falmer Press.

Apple, M. W. (1992). Education, culture, and class power: Basil Bernstein and the neo-Marxist sociology of education—beyond the automaticity thesis. *Educational Theory, 42*(2), 127–145.

Apple, M. W. (1995). *Education and power* (2nd ed.). New York: Routledge.

Apple, M. W. (2000). *Official knowledge: Democratic education in a conservative age* (2nd ed.). New York: Routledge.

Apple, M. W. (2002). Does education have independent power? Bernstein and the question of relative autonomy. *British Journal of Sociology of Education, 23*(4), 607–616.

Apple, M. W. (2006a). *Educating the "right" way: Markets, standards, god, and inequality* (2nd ed.). New York: Routledge.

Apple, M. W., & Beane, J. A. (Eds.). (2007). *Democratic schools* (2nd ed.). Portsmouth, NH: Heinemann.

Apple, M. W., & Buras, K. L. (Eds.). (2006b). *The subaltern speak: Curriculum, power, and educational struggles.* New York: Routledge.

Apple, M. W., & Pedroni, T. C. (2005). Conservative alliance building and African American support of vouchers: the end of *Brown's* promise or a new beginning? *Teachers College Record, 107*(9), 2068–2105.

Arnot, M., & Whitty, G. (1982). From reproduction to transformation: Recent radical perspectives on the curriculum from the USA. *British Journal of Sociology of Education, 3*(1), 93–103.

Au, W. (2005a). Power, identity, and the third rail. In P. C. Miller (Ed.), *Narratives from the classroom: An introduction to teaching* (pp. 65–85). Thousand Oaks, CA: Sage.

Au, W. (2006a). Against economic determinism: Revisiting the roots of neo-Marxism in critical educational theory. *Journal for Critical Education Policy Studies, 4*(2). Retrieved December 12, 2006, from http://www.jceps.com/?pageID=article&articleID=66

Au, W. (2007a). Epistemology of the oppressed: the dialectics of Paulo Freire's theory of knowledge. *Journal for Critical Education Policy Studies, 5*(2). Retrieved November 2, 2007, from http://www.jceps.com/index.php?pageID=article&articleID=100

Au, W., & Apple, M. W. (2007). Freire, critical education, and the environmental crisis. *Educational Policy, 21*(3), 457–470.

Barton, P. E. (2003). *Parsing the achievement gap: Baselines for tracking progress.* Princeton, NJ: Policy Information Center, Educational Testing Service.

Beatty, A., Neisser, U., Trent, W. T., & Heubert, J. P. (2001). *Understanding dropouts: Statistics, strategies, and high-stakes testing.* Retrieved September 27, 2005, from http://www.nap.edu/catalog/10166.html

Berlak, H. (2000). Cultural politics, the science of assessment and democratic renewal of public education. In A. Filer (Ed.), *Assessment: Social practice and social product* (pp. 189–207). New York: RoutledgeFalmer.

Bernstein, B. B. (1990). *The structuring of pedagogic discourse* (1st ed., Vol. IV). New York: Routledge.

Bernstein, B. B. (1996). *Pedagogy, symbolic control, and identity: Theory, research, critique.* London: Taylor & Francis.

Bourdieu, P., & Passeron, J. (1977). *Reproduction in education, society, and culture.* Beverly Hills, CA: Sage.

Bowles, S., & Gintis, H. (1976). *Schooling in capitalist America: Educational reform and the contradictions of economic life.* New York: Basic Books.

Bowles, S., & Gintis, H. (1988). Schooling in capitalist America: Reply to our critics. In M. Cole (Ed.), *Bowles and Gintis revisted: Correspondence and contradiction in educational theory.* Philadelphia: The Falmer Press.

Brown, P., & Lauder, H. (2006). Globalisation, knowledge and the myth of the magnet economy. *Globalisation, Societies and Education, 4*(1), 25–27.

Carlson, D. L. (1988a). Beyond the reproductive theory of teaching. In M. Cole (Ed.), *Bowles and Gintis revisited: Correspondence and contradiction in educational theory* (pp. 158–173). New York: The Falmer Press.

Carlson, D. L. (1988b). Curriculum planning and the state: the dynamics of control in education. In L. E. Beyer & M. W. Apple (Eds.), *The curriculum: Problems, politics, and possibilities* (pp. 98–115). Albany: State University of New York Press.

Carnoy, M., & Levin, H. M. (1985). *Schooling and work in the democratic state.* Stanford, CA: Stanford University Press.

Cole, M. (Ed.). (1988). *Bowles and Gintis revisited: Correspondence and contradiction in educational theory.* Philadelphia: The Falmer Press.

Coleman, J. S., Campbell, E. Q., Hobson, C. J., McPartland, J., Mood, A. M., & Weinfield, F. D. (1966). *Equality of educational opportunity.* Washington, DC: U.S. Government Printing Office.

Creaven, S. (2000). *Marxism and realism: A materialistic application of realism in the social sciences.* London: Routledge.

Dance, J. L. (2002). *Tough fronts: the impact of street culture on schooling.* New York: RoutledgeFarmer.

Darder, A., & Torres, R. D. (2004). *After race: Racism after multiculturalism.* New York: New York University Press.

Darling-Hammond, L. (2004). From "separate but equal" to "no child left behind": the collision of new standards and old inequalities. In D. Meier & G. Wood (Eds.), *Many children left behind: How the no child left behind act is damaging our children and our schools* (pp. 3–32). Boston: Beacon Press.

Darling-Hammond, L. (2007). Race, inequality and educational accountability: The irony of 'no child left behind'. *Race, Ethnicity, and Education, 10*(3), 245–260.

Darling-Hammond, L., McClosky, L., & Pecheone, R. (2006). *Analysis and recommendations for alternatives to the Washington Assessment of Student Learning*. Palo Alto, CA: School Redesign Network, Stanford University School of Education.

Du Bois, W. E. B. (1903). The talented tenth. In *The Negro problem* (pp. 31–76). New York: James Pott and Company.

Edwards, T. (1980). Schooling for change: Function, correspondence and cause. In L. Barton, R. Meighan, & S. Walker (Eds.), *Schooling, ideology, and the curriculum* (pp. 67–79). Sussex, UK: The Falmer Press.

Engels, F. (1968c). Ludwig Feuerbach and the end of classical German philosophy. In I. Publishers (Ed.), *Karl Marx & Frederick Engels selected works* (pp. 596–618). New York: International Publishers.

Evers, W. M., & Walberg, H. J. (2004). Introduction and overview. In W. M. Evers & H. J. Walberg (Eds.), *Testing student learning, evaluating teaching effectiveness* (pp. vii–xiii). Stanford, CA: Hoover Institution Press.

Fritzell, C. (1987). On the concept of relative autonomy in educational theory. *British Journal of Sociology of Education, 8*(1), 23–35.

Gibson, R., Queen, G., Ross, E. W., & Vinson, K. D. (2007). "I participate, you participate, we participate … they profit," notes on revolutionary educational activism to transcend capital: the Rouge Forum. *Journal for Critical Education Policy Studies, 5*(2). Retrieved November 2, 2007, from http://www.jceps.com/index.php?pageID=article&articleID=97

Giroux, H. A. (1980). Beyond the correspondence theory: Notes on the dynamics of educational reproduction and transformation. *Curriculum Inquiry, 10*(3), 225–247.

Giroux, H. A. (1983a). Ideology and agency in the process of schooling. *Journal of Education, 165*(1), 12–34.

Giroux, H. A. (1983b). Theories of reproduction and resistance in the new sociology of education: A critical analysis. *Harvard Educational Review, 53*(3), 257–293.

Gramsci, A. (1971). *Selections from the prison notebooks* (Q. Hoare & G. N. Smith, Trans.). New York: International Publishers.

Groves, P. (2002). 'Doesn't it feel morbid here?': High-stakes testing and the widening of the equity gap. *Educational Foundations, 16*(2), 15–31.

Hampton, E. (2005). Standardized or sterilized? Differing perspectives on the effects of high-stakes testing in West Texas. In A. Valenzuela (Ed.), *Leaving children behind: How 'Texas-style' accountability fails Latino youth* (pp. 179–199). Albany: State University of New York.

Haney, W. (2000). The myth of the Texas miracle in education. *Education Policy Analysis Archives, 8*(41). Retrieved October 8, 2005, from http://epaa.asu.edu/epaa/v8n41

Hoffman, B. (1962). *The tyranny of testing*. New York: The Crowell-Collier Press.

Hunter, R. C., & Bartee, R. (2003). The achievement gap: Issues of competition, class, and race. *Education and Urban Society, 35*(2), 151–160.

Jennings, J. F. (2000). Title I: its legislative history and its promise. *Phi Delta Kappan, 81*(7), 516–522.

Kane, T. J., & Staiger, D. O. (2002). Volatility in school test scores: Implications for test-based accountability systems. In D. Ravitch (Ed.), *Brookings papers on education policy 2002* (pp. 235–284). Washington, DC: Brookings Institution Press.

Karp, S. (2006b). Leaving public education behind: The Bush agenda in American education. *Our Schools/Our Selves, 15*(3), 181–196.

Kim, J. S., & Sunderman, G. L. (2005). Measuring academic proficiency under the no child left behind act: Implications for educational equity. *Educational Researcher, 34*(8), 3–13.

Kornhaber, M. L., & Orfield, G. (2001). High-stakes testing policies: examining their assumptions and consequences. In G. Orfield & M. L. Kornhaber (Eds.), *Raising standards or raising barriers?: Inequality and high-stakes testing in public education* (pp. 1–18). New York: Century Foundation Press.

Ladson-Billings, G. (2006). From the achievement gap to the education debt: Understanding achievement in U.S. schools. *Educational Researcher, 35*(7), 3–12.

Laird, J., Lew, S., DeBell, M., & Chapman, C. (2006). *Dropout rates in the United States: 2002 and 2003* (No. NCES 2006-062). Washington, DC: U.S. Department of Education: National Center for Education Statistics.

Lankshear, C. (1997). Language and the new capitalism. *The International Journal of Inclusive Education, 1*(4), 309–321.

Lemann, N. (1999). *The big test: The secret history of the American meritocracy*. New York: Farrar, Straus, and Giroux.

Lenin, V. I. (1975). *What is to be done?: Burning questions of our movement*. Peking: Foreign Language Press.

Lomax, R. G., West, M. M., Harmon, M. C., Viator, K. A., & Madaus, G. F. (1995). The impact of mandated standardized testing on minority students. *Journal of Negro Education, 64*(2), 171–185.

Madaus, G. F., & Clarke, M. (2001). The adverse impact of high-stakes testing on minority students: evidence from one hundred years of test data. In G. Orfield & M. L. Kornhaber (Eds.), *Raising standards or raising barriers?: Inequality and high-stakes testing in public education* (pp. 85–106). New York: Century Foundation Press.

Maran, M. (2000). *Class dismissed: A year in the life of an American high school, a glimpse into the heart of a nation*. New York: St. Martin's Griffin.

Marchant, G. J., & Paulson, S. E. (2005). The relationship of high school graduation exams to graduation rates and SAT scores. *Education Policy Analysis Archives, 13*(6). Retrieved February 8, 2006, from http://epaa.asu.edu/epaa/v13n6/

Marx, K. (1968a). Preface to a contribution to the critique of political economy. In *Karl Marx & Frederick Engels: Their selected works* (pp. 181–185). New York: International Publishers.

Marx, K. (1968b). The eighteenth brumaire of Louis Bonaparte. In *Karl Marx & Frederick Engels: Their selected works* (pp. 95–180). New York: International Publishers.

Marx, K., & Engels, F. (1848/1977). *Manifesto of the communist party*. Peking: Foreign Language Press.

McLaren, P., & Farahmandpur, R. (2005). *Teaching against global capitalism and the new imperialism: A critical pedagogy*. New York: Rowman and Littlefield.

McNeil, L. M. (1986). *Contradictions of control: School structure and school knowledge*. New York: Routledge & Kegan Paul.

McNeil, L. M. (2000). *Contradictions of school reform: Educational costs of standardized testing*. New York: Routledge.

McNeil, L. M. (2005). Faking equity: High-stakes testing and the education of Latino youth. In A. Valenzuela (Ed.), *Leaving children behind: How 'Texas-style' accountability fails Latino youth* (pp. 57–112). Albany: State University of New York.

McNeil, L. M., & Valenzuela, A. (2001). The harmful impact of the TAAS system of testing in Texas: Beneath the accountability rhetoric. In G. Orfield & M. L. Kornhaber (Eds.), *Raising standards or raising barriers?: Inequality and high-stakes testing in public education* (pp. 127–150). New York: The Century Foundation Press.

Moe, T. M. (2003). Politics, control, and the future of school accountability. In P. E. Peterson & M. R. West (Eds.), *No child left behind?: The politics and practice of school accountability* (pp. 80–106). Washington, DC: Brookings Institution Press.

Moore, R. (1988). The correspondence principle and the Marxist sociology of education. In M. Cole (Ed.), *Bowles and Gintis revisited: Correspondence and contradiction in educational theory* (pp. 51–85). New York: The Falmer Press.

Nichols, S. L., & Berliner, D. C. (2007). *Collateral damage: How high-stakes testing corrupts America's schools*. Cambridge, MA: Harvard Education Press.

Nichols, S. L., Glass, G. V., & Berliner, D. C. (2005). *High-stakes testing and student achievement: Problems for the no child left behind act* (No. EPSL-0509-105-EPRU). Tempe: Education Policy Research Unit, Education Policy Studies Laboratory, College of Education, Division of Educational Leadership and Policy Studies, Arizona State University.

Noguera, P. (2001). Racial politics and the elusive quest for excellence and equity in education. *Education and Urban Society, 34*(1), 18–41.

Noguera, P. (2003a). *City schools and the American dream: Reclaiming the promise of public education*. New York: Teachers College Press.

Orfield, G., & Wald, J. (2000). Testing, testing: The high-stakes testing mania hurts poor and minority students the most. *The Nation, 270*(22), 38–40.

Pedroni, T. C. (2007). *Market movements: African American involvement in school voucher reform*. New York: Routledge.

Popham, W. J. (2001). *The truth about testing: an educator's call to action*. Alexandria, VA: Association for Supervision and Curriculum Development (ASCD).

Rethinking Schools. (2008). Homepage. Retrieved January 1, 2008, from http://www.rethinkingschools.org

Roderick, M., & Nagaoka, J. (2005). Retention under Chicago's high-stakes testing program: helpful, harmful, or harmless? *Educational Evaluation and Policy Analysis, 27*(4), 309–340.

Sayers, S. (1990). Marxism and the dialectical method: A critique of G.A. Cohen. In S. Sayers & P. Osborne (Eds.), *Socialism, feminism, and philosophy: A radical philosophy reader* (pp. 140–168). New York: Routledge.

Schneider, A. L., & Ingram, H. (1997). *Policy design for democracy*. Lawrence: University of Kansas.

Shor, I. (1987). *Critical teaching & everyday life*. Chicago: The University of Chicago Press.

Shor, I. (1992). *Empowering education: Critical teaching for social change*. Chicago: The University of Chicago Press.

Sirin, S. R. (2005). Socioeconomic status and student achievement: A meta-analytic review of research. *Review of Educational Research, 75*(3), 417–453.

Sloan, K. (2005). Playing to the logic of the Texas accountability system: How focusing on 'ratings'—not children—undermines quality and equity. In A. Valenzuela (Ed.), *Leaving children behind: How 'Texas-style' accountability fails Latino youth* (pp. 153–178). Albany: State University of New York.

Smith, M. L. (2004). *Political spectacle and the fate of American schools*. New York: RoutledgeFalmer.

The Education Trust. (2004). *Education watch: The nation: Key education facts and figures: achievement, attainment, and opportunity from elementary school through college*. Washington, DC: The Education Trust.

U.S. Department of Education. (2002). *No child left behind: A desktop reference*. Washington, DC: U.S. Department of Education, Office of the Under Secretary.

Valenzuela, A. (Ed.). (2005b). *Leaving children behind: How 'Texas style' accountability fails Latino youth*. Albany: State University of New York Press.

Vygotsky, L. S. (1978). *Mind in society*. Cambridge, MA: Harvard University Press.

Vygotsky, L. S. (1987). Thinking and speech (N. Minick, Trans.). In R. W. Rieber & A. Carton (Eds.), *The collected works of L.S. Vygotsky: Problems of general psychology including the volume thinking and speech* (Vol. 1, pp. 37–285). New York: Plenum.

Washington, B. T. (1903). The industrial education of the Negro. In *The Negro problem* (pp. 7–30). New York: James Pott and Company.

Willis, P. (1977). *Learning to labor: How working class kids get working class jobs*. New York: Columbia University Press.

Winick, D. M., & Kress, S. (2004). Accountability works in Texas. In W. M. Evers & H. J. Walberg (Eds.), *Testing student learning, evaluating teaching effectiveness* (pp. 303–322). Stanford, CA: Hoover Institution Press.

Woodson, C. G. (1990). *The mis-education of the negro*. Trenton, NJ: Africa World Press. (Original published 1933)

Zabala, D. (2007). *State high school exit exams: Gaps persist in high school exit exam pass rates—policy brief 3*. Washington, DC: Center on Education Policy.

Post-Reading Questions

1. According to the author, how does standardized testing contribute to existing social inequalities?
2. Which groups are most likely to succeed at standardized testing? Which groups are most likely to struggle with standardized testing? Why do you think these differences exist?
3. What policies do you think would make schools more equitable to everyone? How do you think student performance should be measured? Do you agree with standardized testing? Why or why not?

UNIT VII

POPULATION AND THE ENVIRONMENT

Key Terms and Definitions

Review the key terms and definitions below to strengthen your understanding of the readings in this unit.

Climate Change: Shifts in weather conditions that last over a sustained period due to increased carbon dioxide levels in the atmosphere. This results from coal and gas emissions with the use of fossil fuels.

The Climate Change Countermovement: A reactionary social movement that seeks to downplay global warming and deny the trend toward climate change. This movement is often led by conservative think tanks and the fossil fuel industry (Brulle and Roberts 2017).

The Feminization of Poverty: The increasing economic divide between men and women, resulting in higher rates of poverty for females, and especially for those who are single mothers.

Global Warming: The rising average temperature on earth observed since the mid-twentieth century.

Introduction

Each of these readings reveals how the environment is an important sociological issue. The authors in each piece show how **global warming** and **climate change** are enormous threats to human existence and well-being. In the first reading for unit 9, "Climate Misinformation Campaigns and Public Sociology," Robert J. Brulle and J. Timmons Roberts highlight how sociological research about climate misinformation campaigns has informed public debate. The scientific data overwhelmingly reveal that **global warming** is caused by humans and that immediate intervention is necessary to protect our planet and its people. However, politicians, policymakers, and industry leaders disagree on the gravity of this issue. On the one hand, advocates for climate justice call for a rapid switch from fossil fuels to renewable forms of energy. Many are making appeals for drastic, immediate changes. On the other hand, people within the **climate change countermovement** downplay the problem of global warming and deny the realities of **climate change**.

Since the 1990s, sociologists have been researching the **climate change countermovement**. This movement is largely driven by conservative think tanks and people who have a financial stake in the fossil fuel industry (Brulle and Roberts 2017). Partisan debates about **climate change** happen regularly on the Senate floor and other political arenas. Recent debates, spearheaded by senators on the political left, have shifted focus from simply illuminating the problem of **climate change** to directly challenging climate misinformation. The authors show how sociological research can inform these debates, contributing to public knowledge and policy changes (Brulle and Roberts 2017).

In the second article, titled "Greater New York: Urban Anxiety," Jim Motavalli and Sherry Barnes reveal some troubling patterns to show how New York City is already facing the ill effects of **climate change**. For example, sea levels are rising, temperatures are increasing year to year, and snowfall levels are decreasing. Major economic problems could surface if the city were to face flooding from **climate change**. This problem is certainly not unique to the New York metro area. In nearby New Jersey, properties built close to the water may face flooding in the future, alongside the erosion of beaches and shifting shorelines. This can also widen the divide between the rich and the poor, as wealthy homeowners with beach property scramble to protect their own land but neglect maintaining and preserving public beach areas. Private jetties can contribute to the risk of erosion with rising sea levels. The few beachside neighborhoods that seem to have avoided property development are now being rapidly transformed, despite the environmental costs.

In the final reading in this unit, "Women: In the Shadow of Climate Change," Balgis Osman-Elasha highlights how **climate change** amplifies existing inequalities in society. Those in difficult economic situations are likely to face the most devasting consequences from **climate change**, and research from the United Nations shows that women may also be disproportionately impacted. As you learned in unit 7, in the United States, women face stark economic inequalities compared to men. Women are therefore more likely to face poverty than men, leading to a pattern that sociologists call the **feminization of poverty**. This same pattern happens on a global scale, where women make up the world's largest share of poor people. Women are responsible for most of the world's food production, but men own most of the land. Many women work in subsistence farming but are rarely involved in distribution and other forms of economic decision-making. When environmental disasters strike, domestic responsibilities often prevent women from migrating to seek refuge. On top of this, the author points out that in times of disaster, women face a higher risk of domestic violence, sexual intimidation, human trafficking, and rape. To address these massive gender inequalities, the author calls for several changes. She asks that we account for gender disparities as we address **climate change** to make overall progress on this important matter.

In each of these readings, the authors reveal that to make progress on environmental justice issues, we must expose and displace climate misinformation campaigns. We also must acknowledge how property development, without the proper environmental considerations, is damaging our beaches and shorelines.

Finally, we need to acknowledge that some groups in society face increased risks of **climate change**, including poor people, females, and people of color. On a worldwide scale, we have a lot of work to do to enhance environmental sustainability and prevent any further damage to our planet.

References

Brulle, Robert J., and J. Timmons Roberts. "Climate Misinformation Campaigns and Public Sociology." *Contexts* 16, no. 1 (2017): 78–79. https://doi.org/10.1177/1536504217696081.

Climate Misinformation Campaigns and Public Sociology

Robert J. Brulle and J. Timmons Roberts

Robert J. Brulle and J. Timmons Roberts, "Climate Misinformation Campaigns and Public Sociology," *Contexts: Understanding People in Their Social Worlds*, vol. 16, no. 1, pp. 78–79. Copyright © 2017 by SAGE Publications. Reprinted with permission.

On July 11, 2016, Senate Minority Leader Harry Reid (D-Nevada) took to the floor of the Senate to discuss climate change. Rather than focusing on the well-known science of climate change, he focused on the "Web of Denial"—the network of think tanks and foundations that promote misinformation in order to delay action on climate change. Following Reid, Senator Sheldon Whitehouse (D-Rhode Island) delivered his 143rd speech about how it is "Time to Wake Up" about climate change as he provided an overview of the seventeen other Senators' speeches to come in this organized, two-day "Web of Denial" marathon speech event.

> The movement of ideas from academia to the Senate floor shows the important role that the sociological community can play in the generation of new cultural perspectives and informing democratic deliberations.

Senator Whitehouse notably acknowledged the contributions of sociological scholarship in bringing this issue to public scrutiny. He mentioned Riley Dunlap, Aaron McCright, and Justin Farrell by name before saying, "The scholarship of all these academics, all these organizations, and all these authors—the detectives who are exposing the Web of Denial—have shined a bright light into its dark corners and illuminated its concerted effort to dupe the American public and sabotage climate action in America, all to protect the fossil fuel industry that funds it."

The sociological literature on climate misinformation efforts has provided intellectual space to reflexively critique, and potentially move beyond, the limited perspectives pushed by the Web of Denial. These speeches, however, represent public sociology, a debated term but one that involves expanding sociological analysis to encompass and inform the public about issues of common moral and political concern.

What ideas are normal and acceptable in society? Which are deviant and radical? This is the terrain of continual conflict between and among social groups as described by cultural sociologists. Based on a linguistic perspective, this approach focuses on the construction of different framings of the social worlds within which institutional practices are defined. Sociologists have observed that groups try to maintain particular framings that define the appropriate practices in a specific policy area, setting the conditions of appropriate and inappropriate institutional practices—and ultimately legal and illegal conduct in a policy arena. Struggle over the governing frame is thus a critical component in power contests between those who seek to maintain the status quo and those who seek social change and advocate for a different governing frame. Cultural sociologists' analyses of such contests provide insight into the nature of political action and social change.

From a cultural perspective, then, environmental politics is organized around the interaction between groups supporting the dominant framing of a particular policy arena and alternative challengers. The main dominant actors usually include industry organizations and their trade associations, professional bodies, government actors, and advocacy organizations. Alternative challengers might include social justice activists and environmentalists. Struggles over public policy take the form of a contest over the appropriate field framing and involve building institutions (such as cultural, educational, and media organizations) that can act to maintain or transform the popular mentality so that the desired framing is accepted as common sense in that particular arena.

It needs to be understood that climate change policy debates are quite separate from the scientific findings regarding climate change. The most recent Intergovernmental Panel on Climate Change (IPCC) report shows that global warming is happening and is caused by humans. For nearly all scientists, as well as for populations and governments around the world, the debate about the *existence* of climate change is over. However, in the United States, the policy debate continues. On one side there is the climate movement that seeks to move the U.S. to take rapid and ambitious actions to address climate change by shifting quickly from fossil fuels to efficiency, conservation, and renewable energy. On the other side is the climate countermovement. Mostly funded by conservative foundations and fossil fuel interests, its strategy is to deny the scientific findings regarding the human cause of climate change, confound the public, and downplay the seriousness of this issue and the need for action. It is a long-standing framing dispute, with vast profits and the stability of Earth's life support systems at stake.

IMAGE 20.1

Courtesy Sen. Whitehouse

The Senate is the site of frequent speeches and events that highlight the issue of climate change. For example, in February 2015, Senator James Inhofe (R-Oklahoma) brought a snowball to the floor of the Senate to demonstrate that climate change was a hoax (see "Not a Snowball's Chance for Science," *Contexts* Fall 2015).

The marathon speeches about climate misinformation efforts in July 2016 were entirely different. Senator Reid's speeches on the the Web of Denial were informed by extensive, peer-reviewed sociological research. The senators sought to show that the organized efforts at climate misinformation are grounded in organizations funded by vested interests (huge fossil fuel corporations) aiming to block government actions that would require rapid shifts in U.S. energy production. These senators are attempting to shift the debate away from the dangerous distortions of climate denial by revealing how the fossil fuel industry uses their political and economic power to systematically undermine our ability to act before it is too late.

Sociological research studying the development of misinformation and climate denial efforts has been crucial in this counter-effort. Beginning in the mid-1990s, sociologists began to analyze the nature of what they called the emerging "climate change countermovement." In a series of papers, starting in 2000, Riley Dunlap and Aaron McCright provided critical insights into how conservative think tanks developed sophisticated strategies to promulgate doubt and misinformation about climate change science. In 2010, Naomi Oreskes published *Merchants of Doubt*, which documented the historical efforts of a small group of individuals similarly sowing doubt.

After these path-breaking works, scholarship in this area rapidly expanded. This research enabled the National Academy of Science to conclude in 2012 that the concerted campaign to promote scientific misinformation about climate science had affected media coverage of this issue. Concerted political effort had created the impression that there was a serious debate over climate change when, in fact, there was none. It contributed to the party-line polarization over the serious science of climate change.

Yet this well-developed scholarship was not represented in public debates. How did it manage to move out of sociological journals and books to the Senate floor, informing political debates in such an extensive and powerful manner? In the case of climate change, the community of scholars focused on an area of the climate countermovement and developed a robust sociological analysis of a new social phenomenon. The key to its diffusion from the academic community and into the public sphere was the activity of intermediary figures both familiar with the academic research and able to communicate these results. We were proud to participate in this important effort. Timmons Roberts met regularly Senator Whitehouse and his staff, and when they expressed interest in uncovering the roots of influence over Senate peers, was able to provide research like McCright, Dunlap, and Brulle's 2014 article on the funding relationships between foundations and conservative think tanks. Senator Whitehouse subsequently utilized this material in his weekly floor speeches about climate change, and it served as a key resource in developing the collective Web of Denial speech event (one of the key graphics from Brulle's 2014 paper was repeatedly displayed throughout).

Sociology is both an academic and public discipline. In this case, sociologists worked out new insights about the social phenomena of the climate countermovement and developed a robust literature. This knowledge diffused through the media and into the political sphere, informing an ongoing political effort to move the U.S. toward addressing climate change. This movement of ideas shows the important role that the sociological community can play in generating new cultural perspectives and informing democratic deliberations.

Post-Reading Questions

1. According to the authors, which groups in society make up the climate change countermovement? What stakes do these groups have in this movement?
2. Why do some politicians and industry leaders promote climate misinformation? Whose interests are they protecting?
3. Why is climate change often treated as a partisan issue? Doesn't it impact everyone?
4. How can sociological research be used publicly to prevent the spread of climate misinformation?

Greater New York

Urban Anxiety

Jim Motavalli and Sherry Barnes

From a sea kayak floating off Pier 40 in lower Manhattan, you get a whole new perspective on New York City. The bustling metropolis falls away, and you are alone except for the sporadic barge traffic and the incongruity of students walking the high wire as part of a trapeze school in the Hudson River Park just beyond the seawall.

If the Hudson rises, it is most immediately noticeable to people like Randall Henriksen, who has led sea-kayaking expeditions here since 1994. From his perch in the front of the kayak, Hendriksen points to a green-and-white state Department of Environmental Conservation sign on the seawall. "The algae there shows the mean high water line," he says. "It's been slowly but steadily moving up against that sign. The water has certainly been rising over the last few years, though you may not notice the change on a day-to-day basis," he says.

New York City, with more than seven million people, spills out over 378 square miles of land separated by the Hudson, East, and Harlem Rivers, Long Island Sound, and the Atlantic Ocean. The city, one of America's most diverse urban centers, is held together by a complex network of public works infrastructure, including roads, toll bridges, subway tunnels, water mains, gas lines, and millions of miles of telephone and television cables and electrical conduit.

It is a difficult city to run on a good day: In 1996, a "report card" prepared by the city's former U.S. Army Corps of Engineers chief gave New York's infrastructure failing grades, particularly for its aging water mains and solid waste treatment system, which dumps raw sewage into city harbors during storms.

So what happens when things get really bad? On December 11, 1992, a nor'easter storm hit the great city head-on. With wind gusts of up to 90 miles per hour and water surges 8 1/2 feet above mean sea level, New York's transportation infrastructure sputtered to a halt. Four million subway riders were stranded. The FDR Drive, the main highway along the east side of Manhattan, flooded up to 4 1/2 feet in some areas, and LaGuardia Airport, only 7 feet above sea level, grounded flights for the day. In the end, the federal disaster assistance totaled $233.6 million, according to Environmental Defense.

Was the storm a once-in-a-century fluke? Unlikely. Consider the summer of 1999, when high temperatures reigned over most of the eastern United States New York City experienced 27 days with temperatures of 90° F or more—double the number in an average year. Stores sold out of air conditioners, and 200,000 Manhattanites suffered a 19-hour blackout on July 7 because of excess power demand. Water consumption broke records, and thirty-three people died of heat-related causes in the city. The heat was accompanied by the worst American drought since the Dust Bowl of the late 1930s—rainfall in New York was 8 inches below normal for the summer.

But after the drought, a deluge occurred. Heavy rains soaked the city in late August that year, once again flooding the FDR Drive and the West Side Highway, and drowning some subway tracks in 5 feet of water. The big rainstorm was followed in September by Hurricane Floyd. The worst of the hurricane just bypassed the city, but total regional property damage was estimated at $1 billion. Since global warming brings with it the certainty of rising sea level and stormier weather, the city's aging infrastructure and delicate natural balance face unheard-of challenges.

Vivien Gornitz, associate research scientist at NASA's Goddard Institute for Space Studies, points toward a rectangular box jutting out of the Hudson in lower Manhattan, near a guarded U.S. Coast Guard booth. "That tide gauge uses an acoustic device to record the level of the sea's surface," she explains. "It takes a reading every six minutes." Gornitz and other researchers from Columbia University, New York University, and Montclair State University in New Jersey conducted an exhaustive study of the Metro East Coast (MEC) Region, which includes greater New York, Northern New Jersey, and Southern Connecticut, for the "U.S. National Assessment of the Potential Consequences of Climate Variability and Change for the Nation." The MEC findings were published by the Columbia Earth Institute in 2001.

One of the things that troubles Gornitz is all the recent construction at the water's edge. "Look, you can see it's on both sides of the river," she gestures, her arm taking in both sides of the Hudson just north of the former World Trade Center site. Gornitz fears that all the luxurious waterfront condominiums and commercial businesses are taking a risk that will increase dramatically as the new century progresses.

The most conservative climate change model used for the MEC study does not allow for rising greenhouse gas emissions; it merely projects the effects of the current rate of sea-level rise. By the end of the century, it says, we will be seeing 100-year floods every 50 years. "In the worst-case scenario, it could be as often as every four to five years," Gornitz adds. "It wouldn't mean the whole city under water, just the low-lying areas, including beach communities, coastal wetlands and some of the airports." And to further exacerbate the problem, the greater New York area is still experiencing land subsidence triggered by the glacial retreat that occurred more than 10,000 years ago.

New York City is not waiting for climate change: It is already experiencing much warmer years and reduced snowfall. Gornitz notes anecdotal effects, including the Central Park pond that people skated on in the 1970s that now often remains unfrozen all winter. "The cherry blossoms come into leaf a lot earlier now," she adds, "and the leaves stay on the trees a lot longer in the fall."

Janine Bloomfield is a senior scientist at Environmental Defense and author of the report "Hot Nights in the City: Global Warming, Sea-Level Rise and the New York Metropolitan Area." Her report, based on MEC research, makes frightening reading. By 2100, she writes, New York City will have as many 90-degree days as Miami does today. "Sealevel rise will contribute to the temporary flooding or permanent inundation of many of New York City's and the region's coastal areas. ... A large part of lower Manhattan would be at risk from frequent flooding by the end of the [twenty-first] century. ... The East River would flood Bellevue Medical Center, the FDR Drive and East Harlem between 96th and 114th Street," the report says. In a poignant note, the pre-9/11 report notes that the foundations of the World Trade Center would be vulnerable to nearly annual flooding at the end of the century. Droughts that now occur once in a hundred years could occur every 3 to 11 years by 2100.

"The tragedy of this is that we could do something about this now so the scenarios I wrote about won't come to pass," says Bloomfield, who now lives in Boston. "Unfortunately, we won't react until the crises become obvious."

The coming changes will do more than make people swelter or get their feet wet occasionally. "It really could become a serious economic burden for the city," says Klaus Jacob, senior research scientist at Columbia University's Lamont-Doherty Earth Observatory. "The current flood insurance program doesn't account for 100 years from now, and that's no way to plan for the future, especially a sustainable one."

Coordinated planning for these eventualities has been minimal, and actual action even less. Some airport runways and seawalls have been raised. Rae Zimmerman, a New York University professor and director of the Institute for Civil Infrastructure Systems, complains that there is little cooperation between city agencies affected by climate change, and long-range planning is often the first thing cut from budgets that need to be slashed. Federal action has been nonexistent, with the Bush administration and Congress refusing to commit to anything more than redundant studies. But Jacob notes sardonically, "Whether Congress wants to address it or not, the sea level will rise." [...]

New Jersey's Beaches on Shifting Sands

On stormy days, the wind at the tip of Fort Hancock, a former military base that is now part of the bustling Gateway National Recreation Area at the entrance to lower New York Bay, is enough to knock you down, and it churns the Atlantic into a froth favored by surfers but anathema to the embattled homeowners on this exposed coast.

Climate scientists predict that the sea level in New Jersey could rise an additional 2 feet in the next 100 years, with predictable havoc wrought on that priceless real estate. Beach erosion is likely to accelerate dramatically, too. But despite ominous reports of sea-level rise, and horrific damage caused by ever-increasing storms, proximity to New York City has meant rapidly escalating land values for this region, and a determination to build right to the water's edge. Even Fort Hancock, which can appear eerily deserted on a winter afternoon, is about to undergo a chic makeover.

Sandy Hook, where Fort Hancock is located, is like a finger pointed into the ocean toward Brooklyn, a beacon for the great New York/New Jersey estuary. The national park is a rare respite from a landscape dominated by beach communities and chock-a-block strip development. A former officer's quarters in the park, not far from nineteenth-century coastal defense emplacements, now serves as home to two organizations that are trying to protect this prosperous region from itself. The American Littoral Society and New York/New Jersey Baykeeper work together trying to preserve what is left of a natural environment laid low by dredging, filling, and construction.

Dery Bennett, the Littoral Society's friendly and grizzled director, takes visitors on a tour of nearby Sea Bright, where relatively modest vacation homes hide behind a protective seawall built in the 1930s. There is a 100-foot-wide beach behind the wall, built not over the millennia by the workings of the tides but beginning in 1996 by the U.S. Army Corps of Engineers as part of a $9 billion plan to "replenish" the beaches along the 127-mile New Jersey shore. The new sand is dredged from an offshore "borrow" site.

New Jersey is the poster boy for beach replenishment, since it is the only state in the union to pay its share not out of general funds but from a dedicated $25 million purse taken from realty transfer fees. Noreen Bodman, president of the business-oriented Jersey Shore Partnership, calls replenishment "a return on investment that benefits the state in terms of tax dollars, and ultimately benefits every resident in terms of quality of life and recreational values. It also protects businesses and utilities from the impact of some of these storms."

The luncheonette in downtown Sea Bright displays some starkly revealing aerial photos. One, taken in the early 1990s, shows a town with no beach to speak of, thanks largely to the effects of that seawall. The other, from 1999, shows a wide expanse of sand. The photos appear to offer stark proof that what human folly destroys, human ingenuity can repair. But many local environmentalists, including Bennett, Baykeeper Andy Willner, and Surfers' Environmental Alliance co-regional director Brian Unger, oppose the beach replenishment work. They say the massive effort to pump in sand benefits only a few wealthy homeowners, and also encourages even more dangerous shoreline development. And, they add, it is ultimately folly because global-warming-induced storms and rising tides will likely wash it all away in the next decade.

Orrin Pilkey's classic book *The Corps and the Shore*, written with Katharine Dixon, details how jetties, seawalls, groins, and other desperate maneuvers offer only temporary respite from the natural effects of erosion and shifting coastline—and eventually make things worse. The same thing is true of imported sand. New Jersey's replenished beaches, the authors wrote, could expect only a 1- to 3-year lifespan, at a cost of damage to coral, water clarity, and bottom-dwellers. In actual fact they have already outlived that prediction, though the sand is receding.

The East Coast was created in a collision between two tectonic plates, the American and Atlantic. Their coming together produced the Appalachian Mountains, and also the longest stretch of thin barrier islands in the world, extending from New England to Mexico. As Cornelia Dean notes in *Against the Tide: The Battle for America's Beaches*, "When these barrier islands are attacked by rising seas, their natural defense is to back out of the way." In other words, they are constantly shifting and reforming. Pilkey points out that barrier islands differ from any other topographic feature on earth because of "their ability to maintain themselves as a unit as they roll across a flooding coastal plain in response to a rise in sea level."

When this natural phenomenon meets global warming and the devastating effects of nonstop coastal development, rapid erosion is the result. "There's a natural process called littoral drift," explains Willner as he provides a pickup-based tour of Sandy Hook's windswept charms. "Sand from ancient granite mountains like the Appalachians was carried down by glacial action to create the beaches. Once here, it moves north in a predictable, inexorable fashion, reshaping the coast as it goes. What you see today is the result of millions of years of geological evolution, but people expect that process to stop when human infrastructure is introduced. They're putting homes and beach clubs on mobile land. And they're taking a crapshoot that those natural processes won't happen in their lifetimes. When it does, they're always surprised."

The speed with which the ocean reclaims its own is exacerbated by rising tides. According to Norbert Psuty, a coastal geomorphologist with the Department of Marine and Coastal Sciences at Rutgers University, deeper in-shore waters means more powerful waves, which move more quickly and retain more energy. In the last 100 years, the New Jersey coast has sunk 16 inches, through a combination of tectonic plate depression and sea-level rise. "Almost everything we have along the coast is at risk sooner or later," says Psuty. "We've been fortunate not to have taken any direct hits lately." Stephen Leatherman, who directs the Hurricane Center at Florida International University, puts it another way: "The erosion rates are going to accelerate in the future, which means the cost is going to go up exponentially to maintain these beaches. And no one seems to have figured it out yet. It's like a great big secret."

Subsidized Privacy

There are no easy answers on the Jersey shore. According to the *Philadelphia Inquirer*, property that was worth $8.7 billion in 1962 is now worth $34.3 billion when adjusted for inflation. In 1945, George Lippincott bought a house with 1.2 acres in coastal Avalon for $500, raising the money by selling a single rare stamp. In 2000, Lippincott's descendants put the property on the market for $3.5 million. The coast is now fully developed, with the result that a "100-year storm" would be far more devastating today than it would have been 50 years ago. Taxpayers will foot much of the bill for any rebuilding, since flood insurance is federally guaranteed.

The public trust doctrine, derived from English common law, says that states hold lands under tidal and navigable waterways in trust for their citizens. The concept has been incorporated into many state constitutions, and is generally interpreted as guaranteeing public access to shorelines up to the mean high tide mark. The town of Greenwich, Connecticut, fought a long and ultimately losing battle to maintain the exclusivity of its beaches that went as far as the State Supreme Court. It began when local attorney Brenden Leyden was turned away from jogging at a Greenwich beach, and it continued for 6 years. Fortunately for citizens not lucky enough to live in one of the United States's wealthiest towns, the public trust and First Amendment (claiming that the beach is a "traditional public forum") arguments eventually prevailed.

What does global warming have to do with beach access? Quite a lot, actually. The northern New Jersey coast is now mostly in private hands, and the public has only limited access to surf and sand. The scene is set for self-interest. The property owners who benefit the most from beach replenishment use their political clout not to enrich the shoreline commons, but to protect their own land values, sometimes with the active assistance of community leaders.

The I'm-in-it-for-myself mentality dictates more privately built jetties and seawalls, which accelerate the erosion damage caused by rising sea levels. And it means security guards and high fences on what was once open shore. Meanwhile, the public, by the very fact of their exclusion, loses its interest and its stake in protecting a coastal resource it can only see through locked gates. Sixty-seven-year-old Sea Girt resident Bob Devlin told the *Philadelphia Inquirer*, "I gave up going to the beach there a long time ago."

Public access and beach replenishment collide head on in Long Beach Township communities such as Loveladies and North Beach. To be eligible for federal funding, the towns are nominally required to provide open beach access every quarter mile, but endless rows of closely built houses, without the "street ends" that allow parking and foot traffic, dictate that the actual distance between access points is more like a mile and a half. And even where access does exist, the scarcity of parking (in some cases by design) limits its value to out-of-towners.

One of the groups that have suffered both because of beach replenishment and lost public access is the surprisingly strong northern New Jersey surfing community. The attraction is clear: It is state-of-the-art surfing almost within sight of New York City. As Surfline.com points out, "Sandy Hook boasts one of the few point breaks in New Jersey." Brian Unger, a graying but fit surfer turned environmentalist and access activist, takes visiting journalists on a tour through some of the exclusive beach towns near Sandy Hook that benefit from both beach replenishment and storm insurance, but make it as difficult as possible for the taxpaying nonresident to enjoy the imported sand.

The tour began on a blustery day in Elberon, an exclusive section of Long Branch just north of Bruce Springsteen's Asbury Park. Surfers fear that a pending beach replenishment in Elberon will smooth out the beach, remove natural rock formations, and affect surf-friendly wave formation by bringing deeper water closer to shore. They are arguing for a more nuanced approach that might use offshore reefs, different sand designs, and a much more gradually sloping underwater contour than the Army Corps of Engineers and the New Jersey Department of Environmental Protection had planned.

Elberon was once an ocean resort town for U.S. presidents and known as the Hamptons of the nineteenth century. James Garfield died there in 1881, and the spot is marked with a plaque. The Church of the Presidents, summer worship center for Presidents Ulysses S. Grant, Rutherford B. Hayes, James Garfield, Chester A. Arthur, Benjamin Harrison, and Woodrow Wilson, is now in disrepair, but it remains in a very upscale neighborhood.

It is unlikely the presidents were drawn by Elberon's great surfing, but they would have had no problem getting to the water if they wanted to try out a board. Today, it is far more difficult. In nearby Deal, summer home to many wealthy Sephardic Jews, huge estates have names like "Chez Fleur" and "Belle Mer." The Deal Casino Beach Club offers free parking but is restricted to residents. Meanwhile, the police are kept busy writing tickets on the nearby beach streets, where 2-hour limits are strictly enforced.

Many streets that once ended in public beach access are now off-limits, Unger says, because the municipality sold off the street ends to homeowners (a practice that was stopped only after state intervention). Despite the exclusivity, Deal is also slated for federally subsidized beach replenishment.

It is probably safe to say that wealthy property owners want to limit the invasion of young surfer kids and grizzled fishermen with their bait buckets and six packs of Budweiser. Many immigrant families from Newark or Paterson cannot afford the $5 and $8 daily fees at the lifeguard beaches, so some wait until late afternoon when the money collectors, mostly college students employed for the summer, leave for the day.

The few remaining free public access points between the million-dollar homes are hard to find and fairly forbidding. Unger led the way down a dangerous pile of construction debris that is the only public entry point to one lovely stretch at Darlington Beach. "Attention: Unprotected Beach. No Swimming," reads a sign. It was plain we were not welcome, but it was also plain that this nearly empty stretch of contested sand was worth the effort we made to reach it.

The Jersey shore town of Point Pleasant Beach developed a particularly bad reputation for harassing beach users in the 1990s: Surfers were told to get out of the water by private security guards, and people walking along the high tide line were ordered to leave the "private beach." Curbs were painted yellow to deter would-be parkers. The residents even posted signs that proclaimed: "Private Property. No Trespassing" (followed by, in tiny letters, "When Beach Is Closed").

But in 2002, spurred by the local activism of groups such as Citizens Right to Access Beaches (CRAB), the State Attorney General's office stepped in and forced a settlement that opens the entire beach "from the water to the edge of the dune" to the public. "The case law is very advanced," says Deborah A. Mans, an attorney for the New York/New Jersey Baykeeper. "There has to be access to the mean high tide line, and as intervenors in these cases we're asking for 30 feet above that."

"The homeowners are just trying to make it as hard as possible," says Unger, who has run for the State Senate on the Green Party ticket. "But at some point you have to take a philosophical stand and say, 'No, I won't buy a beach pass because the beaches belong to the people.' But from Deal to Sandy Hook you have to really work hard to get on the beach without paying." [...]

The Big Makeover

Sandy Hook's quiet Fort Hancock looks like the one place northern New Jersey's developers forgot, but appearances are deceiving—plans are well under way to turn time-forgotten Fort Hancock from a quiet corner into a bustling conference center.

The developers, Sandy Hook Partners, share rent-free office space at Fort Hancock with the Jersey Shore Partnership, which is perhaps the biggest civic booster for beach replenishment. James Wassel, president of the Partners and of the larger Wassel Realty, has the kind of self-confidence that comes from a lifetime of standing in front of skeptical town boards and showing them plans for big buildings. A veteran of the Rouse Company (creators of Faneuil Hall in Boston and the South Street Seaport in New York) and commercial realtor Cushman Wakefield, Wassel insists he is not supporting the kind of big-ticket mall development that his résumé might suggest.

Wassel makes historically informed presentations even when his audience is only one wet reporter with a notebook. "This property was an Indian reservation in the early 1800s," he said. "A lighthouse [now the oldest continuously operating lighthouse in the U.S.] was built in 1764. The military started using it as a proving ground for new weapons in 1870. They used to put dilapidated ships offshore and blast away at them to test the range and accuracy of their guns." In the 1890s, as those guns developed longer ranges, Fort Hancock became the first line of defense for New York City.

The fort sits on 140 acres, with 110 buildings still standing. Sandy Hook Partners plans to spend $80 to $90 million rehabilitating the fort properties, though its agreement with the National Park Service means it cannot build so much as one new taco stand. Still, some of the dilapidated buildings will become gleaming restaurants and quaint inns, complete with manicured lawns, and some people are objecting to it.

"This is the last undeveloped stretch of shoreline in New Jersey," says Brian Unger. "I don't think it needs conference centers, restaurants and all that stuff." Cindy Zipf of Clean Ocean Action worries about a public space becoming private, "even though the developers say they won't change a hair on the buildings' chinny chin chins. The pressure to make money will be huge, and we don't want a multi-million dollar mogul to repair buildings and turn the place into a mini–Woods Hole."

But while most local environmentalists would probably prefer for the fort to remain wild and free, the buildings are crumbling rapidly and need emergency intervention. With only $250,000 in annual federal funding, the Park Service estimates that within 5 years many of the historic buildings at Fort Hancock "would likely deteriorate to a condition beyond repair."

Given the development restrictions, what Wassel and his colleagues envision is not a nautically themed mall but an environmentally oriented learning and conference center that would attract corporate clients interested in, among other things, the effects of global warming on coastal America. Instead of Starbucks, there will be low-key bed and breakfasts. It may open for business in 2008.

Wassel does not seem too concerned that flooding is a regular headache at Fort Hancock, and that rising tides have forced the Park Service to raise the roads 24 inches. "It's an area that gets submerged," he admits, but it is unlikely that climate change looms large in the Sandy Hook Partners' planning.

Outside the office window, a flock of Atlantic brants, winter residents of New Jersey before their summer flight to the Arctic Circle, were marching around the parade ground. The geese have no reason to fear global warming, or shifting sands either. A wetter, wilder New Jersey will probably be to their liking.

Janine Bloomfield's "Hot Nights in the City" report for Environmental Defense offers a grim scenario for New York in 2100: almost as hot as Houston, swept by floods, wracked by infectious diseases and respiratory distress, and torn asunder at the coastline by erosion and frequent nor'easter storms.

New York has nearly 600 miles of coastline. Four of its five boroughs are located on islands, linked by vulnerable bridges, tunnels, and a subway system that, like the city's three airports, lies less than 10 feet above sea level. Greater New York is the most densely populated region in the United States and a major travel hub; if its airports are even temporarily closed by high water, air travel all over the United States will be disrupted. Low-lying highways that pass through the New York region, including I-95 and I-80, carry much of the nation's truck-based freight. In a sense, then, we are all New Yorkers, and we need to pay close attention to a looming crisis that could affect the city as profoundly as the toppling of its twin towers.

Discussion Questions

1. How does developing on wetlands increase the risk of flood?
2. Why is "heat stress" a major health hazard in developed areas like New York City?
3. How is global warming related to beach ecology, according to the author?
4. Why might environmentalists be opposed to shoreline stabilization projects like the ones in North Carolina's Outer Banks?

Notes

Jim Motavalli would like to thank the scientists Dr. Paul Epstein of Harvard University, Dr. Janine Bloomfield of Environmental Defense, Vivien Gornitz and Cynthia Rosenzweig of NASA's Goddard Institute for Space Studies, Dr. Dickson Despommier of Columbia University, and Orrin Pilkey of Duke University. Also invaluable in preparing the [reading] were Dery Bennett of the American Littoral Society (on the web at http://www.alsnyc.org); Brian Unger of the Surfers' Environmental Alliance (http://www.damoon.net/sea); Scott L. Douglass of the University of South Alabama (author of the useful *Saving America's Beaches*); Andy Wilner and attorney Deborah A. Mans of the NY/NJ Baykeeper (732-291-0176, http://www.nynjbaykeeper.org); the many-hatted Noreen Bodman, president of the businessoriented Jersey Shore Partnership; and kayaker supreme Randall Henriksen. Information on kayaking around Manhattan is available from Henriksen's New York Kayak at 212-924-1327 or online at http://www.nykayak.com.

Useful books on global warming and the coast include Cornelia Dean's *Against the Tide: The Battle for America's Beaches* (New York: Columbia University Press, 1999); Orrin H. Pilkey and Katharine L. Dixon's *The Corps and the Shore* (Washington, D.C.: Island Press, 1996); Pilkey and Wallace Kaufman's *The Beaches Are Moving: The Drowning of America's Shoreline* (Durham, N.C.: Duke University Press, 1979); Lynne T. Edgerton's *The Rising Tide: Global Warming and World Sea Levels* (Washington, D.C.: Natural Resources Defense Council/ Island Press, 1991); and *Saving America's Beaches: The Causes of and Solutions to Beach Erosion* by Scott L. Douglass (River Edge, N.J.: World Scientific Publishing, 2002).

A draft of the report "A Wetlands Climate Change Impact Assessment for the Metropolitan East Coast Region" by Ellen Kracauer Hartig, Frederick Mushacke, David Fallon, and Alexander Kolker and prepared for the Center for Climate Systems Research at Columbia University is available online in PDF format at http://metro-east_climate.ciesin.columbia.edu/reports/wetlands.pdf.

The homepage for the 2001 "Climate Change and a Global City: An Assessment of the Metropolitan East Coast Region" report is at Columbia University, http://metro-east_climate.ciesin.columbia.edu. The executive summary and full synthesis report can be downloaded from there.

The Environmental Protection Agency's James G. Titus is author of the study "Greenhouse Effect, Sea-Level Rise and Barrier Islands: Case Study of Long Beach Island, New Jersey," available online at http://users.erols.com/jtitus/NJ/CM.html.

The Environmental Defense report "Global Warming: Sea-Level Rise and the New York Metropolitan Region" by staff scientist Janine Bloomfield (with Molly Smith and Nicholas Thompson) can be downloaded in PDF form at http://www.environmentaldefense.org/pdf.cfm?ContentID=493&FileName=HotNY.pdf.

Harvard University's Center for Health and the Global Environment may be contacted at 617-384-8530, or online at http://www.med.harvard.edu/chge. The interested reader can reach Clean Ocean Action, which focuses on ocean dumping, in Sandy Hook at 732-872-0111, or online at http://www.cleanoceanaction.org.

Post-Reading Questions

1. What are some of the environmental dangers that New York City is facing? How have these dangers been amplified in recent years?
2. How do beachside real estate developments in New Jersey contribute to the risks of flooding and erosion?
3. What do you believe must be done to prevent further damage from climate change and other environmental problems?

Women

In the Shadow of Climate Change

Balgis Osman-Elasha

Climate change is one of the greatest global challenges of the twenty-first century. Its impacts vary among regions, generations, age, classes, income groups, and gender. Based on the findings of the Intergovernmental Panel on Climate Change (IPCC), it is evident that people who are already most vulnerable and marginalized will also experience the greatest impacts. The poor, primarily in developing countries, are expected to be disproportionately affected and consequently in the greatest need of adaptation strategies in the face of climate variability and change. Both women and men working in natural resource sectors, such as agriculture, are likely to be affected.[1] However, the impact of climate change on gender is not the same. Women are increasingly being seen as more vulnerable than men to the impacts of climate change, mainly because they represent the majority of the world's poor and are proportionally more dependent on threatened natural resources. The difference between men and women can also be seen in their differential roles, responsibilities, decision making, access to land and natural resources, opportunities and needs, which are held by both sexes.[2] Worldwide, women have less access than men to resources such as land, credit, agricultural

1. ILO, 2008. Report of the Committee on Employment and Social Policy, Employment and labour market Implications of climate change, Fourth Item on the Agenda, Governing Body, 303rd Session (Geneva), p. 2.
2. Osman-Elasha, 2008 "Gender and Climate Change in the Arab Region", Arab Women Organization p. 44.

inputs, decision-making structures, technology, training and extension services that would enhance their capacity to adapt to climate change.[3]

> Worldwide, women have less access than men to resources such as land, credit, agricultural inputs, decision-making structures, technology, training and extension services that would enhance their capacity to adapt to climate change, including

Why Women Are More Vulnerable

Women's vulnerability to climate change stems from a number of factors—social, economic and cultural.

Seventy per cent of the 1.3 billion people living in conditions of poverty are women. In urban areas, 40 per cent of the poorest households are headed by women. Women predominate in the world's food production (50-80 per cent), but they own less than 10 per cent of the land.

Women represent a high percentage of poor communities that are highly dependent on local natural resources for their livelihood, particularly in rural areas where they shoulder the major responsibility for household water supply and energy for cooking and heating, as well as for food security. In the Near East, women contribute up to 50 per cent of the agricultural workforce. They are mainly responsible for the more time-consuming and labour-intensive tasks that are carried out manually or with the use of simple tools. In Latin America and the Caribbean, the rural population has been decreasing in recent decades. Women are mainly engaged in subsistence farming, particularly horticulture, poultry and raising small livestock for home consumption.

Women have limited access to and control of environmental goods and services; they have negligible participation in decision-making, and are not involved in the distribution of environment management benefits. Consequently, women are less able to confront climate change.

During extreme weather such as droughts and floods, women tend to work more to secure household livelihoods. This will leave less time for women to access training and education, develop skills or earn income. In Africa, female illiteracy rates were over 55 per cent in 2000, compared to 41 per cent for men.[4] When coupled with inaccessibility to resources and decision-making processes, limited mobility places women where they are disproportionately affected by climate change.

In many societies, socio-cultural norms and childcare responsibilities prevent women from migrating or seeking refuge in other places or working when a disaster hits. Such a situation is likely to put more burden on women, such as travelling longer to get drinking water and wood for fuel. Women, in many developing countries suffer gender inequalities with respect to human rights, political and economic status, land ownership, housing conditions, exposure to violence, education and health. Climate change will be an

3. Aguilar, L., 2008. "Is there a connection between gender and climate change?", International Union for Conservation of Nature (IUCN), Office of the Senior Gender Adviser.
4. Rena, Ravinder and N. Narayana (2007) "Gender Empowerment in Africa: An Analysis of Women Participation in Eritrean Economy", New Delhi: International Journal of Women, Social Justice and Human Rights, Vol. 2. No. 2., pp. 221–237 (Serials Publishers).

added stressor that will aggravate women's vulnerability. It is widely known that during conflict, women face heightened domestic violence, sexual intimidation, human trafficking and rape.[5]

According to the-IPCC in Africa, an increase of 5–8% (60–90 million hectares) of arid and semiarid land is projected by the 2080s under a range of climate change scenarios.

Oxfam International reported disproportional fatalities among men and women during the tsunami that hit Asia at the end of 2004. According to an Oxfam briefing, females accounted for about three quarters of deaths in eight Indonesian villages, and almost 90 per cent of deaths in Cuddalore, the second most affected district in India. Of the 140,000 who died from the 1991 cyclone disasters in Bangladesh, 90 per cent were women.[6]

Women and girls in many rural societies spend up to three hours per day fetching water and collecting firewood. Droughts, floods and desertification exacerbated by climate change make women spend more time on these tasks, diminishing their ability to participate in wage-earning activities.[7]

Gender Action, 2008. Gender Action Link: Climate Change (Washington, D.C.), http://www.genderaction.org/images/ Gender%20Action%20Link%20-%20Climate%20Change.pdf

Third Global Congress of Women in Politics and Governance, 2008. Background and Context Paper for the Conference, Manila, Philippines, 19–22 October, www.capwip.org/ 3rdglobalcongress.htm

IUCN 2007, "Gender and Climate Change: Women as Agents of Change".

During natural disasters, more women die (compared to men) because they are not adequately warned, cannot swim well or cannot leave the house alone.

Moreover, lower levels of education reduce the ability of women and girls to access information including early warning, and resources, or to make their voices heard. Cultural values could also contribute to women's vulnerability in some countries, for example in Bangladesh, women are more calorie-deficient than men (the male members in a family hate the "right" to consume the best portions of the food, and the female members have to

5. Davis, I. et. al. 2005, "Tsunami, Gender, and Recovery".
6. IUCN 2004 (a), "Climate Change and Disaster Mitigation: Gender Makes the Difference". Intergovernmental Panel on Climate Change, 2001. Climate Change: Impacts, Adaptation and Vulnerability, Contribution of Working Group II to the Third Assessment Report of the IPCC.
7. IUCN 2004 (b), "Energy: Gender Makes the Difference".

content themselves with the left-overs) and have more problems during disasters to cope with.

In Sudan the increase in the migration of men from the drought-hit areas of western Sudan increased the number of female-headed households and consequently their responsibilities and vulnerabilities during natural disasters.

—Balgis Osman-Elasha

Improving Women's Adaptation to Climate Change

In spite of their vulnerability, women are not only seen as victims of climate change, but they can also be seen as active and effective agents and promoters of adaptation and mitigation. For a long time women have historically developed knowledge and skills related to water harvesting and storage, food preservation and rationing, and natural resource management. In Africa, for example, old women represent wisdom pools with their inherited knowledge and expertise related to early warnings and mitigating the impacts of disasters. This knowledge and experience that has passed from one generation to another will be able to contribute effectively to enhancing local adaptive capacity and sustaining a community's livelihood. For this to be achieved, and in order to improve the adaptive capacity of women worldwide particularly in developing countries, the following recommendations need to be considered:

1. Adaptation initiatives should identify and address gender-specific impacts of climate change particularly in areas related to water, food security, agriculture, energy, health, disaster management, and conflict. Important gender issues associated with climate change adaptation, such as inequalities in access to resources, including credit, extension and training services, information and technology should also be taken into consideration.
2. Women's priorities and needs must be reflected in the development planning and funding. Women should be part of the decision making at national and local levels regarding allocation of resources for climate change initiatives. It is also important to ensure gender-sensitive investments in programmes for adaptation, mitigation, technology transfer and capacity building.
3. Funding organizations and donors should also take into account women-specific circumstances when developing and introducing technologies related to climate change adaptation and to try their best to remove the economic, social and cultural barriers that could constrain women from benefiting and making use of them. Involving women in the development of new technologies can ensure that they are adaptive, appropriate and sustainable. At national levels, efforts should be made to mainstream gender perspective into national policies and strategies, as well as related sustainable development and climate change plans and interventions.

Post-Reading Questions

1. According to the author, why are women at higher risk of facing the negative consequences of climate change?
2. How does climate change contribute to environmental disasters? How do environmental disasters create more risks for women?
3. What policy changes are needed to address the gender inequalities amid climate change?

UNIT VIII

SOCIAL CHANGE, SOCIAL JUSTICE, AND SOCIAL MOVEMENTS

Key Terms and Definitions

Review the key terms and definitions below to strengthen your understanding of the readings in this unit.

Broken Windows Approach: An approach to criminology that assumes that to create social order, it is necessary to clear neighborhoods of any sign of disrepair or disorder. At its extreme, this can result in the forcible removal of people experiencing homelessness to make a neighborhood appear functional.

Collective Bargaining Agreements: Contracts between a union and a company that help to establish fair labor practices and terms of employment.

Collective Behavior: Patterns of group behavior in which people act spontaneously, often violating social norms. This can happen in crowds, fashion, disasters, riots, mobs, public opinion, moments of mass hysteria, and the spread of rumors and other social patterns.

Colorblind Narratives: A common social attitude and practice that involves taking a blind eye to the role that race plays in social dynamics. This usually involves an effort to downplay how race has informed social attitudes and practices. Colorblind narratives often rest on the assumption that if we do not acknowledge race, then we can somehow reach equality, even though experts do not believe this is possible or desirable.

Gentrification: Neighborhood renovation and revitalization efforts that result in higher property values and increasing rents and mortgages in the area. Gentrification can push long-term residents out of the area in search of new housing as housing affordability in their own neighborhood dwindles and wealthy outsiders move into the area.

ICT: Information communication technology, such as email, texting, social media, and other forms of technology and online platforms.

Mobile Journalists (Mojos): Freelance journalists who use media technology such as digital cameras and recording devices to document events in society.

Neoliberalism: An economic model that favors privatization and unregulated free-market capitalism and seeks to drastically limit or prevent government intervention in the affairs of businesses. It also often coincides with limits on welfare state provisions.

Racialization: When people in society or institutions extend racial meaning to a group, organization, or social practice. This can often have harmful outcomes, depending on the context.

Repertoires of Contention: The various tactics that social movement actors may use to build their movement, including but not limited to civil disobedience, rallies, protests, public vigils, and armed struggle.

Social Control: Efforts at maintaining law and order through encouraging conformity to social norms and prevent acts of deviance.

Social Movements: Prolonged collective behavior that is organized under a common purpose and aimed at provoking social change or preserving the status quo.

Union Busters: Anti-union groups that seek to halt the development of unions or to disrupt or weaken union activity in the workplace.

Introduction

In the first reading for unit 10, "The Digital Impact on Social Movements," Victoria Carty writes about how **social movements** have proliferated in the online environment as millennials, born roughly between 1980 and 2000, have engaged in increased activism over the internet. New generations are following suit, using social media and other forms of online communication to create a space for **collective behavior**, sometimes leading to the development of **social movements**.

In recent years, researchers have noticed an upsurge in social movement activity online. People are increasingly using **ICT**, or information communication technology, to organize for various causes. Technology and the internet can be implemented in both progressive and reactive social movements. In other words, individuals may seek changes in society, or they may fight to preserve the status quo. Importantly, the author also points out how social movement activity online can be met with **social control**, as government surveillance and other forms of social monitoring can prevent collective efforts at social change.

Scholars have identified that activists in social movements often make efforts to prove to the public that their cause is worthy of attention. They also engage in what Charles Tilly (2004) called **repertoires of contention**, or various tactics to help drive the movement forward. Now that many social movements are emerging and growing in the online context, media has become a tactical tool that movements use to gain momentum. New media, such as the internet and social media, is unique from old forms of media because it is a two-way channel of communication. Activists can create and distribute their messages to wide audiences, rather than just being passive consumers of information. They can implement the support of **mobile journalists**, sometimes referred to as mojos, to disseminate information. Mobile journalists may use advanced technology, such as cameras and recording software on smartphones, to document events, including social movement activity. Mobile journalists (and sometimes ordinary people) are often on the scene, capturing and documenting an event before mainstream press outlets. These images and recordings can go viral and reach masses of people. Under these circumstances, activists can gain the rapid support of people online and compel them to sign petitions and post content related to the movement. Unlike traditional social movements, new social movement activity in the digital world does not always have a top-down organizational structure. Instead, it has a horizontal organizational structure, which has produced a grassroots civil society that can disseminate information. This can lead, in some cases, to the development of more participatory and democratic social movements.

In the second reading, "Food Workers and Consumers Organizing Together for Food Justice," Joann Lo and Biko Koenig introduce us to Taylor Farms, the largest processor in the world for salads and many organic vegetables. In one of their ten facilities, located in Salinas, California, workers are represented by the Teamsters Local 890 union. This means that unlike most workers in the food system, they receive regular raises, health insurance, and sick time. Many temporary workers in this facility become eligible for full-time employment after a thirty-day period. However, the situation looks much different in Tracy, in California's Central Valley. In this facility, most workers are temporary employees and do not have the opportunity to gain full-time employment. Most earn minimum wage and are paid less than workers in the Salinas facility. This facility also faces many labor abuses, including OSHA violations and dangerous work conditions that can lead to workplace injuries. Furthermore, workers at the facility have been fired for reporting injuries.

In 2013, workers at the Tracy facility organized to join the Teamsters Local 601 union. Taylor Farms responded by hiring **union busters**, or anti-union groups that undermined labor organizing at the facility. As part of this campaign to disrupt union activity, employers threatened undocumented workers involved in unionization efforts with the potential of immigration enforcement. Taylor Farms began to make internal improvements to working conditions at the Tracy facility to detract union activity. Unfortunately, these various efforts ultimately halted several **collective bargaining agreements** between the union and Taylor Farms. However, employees at the Tracy facility shifted their focus to a new social movement campaign. Now, they work to urge consumers not only to support businesses that make claims to be environmentally sustainable, ethical to animals, and healthy for consumers but also to support businesses that treat their employees with dignity. Teamsters at Taylor Farms continue to organize to hold companies accountable to quality standards and fair labor.

In the third excerpt for unit 10, "Shut 'Em Down: Social Movements Confront Mass Homelessness and Mass Incarceration in Los Angeles," Jordan T. Camp describes social movement efforts to secure the right to housing for all people in Los Angeles's Skid Row. Camp shows how **gentrification** and mass incarceration have contributed to the problem of homelessness. In 2012, a music festival called Operation Skid Row took place in the Skid Row district of downtown Los Angeles, which contains the highest concentration of people experiencing homelessness in the United States. During the music festival, artists and **social movement** actors converged together to highlight the struggles of poverty, housing insecurity, and invasive and violent policing as well as the effects of gentrification and unfettered global capitalism under **neoliberalism**.

Residents of Skid Row are mostly people of color who face various social inequalities and disadvantages that are compounded by poverty and homelessness. Mass evictions drive more and more people into the streets, and policing in the area is both heavy and unregulated. Instead of strategizing to house the population, the tactic has been a **broken windows approach** to homelessness, whereby people experiencing homelessness are forcibly removed from one place and relocated to another, which sometimes lands them in jails and prisons. Policies on people experiencing homelessness are informed both by **racialization**, a process you learned about in unit 4, and **colorblind narratives**. Colorblind narratives deny the importance of race in society. Policies informed by colorblindness tend to wash over the fact that Black people, Latinx people, and other minoritized racial groups are disproportionately impacted by poverty, homelessness, and mass incarceration. The author discusses how Skid Row in Los Angeles has become an "open-air prison," where society's most disadvantaged members are located. As downtown Los Angeles has become gentrified in recent years, the people of Skid Row face increased criminalization and mass incarceration. Instead of trying to solve the housing crisis by providing housing, officials are displacing the most vulnerable residents and funneling them into the prison system.

To address these inequalities, social movement leaders in groups such as the LA Community Action Network (CAN) and the Western Regional Advocacy Project (WRAP) work to provide viable housing solutions and safe urban spaces for people experiencing homelessness and fight against policing and criminalization in Skid Row. Through protests, community meetings, and public exposure, the group exposes the inequalities in Skid Row and advocates on behalf of and alongside Latinx and Black residents, the poor, and people experiencing homelessness to fight for equality.

Each of the readings in this unit focuses on different elements of social injustice and social movement activity. The first excerpt centers around how new technology can provide a forum for collective behavior and social movements. The second reading looks at a social justice struggle in a California facility that processes vegetables. Workers have organized alongside consumers to demand equitable labor practices. In the third reading, you are introduced to social justice efforts in Los Angeles's Skid Row that focus on ending homelessness, negative police practices, and mass incarceration among the most disadvantaged groups in society. Each reading provides a window into some of the contemporary struggles for rights and equality in the United States. They also highlight some of the collective action and social movements that push for widescale changes in society.

References

Tilly, C. (2004). *Social Movements, 1768-2004* (1st ed.). Paradigm Publishers.

The Digital Impact on Social Movements

Victoria Carty

Victoria Carty, Selections from "Introduction: The Digital Impact on Social Movements," *Social Movements and New Technologies*, pp. 1–7, 9–15, 189–213. Copyright © 2015 by Taylor & Francis Group. Reprinted with permission.

Digital natives, millennials, Gen Y, Gen 2.0: however you label them, the generation born roughly between 1980 and 2000 has been immersed in revolutionary digital technologies since birth. For those of you who fit into this age cohort, life was experienced very differently in the 1990s, and these technological novelties have had vast repercussions at the individual and societal level. The way people communicate has fundamentally changed with the advent of new information communication technologies (**ICTs**), from e-mail to Snapchat. Not only can messages, photos, and videos be sent instantly, they have the potential to be spread far and wide through social networks—and the ramifications have been felt in all areas of society.

On a personal level, new technology has resulted in a radical shift in the way individuals view themselves and their social ties. Students of previous generations, for example, interacted in a much more limited though intimate way. Friendships and ways of communicating consisted of conversations in the cafeteria at lunch, bonding through sports or other extracurricular activities, sitting next to someone in class and passing secret notes (on paper!), or having neighborhood playmates. The main vehicle of communication was physically going to friends' houses to see whether they were free to play or using the telephone—the one or two stationary phones inside the house that the whole family shared. In sum, communication was initiated, shared, and sustained among people who knew each other personally, and it took effort on the part of the receiver and sender of information. This has changed in many ways as communication now, for many people, takes place to a great extent through digital venues, especially among youth. For example, in 2009 the average US teenager, on Twitter alone, was receiving or sending more than 3,000 messages a month (Parr 2010). In 2010 researchers at the University of Maryland conducted a study of two hundred students who were asked to abstain from using electronic media for twenty-four hours. Though everything else about their college experience was the same—they were surrounded by other students and their identity was intact—not being connected *virtually* to others horrified the participants. One student stated that he had never felt so "alone and secluded from my life." Another reported, "Although I go to a school with thousands of students, the fact that I was not able to communicate with anyone via technology was almost unbearable" (Ottalini 2010).

Many long-standing, profitable, and dominant businesses are now obsolete as digitized industries have replaced analog ones: Polaroid declared bankruptcy with the introduction of digital cameras in 2001, iTunes replaced Tower Records as the largest music retailer in United States, and the chain bookstore Borders, which at one point had more than one thousand stores throughout the United States, closed after the rise of e-reading technology such as Amazon's Kindle (Kansaku-Sarmiento 2011). These are just three examples, but the business world is littered with cases like these. Can anybody really be surprised that "Cyber Monday," the Monday after Thanksgiving, has overtaken Black Friday as the biggest sales day of the year (Carr 2011)?

Even religion has not escaped the technological revolution: the Catholic Church, one of the institutions that has traditionally been most resistant to change, has finally succumbed to the digital age. The electronic missal enables users to stream Mass online and has made the paper missalette (which contains prayers and Scripture readings) antiquated (Catholic PR Wire 2011). Instead of prayer cards, there is now a touch-screen "Saint a Day." The Vatican Observatory Foundation recently launched the Vatican-approved iPhone app "Daily Sermonettes with Father Mike Manning," and users can pray the rosary in their own "sacred space" through the "Rosary Miracle Prayer" app. Pope Benedict XVI used Twitter for the first time in June of 2011, announcing the start of a news information portal that aggregates information from the Vatican's various print, broadcast, and online media (Donadio 2012). The Vatican also now has a YouTube channel and a Twitter feed (@pontifex) that has nearly 10 million followers in more than six languages. Pope Francis, the current pope, has embraced new media as well. In a papal statement in 2014 he praised the peer-to-peer sharing quality of new ICTs: "A culture of encounter demands that we be ready not only to give, but also to receive. ... The Internet, in particular, offers immense possibilities for encounter and solidarity. ... This is a gift from God" (Fung 2014).

Though the Vatican has not yet released an official response, in September of 2014 Pope Francis engaged with schoolchildren from Detroit via Facebook when they pleaded with him, through a social media campaign, to visit Detroit during his upcoming tour of the United States slated for 2015. They set up a Facebook page called "Let's Bring Pope Francis to Detroit in 2015," which includes personalized letters to the pope and photos of students attending Catholic schools (Montemurri 2014a). At the all-boys Loyola High School (a school that works in the tradition of the Jesuit Order with an emphasis on service), students created a YouTube video asking the pope to visit the area. One student is videotaped making a plea aligned with social justice stating, "You are exactly what we stand for—men for others" (Montemurri 2014b). Though students and the mayor of Detroit (who has vocally supported the students' campaign) are awaiting an official response from the Vatican, the fact that the students assumed using ICTs was the best method to get the pope's attention reveals their awareness that this is one of the key ways the pope connects to and interacts with people.

New Information Communication Technologies and Protest Politics

Unsurprisingly, the rise of digital technology and social media also deeply affects contentious politics as well as the organization of and participation in social movements. Over the past several years, there has been an explosion of protest activity among young people around the globe as they embrace a new vision of the future and demand radical changes in the existing economic and political systems. *Time* magazine, in fact, named the protester as its Person of the Year in 2011. We can only speculate as to the reasons for this upsurge in social movement activity, but scholar and cultural critic Henry Giroux emphasizes the influence of the communication field on the political environment:

> Alternative newspapers, progressive media, and a profound sense of the political constitute elements of a vibrant, critical formative culture within a wide range of public spheres that have helped nurture and sustain the possibility to think critically, engage in political dissent, organize collectively, and inhabit public spaces in which alternative and critical theories can be developed." (2012, 39)

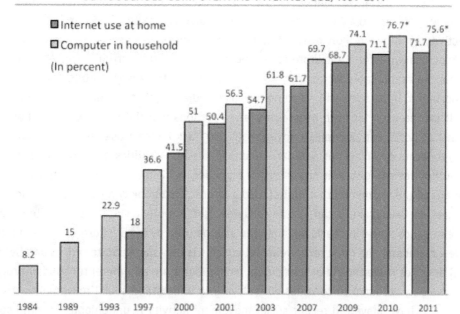

US HOUSEHOLD COMPUTER AND INTERNET USE, 1984–2011

IMAGE 23.1   Smaller changes between 2010 and 2011 were due partly to question wording and other instrument changes. The dramatic and steady increase in computer and internet use over the last three decades has had vast repercussions at the individual and societal level.

Source: US Census Bureau, Current Population Survey, selected years.

In essence, the media ecology can either accelerate—or, conversely, impede—serious political discussion and debate, and ultimately facilitate displays of collective behavior. With new digital technology at their disposal, social movement actors have access to innovative media outlets that help nurture a new political terrain within which they can discuss grievances, disseminate information, and collectively make demands.

There are, of course, many factors to consider when examining recent forms of collective behavior—namely, the austere economic conditions around the globe, political disenfranchisement, and a lack of accountability among political elites. The focus of this book, however, is the use of digital technology in different social movements, communities, and campaigns—from the Indignados in Europe and Mexico, to women seeking social justice, to the Arab Spring in the Middle East and North Africa, to Occupy Wall Street and the DREAMers' quest for immigration reform, to the savvy digital organizing by political groups and communities in the United States. People are challenging political authorities, entrenched dictators, and political and economic systems once taken for granted. On a more micro and individual level, and particularly as it pertains to youth, individuals aided by digital technology are mobilizing to confront skyrocketing debt and current policies regarding immigration through contentious politics.

Indeed, the common thread that runs through all of these case studies in this [reading] is the seminal use of ICTs (this includes the Internet, the World Wide Web, cell phones, texting, Instagram, social media, and social networks) to advance their respective causes. With the recent explosion of e-movements, e-protests, and e-activism, these organizational tools have become an essential component of social movement actors' repertoire. The emergence of social media networking sites is changing the nature of political struggle and social movement activism in the United States and around the world.

This [reading] will explore how new Web 2.0 technologies enable, facilitate, and encourage social movement activity by allowing individual actors to share grievances, accelerate social movement activity, decentralize mobilization efforts, facilitate recruitment efforts through virtual forms of collective identity, and hold authorities accountable for their responses to protest activity with mobile devices.

It is important to remember while reading the case studies [...] that technology is a tool, and therefore it is neutral. It can be used for both progressive and reactionary social movements, and authorities can use ICTs against activists. For example, a government can track Internet use and e-mails and monitor cell phone activity to locate organizers of, and participants in, dissident politics. Corporations can block or limit service, and authorities can discredit protesters by engaging in disinformation or propaganda campaigns, taking advantage of the anonymity that digital media affords. Facebook can be used to build a community around a progressive cause, and it can just as easily be used to bully a classmate. Mobile video recording devices can keep police abuse in check, but they can also be used by terrorist groups to publicize their acts and recruit new members. The most recent example of this is the Islamic State of Iraq and Syria (ISIS) [...]. This [reading] does not make the claim that digital technologies are all inherently good or progressive nor that they are the only resource to consider when trying to understand social movement activity. But the important role ICTs have played in recent social movement activity is undeniable, and the specific ways their use can translate into motivation, interest, and participation among social movement actors are worth examining.

As we will see [...], social movement theory serves as a toolkit to unpack the conceptual ways in which ICTs influence the political landscape. This [reading] analyzes the many ways that ICTs are changing the structure and tactics of social movements, and the case studies serve as illustrative (rather than conclusive) examples that can assist in updating social movement theories. What we will see is that by applying various theoretical frameworks in a comprehensive and holistic way and by updating them to include theories of new media, we can better make sense of contemporary forms of contentious politics. These are exciting times, both for those fighting for social change and those studying social movements!

What Are Social Movements?

It is important to take a moment to clarify exactly what social movements are and how they are different from other forms of collective behavior. A social movement is neither a riot nor electoral politics. Rather, it is a sustained collective articulation of resistance to elite opponents by a plurality of actors with a common purpose (Tarrow 1998). According to Charles Tilly (2004), the three main elements of social movements are campaigns (long-term, organized public efforts that make collective claims on target authorities), repertoires (tactics that a group has at its disposal in a certain sociopolitical environment), and **WUNC** (worthiness, unity, numbers, and commitment). WUNC is an intentional effort by participants in a social movement to publicly present themselves and their supporters as worthy of support from other citizens, which Tilly (2004, 23) encapsulates this way: "Social movements' displays of worthiness may include sober demeanor and the presence of clergy and mothers with children; unity is signaled by matching banners, singing and chanting; numbers are broadcast via signatures on petitions and filling streets; and commitment is advertised by braving bad weather, ostentatious sacrifice, and/or visible participation by the old and handicapped. WUNC matters because it conveys crucial political messages to a social movement's targets and the relevant public."

Key to any social movement are mobilizing strategies—"those collective vehicles, informal as well as formal, through which people mobilize and engage in collective action" (McAdam, McCarthy, and Zald 1996, 3). More specifically, Tilly (2006) introduced the concept of a "**repertoire of contention**," which refers to the tactical forms from which social movement actors can choose at any given moment. Repertoires vary over time and across cultures, but some of the most widely used have included armed struggle, nonviolent civil disobedience, self-immolation, protests, rallies, demonstrations, teach-ins, global witnessing, and public vigils.

With the advent of the digital revolution, which began in 2004, social movement scholars and organizers have turned their attention to the new range of nuanced tools that activists have in their arsenal. As history reveals, every social movement is in part shaped by the technology available at the time and its influences on the tactics that social movement actors will pursue. Activists have always utilized the latest communication device to recruit, distribute information, and mobilize support, whether it be the pen, printing press, telegraph, radio, television, Internet, or high-speed digital technologies. Manuel Castells (2007, 239) summarizes the critical role of media in protest politics in the following way: "power relations ... as well as the processes challenging institutionalized power relations are increasingly shaped and decided in the communication field." [...]

We Are the Message Creators

New media technologies allow users to become not merely receivers of the message but also the *creators* and *distributors* of messages. Indeed, the latest generation has an unprecedented degree of control over the production, distribution, and consumption of information and therefore over their cultural environment, which also has powerful implications for serious social and political change. The distribution of information is now immediate, worldwide, often free, and in the hands of ordinary citizens. New Internet media platforms and social networking sites, web publishing tools, and the proliferation of new mobile devices—there are currently more cellphones in the United States than there are humans (Kang 2011)—are all altering the political atmosphere.

In this new communication and media setting, almost anyone and anything can be recorded and disseminated without the permission of the elites (be they the professional mainstream press, corporate gatekeepers, the police, the military, or campaign managers). Through an emerging indigenous free press reliant on "**mojos**" (mobile journalists), citizens can broadcast unedited live footage from smart phones, flip cameras, and laptops that have digital audio- and video-recording capabilities. In terms of social movement activity, the ubiquity of camera-ready smart phones allows for authentic transparency, as live-streamers serve as journalist mediators between authorities and protesters. Individuals can also send video shots on mobile phones to international news services, which are then beamed via satellite all over the world, thus connecting mobile amateur journalists to the mainstream press. The images can also obviously be posted onto YouTube, Facebook, and other social networking sites where, if they go viral, can instantaneously capture national attention.

IMAGE 23.2   New media technologies allow users to become not merely receivers of the message but also the creators and distributors of messages.

In fact, the very concept of journalism itself is being reconfigured. A perfect example of this happened during the 2011 re-election bid of former senator George Allen (R-VA) against Democratic nominee Jim Webb. As part of its strategy, the Webb campaign had a University of Virginia student follow Allen with a handheld video camera. At one of his rallies Allen introduced the tracker, S. R. Sidarth (who is of Indian American descent) to the crowd as Macaca (considered a racial slur). During the speech Allen interjected, "This fellow over here with the yellow shirt, Macaca, or whatever his name is. He's with my opponent. He's following us around everywhere. ... Let's give a welcome to Macaca, here. Welcome to America and the real world of Virginia" (Sidarth is actually a US citizen, born in Virginia). The video of the "Macaca moment" was played more than 400,000 times on YouTube, and bloggers, especially at the *Daily Kos*, amplified the story (Shear 2011). The incident later appeared in an article in the *Washington Post*, illustrating how stories that originate in alternative media often filter into the mainstream media, thereby increasing the visibility and viewership of events. The taping and circulation of this incident helped to foil Senator Allen's re-election bid, with Webb winning by a narrow margin.

Mojos, as bearers of breaking news, oftentimes beat the mainstream press to highly relevant stories that can have a political impact. For example, amid the hunt for the mastermind behind the 9/11 attacks in the United States, a Twitter user in Pakistan, @ReallyVirtual, tweeted live as Osama bin Laden was being killed: "helicopter hovering above Abbottabad at 1AM (is a rare event)." The news of the assassination circulated on social media immediately and widely. This information was obtainable an hour before President Barack Obama's address from the White House announcing the killing on broadcast television (Patesky 2011). The proliferation of text messages and peer-to-peer sharing of this information via social networks facilitated ad hoc celebratory assemblies at Ground Zero, Times Square, and outside of the White House. This ability for strangers to organize quickly and in real time was facilitated through the several smart phone apps now available.

The Digital Grassrooting of Social Movements

New technologies are changing more than just the way individuals can share and disseminate information. The actual structure of digitally savvy social movement organizations (**SMOs**) is unique. Traditional movements tended to rely more on a hierarchical model of formal, well-established organizations with charismatic leaders and professional experts, which provided a clear set of grievances and demands as the cornerstone of the collective behavior. More recently, however, collective behavior manifests itself through a more horizontal infrastructure of connectivity. This broadens the public sphere, as citizens can now share grievances and express their opinions through peer-to-peer networks, contributing to the "electronic grassrooting of civil society." Castells (2001) coined this term to describe a new type of "informational politics" in which electronic media become the space of politics by framing processes, messages, and outcomes and results in a new kind of civil society.

These new types of communication flows change the organizational process, as collective behavior is now less dependent on professional leadership and expertise and operates at the grassroots level and in ad hoc settings. Unlike past forms of technology, which relied on the one-to-many flow of information, largely controlled by state or corporate interests (for example, heavy, though not exclusive, reliance on newspaper, television, or radio coverage during the civil rights struggle or the women's suffrage movement), the new media ecosystem is a bottom-up approach to communication. Ordinary citizens, equipped with their tech-savvy sense, now organize and hold politically oriented events to effect social change in both cyberspace and in local communities. Many contemporary social movements have an aversion to naming a specific leader or spokesperson, and some are conscientious about avoiding specific demands. Furthermore, social movement actors are often more flexible than activists who have participated in previous forms of mobilization, in that they demonstrate a proclivity to alter their demands and tactics as protest activities unfold. This approach is made possible by up-to-the-minute information sharing and organizing through new media.

This horizontal structure of social movements, made possible by digital technology, emerged in the early 1990s when the Internet was first utilized for protest activity. For example, the 1994 uprising by the Zapatistas (an indigenous and initially armed group in the southern state of Chiapas) against the Mexican federal government in an effort to protect their indigenous rights and access to land surprised the world, and the only way that the world knew about the revolution was because of the Internet. This new media resource disseminated firsthand accounts of developments in this remote region. The rebellion was not organized over the Internet (as access to computers was clearly lacking in this extremely poor and remote area of Mexico), but commentary, suggestions, debate, and reporting was shared in cyberspace on a peer-to-peer basis, which stirred interest and gained them international support (Cleaver 1998). The Zapatistas handwrote communiqués for distribution to the mass media and gave them to reporters or to friends of reporters, which were then typed or scanned and distributed through the Internet (Arquilla and Ronfeldt 2001).

Another early example is the successful attempt to shut down the World Trade Organization (WTO) ministerial meetings in Seattle in 1999. Despite a lack of face-to-interaction before the major demonstrations, organizations and individuals shared ideas and information as to how to best educate citizens about the WTO and its policies that were deemed harmful to both workers and the environment, as well as how to best plan and carry out the rallies. Demonstrators held protests in more than eighty locations in dozens of countries once the information sharing plateaued (Rheingold 2002). They organized these through the website seattle wto.org/N30 (now defunct), which put out action alerts in ten different languages letting those interested know how they could get involved.

Getting the Message Out

New ICTs have made it easier and faster than ever before for activists to gain support for boycotts, garner signatures in petitions, or simply get the message out to people sympathetic to their cause. Effective online petitions and calls for boycotts abound, and this form of e-activism is now an integral part of most people's social media activity. There are websites, such as PetitionOnline.com, that host or link online actions as a free service through which visitors can create and maintain online petitions for any cause. Other sites feature action centers that allow citizens to choose from a menu of a variety of actions such as boycotts; online petitions; virtual sit-ins, rallies, and demonstrations; or e-mail or fax correspondence about a particular cause of concern (Earl et al. 2010).

In one particularly effective case, after a fourth-grade class in Brook-line, Massachusetts, read *The Lorax*, by Dr. Seuss, they discovered on Universal Studio's website that the environmental themes, central to the story, were not going to be addressed in the upcoming film based on the book. The students started a petition on Change.org (host of the world's largest petition platform) demanding the movie company "let the Lorax speak for the trees" (Kristof 2012). The petition went viral and gathered more than 57,000 signatures. The studio, in response to the outcry, updated the movie site with the environmental message (Kristof 2012).

In another example, Molly Katchpople also used Change.org to pursue a cause. She petitioned Bank of America on the site to reconsider its plan to add a five-dollar-per-month fee on its customers' debit cards (Dias 2011). The petition drive was successful. Later, she put up another petition against Verizon, which also intended to raise its fees by five dollars a month. This also resulted in a victory when the corporation relented in less than forty-eight hours (Kim 2011). In both cases this online activism saved Americans billions of dollars.

After airline passengers were trapped on the tarmac for eight hours in Austin, Texas, on an American Airlines flight in 2009, one of the disgruntled passengers began an online petition, also using Change.org. The circumstances were horrid, as food and water supplies ran out, toilets overflowed, and patience wore thin. This individual effort snowballed into a national movement for reform across the entire airline industry. Individuals then collectively lobbied Congress to consider the Airline Passenger's Bill of Rights, which it did as the airlines voluntarily accepted the standards proposed by the petition. The bill, passed by the Senate on February 6, was entitled the FAA Reauthorization Bill (Shirky 2008).

A final example of online activism through the use of petitions is a group called Colorlines.com (a think tank that fights for racial justice). The group undertook a three-year campaign to convince mainstream news outlets to stop using the word "illegal" when referring to immigrants living in the United States without the proper documentation, on the basis that the term is racially charged and dehumanizing. They accomplished a major feat when the Associated Press, the largest news gathering organization, agreed to eliminate the use of the "I" word (Rosenfeld 2013). This is of particular significance because the Associated Press feeds hundreds of local television networks and newspapers and serves as a stylebook for all credentialed journalists.

Although large numbers truly make online campaigns effective, get the attention of those being targeted, and often translate into the perceived worthiness of the cause, it is important to keep in mind that these are more "flash campaigns" and not genuine social movements. They are not persistent mobilizations (an essential component for social movements according to Sidney Tarrow), and there is typically no clear sense of collective identity. Nevertheless, they give us insights into the tactics that those seeking social change can utilize, and online mobilization efforts do have the *potential* to transform into social movements. What the above examples also show is that it has never been easier, cheaper, and faster for activists to get their message out, quickly reach a critical mass, and mobilize into a formidable political campaign.

Because of the digital revolution, individuals now have an unparalleled degree of control over the production, dissemination, and consumption of information, which has a significant impact on their efforts to affect social change through displays of collective behavior. Indeed, the emergence of the Internet, social media networking sites, and e-activism are changing the nature of political struggle and social movement activism in the United States and around the world. As the case studies [...] will show, new ICTs are now an essential component of social movement actors' repertoire in their ability to facilitate and speed up the process of organizing, recruiting, sharing information, and galvanizing support among the public.

References

Arquilla, Hohn, and David Ronfeldt. 2001. *Networks and Netwars: The Future of Terror.* Santa Monica, CA: Rand Corporation.

Carr, Coeli. 2011. "Black Friday vs. Cyber Monday: The Rivalry Is Over." *CNBC,* November 18. Available at http://www.cnbc.com/id/45278120. Accessed December 6, 2013.

Castells, Manuel. 2001. *The Internet Galaxy: Reflections on the Internet, Business and Society.* Malden, MA: Blackwell.

———. 2007. "Communication, Power and Counter-power in the Network Society." *International Journal of Communication* 1: 238–266.

Catholic PR Wire. 2011. "iMissal Launches on iTunes: The First Catholic Missal/Missalette for iPhone and iPod Touch." *Catholic Online,* March 25. Available at http://www.catholic.org/prwire/headline.php?ID=6271. Accessed June 5, 2012.

Cleaver, Harry. 1998. "The Zapatistas Effect: The Internet and Rise of an Alternative Fabric." *Journal of International Affairs* 51(2): 621–640.

Dias, Elizabeth. 2011. "The 22-Year-Old Who Led the Charge Against Bank of America." *Time,* November 7. Available at http://www.time/com/time/nation/article/0,8599,2098715,00.html. Accessed July 4, 2012.

Donadio, Rachel. 2012. "Dear Friends: Pope Takes to Twitter, with an Assist." *The New York Times,* December 12. Available at http://www.nytimes.com/2012/12/12/world/europe/the-pope-now-on-twitter.html. Accessed August 1, 2013.

Earl, Jennifer, Katrina Kimport, Greg Prieto, Carly Rush, and Kimberly Reynoso. 2010. "Changing the World One Webpage at a Time: Conceptualizing and Explaining 'Inter-net Activism.'" *Mobilization* 15(4): 425–446.

Fung, Brian. 2014. "Pope Francis Calls the Internet 'a Gift from God.'" *The Washington Post,* January 23. Available at http://www.washingtonpost.com/blogs/the-switch/wp/2014/01/23/the-pople-calls-the-interent-a-gift-from-God. Accessed April 25, 2014.

Giroux, Henry A. 2012. *The Twilight of the Social.* Boulder, CO: Paradigm Publishers.

Kang, Cecilia. 2011. "Number of Cellphones Exceeds US Population." *The Washington Post,* October 11. Available at http://www.washingtonpost.com/blogs/post-tech/post/number-of-cell-phones-exceeds-us-population-ctia-trade-group/2011/10/11/gIQA RNcEcL_blog.html. Accessed July 3, 2012.

Kansaku-Sarmiento, Alana. 2011. "Borders Bookstores Close Final Chapter." *The Times,* July 21. Available at http://www.tigardtimes.com/news/print_story.php?story_id=131120238899080900. Accessed June 5, 2012.

Kim, Susana. 2011. "Verizon Cancels $2 Fee." *ABC News,* December 30. Available at http://abcnews.go.com/blogs/business/2011/12/verizon-cancels-2-fee/. Accessed August 1, 2013.

Kristof, Nicholas D. 2012. "After Recess: Change the World." *The New York Times,* February 4. Available at http://www.nytimes.com/2012/02/05/opinion/sunday/kristof-after-recess-change-the-world.html. Accessed June 5, 2012.

McAdam, Doug, John McCarthy, and Meyer Zald. 1996. *Comparative Perspectives on Social Movements: Political Opportunities, Mobilizing Structures, and Cultural Framings.* New York: Cambridge University Press.

Montemurri, Patricia. 2014a. "Schoolkids Beckon Pope to Detroit." *USA Today,* September 12, p. 4A.

———. 2014b. "Students Create Video Inviting Pope to Detroit." *Detroit Free Press,* September 23. Available at http://www.freep.com/story/life/2014/09/23/loyola-high-video-papal-invite/16099799. Accessed September 25, 2014.

Ottalini, David 2010. "Students Addicted to Social Media—New UM Study." April 21. University of Maryland press release. Available at http://www.newsdesk.umd/edu/sociss/release.cfm?AritcleD=2144. Accessed May 9, 2012.

Parr, Ben. 2010. "The Average Teenager Sends 3,339 Texts Per Month." October 14. Available at http://www.mashable.com/2010/10/14/nielsen-texting/stats. Accessed July 20, 2012.

Patesky, Mark. 2011. "Osama bin Laden Is Dead: News Explodes on Twitter." *Forbes,* May 1. Available at http://www.forbes.com/sites/markpatesky/2011/05/01/osama-bin-laden-is-dead-news-explodes-on-twitter/. Accessed May 1, 2012.

Rheingold, Howard. 2002. *Smart Mobs: The Next Social Revolution.* Cambridge, MA: Basic Books.

Rosenfeld, Adam. 2013. "AP Press to Drop the Word 'Illegal' in Immigration Coverage." *AlterNet,* April 2. Available at http://www.alternet.org/immigration/AP-to-drop-the-word-illegal. Accessed August 1, 2013.

Shear, Michael D. 2011. "Trailing G.O.P. with Cameras, Seeking Gaffes." *The New York Times,* July 8. Available at http://www.nytimes.com/2011/07/09/us/politics/09trackers.html?pagewanted=all. Accessed June 5, 2012.

Shirky, Clay. 2008. *Here Comes Everybody.* New York: Penguin Press.

Tarrow, Sidney. 1998. *Power in Movement. Social Movements, Collective Action and Politics.* Cambridge, MA: Cambridge University Press.

Tilly, Charles. 2004. *Social Movements.* Boulder, CO: Paradigm.

———. 2006. *Regimes and Repertoires.* Chicago: University of Chicago Press.

Post-Reading Questions

1. According to the author, what is the difference between collective behavior and social movements?
2. How has new technology and the internet created a platform for social movement activity?
3. What are some examples of social movements that are visible online? Who is involved in these movements, and why?

Food Workers and Consumers Organizing Together for Food Justice

Joann Lo and Biko Koenig

Taylor Farms: The Potential of Institutional Strategies

Your average consumer has never heard of Taylor Farms, but they have nonetheless likely eaten their products. Based in California's Central Valley, Taylor Farms makes products for a variety of well-known customers. From organic spinach salad for Trader Joe's to private-label packaged salads for Walmart, Safeway, and Kroger, Taylor Farms is the world's largest processor of salads and fresh-cut produce and a sizable processor of organic vegetables in the United States (Sherry 2009). To put this in perspective, it sells as much salad as its next three competitors, is the largest fresh salad processor in the world, and employs ten thousand workers across its ten plants in the United States and one in Mexico (Berkeley Haas 2012, Murfreesboro Post 2013, Strom 2013, Taylor Farms n.d.).

As a multibillion-dollar corporation, Taylor Farms can set standards in its industry and in the economy—standards around the kind of food it produces, how the food is grown and processed, and how the workers are treated. Combined with the anonymity provided by private labels and institutional buyers, Taylor Farms is a company that exists beyond the influence and knowledge of most individual customers.

A Dr. Jekyll and Mr. Hyde Company

About an hour and a half south of San Francisco, near the California coastline, sits a Taylor Farms facility—modern, shiny, and clean. The 2,500 workers at the Salinas plant have been represented for twenty years by the Teamsters Local 890. With a union contract comes a situation at odds with that of most other workers in the food system: these workers receive regular raises, affordable health insurance, and paid sick days. When workplace issues arise at the plant, there is a fair grievance process in place to help resolve them. And when the company brings in temporary workers, they become permanent employees after they have worked more than thirty days.

In the Central Valley town of Tracy, conditions are much different. There, two Taylor Farms plants on Valpico and MacArthur boulevards exist in a different world than the Salinas plant. About nine hundred workers, mostly Latino, toil at these two Tracy plants, where two-thirds of the workers are employed through two temporary staffing agencies: Slingshot and Abel Mendoza. The use of temporary workers is a growing trend in the food system, from farms and warehouses to food processing plants and distribution companies and even fast-food restaurants, and these plants exemplify the problems of a disposable workforce (McCluskey et al. 2013, Mertl 2014). According to Doug Bloch, political director of the Teamsters Joint Council 7, some of these "temporary" employees have been working at Taylor Farms for up to fourteen years; most are paid the minimum wage; and, on average, the workers in Tracy earn $3 an hour less than workers in the same job classifications in Salinas.

Jose Gonzalez, who has worked for Taylor Farms for over a year through the Slingshot agency, reports of those hired through the agencies: "We work directly next to direct Taylor Farms workers and are fully intermingled in every way with those workers. We do the same work, have the same hours, and have the same supervisors as the Taylor Farms workers." Workers hired directly by the company receive slightly higher pay but still don't earn anything close to the region's living wage of $20.06 per hour for an adult with one child (Glasmeier 2015).

As in many parts of the food system, the problems at Taylor Farms go beyond poor wages to include a troubling record of labor violations. The company has accrued $80,000 in OSHA (Occupational Health and Safety Administration) penalties from 2008 to 2013 and is currently the defendant in a class-action lawsuit for wage theft that was filed in 2011 (Tierney 2014). Multiple workers have suffered injuries that make it difficult for them to work in their regular jobs or to work at all. One of these workers is Victor Borja, who slipped from a machine in 2012. His foot was crushed and he can no longer work. Victor says his first thought after his fall was that he was going to be fired, as he had seen coworkers suffer a full range of injuries, "and one thing always happened if they reported it: they would get fired." He describes a workplace where fear of termination has created an environment where instead of reporting injuries, many workers simply try to fix the problem (Teamsters 2014).

The Union Organizing Campaign

In August 2013, after months of behind-the-scenes organizing, workers at the Taylor Farms plants in Tracy came out publicly that they were organizing to join the Teamsters Local 601. A few workers had approached the union because they were concerned about how the temporary workers were being mistreated. "Workers are segregated in three different categories—the workers hired by two different staffing agencies and the different hires … a lot of conditions that we kept hearing about was around how the different classes were being treated," explains Veronica Diaz, former political coordinator with the Teamsters Joint Council 7, which is supporting the workers' campaign.

Once the worker leaders came out publicly that they were organizing to join the Teamsters, Taylor Farms responded with both carrots and sticks. On the stick side, the company management hired antiunion consultants, also called union-busters. The Teamsters estimate that Taylor Farms spent $500,000 on these consultants, who held meetings with the workers to scare them from supporting the union, part of a strategy that embraced intimidation, harassment, and mistreatment to break the campaign (Teamsters 2014). Marta Barrajas recalls, "They intimidated us that we couldn't vote because immigration was going to come ... to take us away." Armida Galeana vividly remembers the humiliating feeling when one of the antiunion consultants referred to the workers as "Latinos de mierda," or "piece-of-shit Latinos." In case anyone missed the point, a warehouse manager posted images of a donkey wearing a sombrero with the caption "This is what the union means" (ibid.).

The company also fired worker leaders in the organizing campaign, sometimes creating excuses to do so and sometimes not. Victor Borja, whose foot was crushed, is one such fired leader. Another is Edibray Rodriguez. Edibray was receiving thirty cents less per hour than he had been promised when he was hired. In the break room and after work, he began discussing the possibility of organizing into a union with his coworkers. On October 29, 2013, he joined Teamster organizers in handing out fliers outside of his facility. Edibray was then questioned by two supervisors about his conversations with the Teamsters, and he described his desire to correct his pay for the last month and a half. The next day, a director at Abel Mendoza, the agency that hired Edibray for Taylor Farms, came to his house with a check, saying, as Edibray described it, "Here is the check for the thirty cents we owe you for every hour you have worked, but here is also your last paycheck ... today was your last day" (ibid.).

On the "carrot" side, Taylor Farms began making some improvements to working conditions in what appeared to be efforts to try to convince workers they would not need the union. In January 2014, the company started providing direct-hire workers with paid sick days. On Mother's Day, the company gave roses to the women, and on Father's Day, they gave backpacks, jackets, and scarves to the men. The company also now provides transportation between the employee parking lot and the facility, which they had not done before. Taylor Farms also gave out free shirts and hats that said not to vote for the union.

Despite the company's antiunion tactics, the worker leaders and the Teamsters organizers were able to collect enough signatures on union authorization cards to file for an election through the National Labor Relations Board (NLRB). The vote on whether the workers wanted the Teamsters to be their union representative was held on March 27 and 28, 2014. Right after the vote, in an unprecedented move, the NLRB impounded the ballots because the Teamsters had filed hundreds of complaints of unfair labor practices before the vote. However, the long process at the NLRB allowed the company to fire more union supporters since the vote. In December 2015, the NLRB determined that Taylor Farms had committed so many unfair labor practices that a new election could not be conducted fairly. The NLRB issued a bargaining order to Taylor Farms, but talks have not led to a union contract (Teamsters Joint Council 7 2016). "Our campaign has demonstrated almost the complete failure of federal labor law to protect workers to organize and collectively bargain," says Doug.

Building Support from Consumers to Institutions

Since the workers and the union cannot depend on fast action by the federal labor agency and Taylor Farms continues to fight against the workers' organizing efforts, the campaign has turned toward alliances with consumers. In the words of Veronica Diaz,

> We're in a period where people are increasingly conscious of where they get their food. It's very trendy to ask if your lettuce is organic and to be concerned with whether your beef or chicken is free-range and killed humanely. But that movement, so far, I haven't really seen it to be encompassing of also asking whether the people who slaughtered the cow or picked the lettuce in the field were also treated humanely or given a fair salary. I think some of these consumer campaigns, especially with items like organic lettuce that Taylor Farms supplies ... it's an opportune time to make that connection to consumers as well.

When facing companies that have the size, spread, and distribution of Taylor Farms, it can be a challenge to envision clear strategies for consumers to leverage their power on behalf of workers. With anonymous private-label products and large-scale food service customers, individual activist purchasing decisions are easily drowned out amid larger purchasers like schools and grocery stores. Also, it's hard to know where food comes from because of private labels like Trader Joe's. One solution involves flipping the problem on its head: by organizing around institutional buyers, citizens can amplify their individual purchasing power through collective procurement policies on the regional scale.

Advocates of the Taylor Farms campaign are embracing this strategy, utilizing a model embodied by the Good Food Purchasing Policy (GFPP). Adopted in October 2012 by the City of Los Angeles and then by the Los Angeles Unified School District (LAUSD) in November 2012, the GFPP sets purchasing guidelines across five key values: local food economies, environmental sustainability, humane animal treatment, healthy nutrition standards, and fair treatment and compensation of food-chain workers. By leveraging the purchasing power of institutional buyers—including the LAUSD, which serves over 650,000 meals a day—citizens can make major impacts on companies too large to feel the pressure of smaller-scale purchasing decisions (Lo and Delwiche 2016).

A clear example of this power can be seen in the Teamsters' strategy regarding school food. On May 1, 2014, the Teamsters organized an emergency town meeting in Oakland for Taylor Farms workers to talk about what was happening at the Tracy plant. Attendees included California Assemblymember Rob Bonta, members of the Oakland Unified School Board, and representatives of the school district's employee unions and the Oakland Food Policy Council. Without any request from the FCWA or the Teamsters, members of the Oakland Unified School Board announced at this meeting that the school district was no longer buying from Taylor Farms. In short order, a small group of committed activists were able to leverage the institutional power of a school system that serves over thirty thousand meals a day—a substantial pressure point on a company that needs these contracts to remain profitable (Oakland Unified School District n.d.).

With support from the FCWA and the new Center for Good Food Purchasing, the Teamsters are now organizing to ask school districts across California to adopt a comprehensive food-procurement policy that includes labor standards in order to hold companies like Taylor Farms accountable to provide good and safe working conditions. "We ended up looking at the Good Food Purchasing Policy in Los Angeles, which is the best model to support the food chain that we believe—where workers' rights are being respected, where the environment is being respected, local businesses are being supported, and where school districts are being smart about using the resources that they have to support an equitable, just food chain," says Bloch. "Taylor Farms is the perfect example of why school districts need a policy like this." Due to the Teamsters' leadership, both the San Francisco Unified School District (on May 24, 2016) and the Oakland Unified School District (on November 30, 2016) unanimously adopted the GFPP.

In campaigns like Taylor Farms, consumers can punch above their weight through institutional purchasers like school districts, municipalities, corporate cafeterias, and grocery co-ops. Such an approach takes the "voting with your fork" analogy to a much higher level by dramatically multiplying the number of forks in play while requiring political action in city councils and school districts. [...]

References

Berkeley Haas. Spring 2012. "Lettuce Now Praise Farming Men." http://haas.berkeley.edu/groups/pubs/berkeleyhaas/spring2012/yhn04.html.

Glasmeier, Amy. 2015. "Living Wage Calculation for San Joaquin County, California." MIT Living Wage Calculator. http://livingwage.mit.edu/counties/06077.

Lo, Joann, and Alexa Delwiche. 2016. "The Good Food Purchasing Policy: A Tool to Intertwine Worker Justice with a Sustainable Food System." *Journal of Agriculture, Food Systems, and Community Development* 6: 185–194.

McCluskey, Martha, Thomas McGarity, Sidney Shapiro, and Matthew Shudtz. 2013. "At the Company's Mercy: Protecting Contingent Workers from Unsafe Working Conditions." Washington, DC: Center for Progressive Reform.

Mertl, Steve. 2014. "Fast-food Industry's Use of Temporary Foreign Worker Program Suspended Following Damning Report." *The Daily Brew, Yahoo News Canada,* April 24. https://ca.news.yahoo.com/blogs/dailybrew/fast-food-industry-temporary-foreign-worker-program-suspended-014305363.html.

Murfreesboro Post. 2013. "Taylor Farms to Expand Smyrna Operations." *The Murfreesboro Post,* July 7. www.murfreesboropost.com/taylor-farms-to-expand-smyrna-operations-cms-36132.

Oakland Unified School District. n.d. "Nutrition Services: Overview." www.ousd.k12.ca.us/nutritionservices.

Sherry, Kristina. 2009. "Farmers Critical of Food Safety Bill." *Los Angeles Times,* July 17. http://articles.latimes.com/2009/jul/17/nation/na-food-safety17.

Strom, Stephanie. 2013. "Taylor Farms, Big Food Supplier, Grapples with Frequent Recalls." *The New York Times,* August 29. www.nytimes.com/2013/08/30/business/taylor-farms-big-food-supplier-grapples-with-frequent-recalls.html.

Taylor Farms. n.d. "Our Story." www.taylorfarms.com/our-story/.

Teamsters. 2014. "NLRB Impounds Ballots In Taylor Farms Teamster Election." April 1. International Brotherhood of Teamsters Food Processing Division. http://teamster.org/news/2014/04/nlrb-impounds-ballots-taylor-farms-teamster-election.

Teamsters Joint Council 7. 2016. "Supporting the Workers at Taylor Farms." *Joint Council 7 Teamster* 61 (1): 2. http://teamstersjc7.org/newsletter/PDFs/JC7News_16-FMA.pdf.

Post-Reading Questions

1. What were some of the difficult workplace conditions that workers at Taylor Farms faced at the Tracy, California facility?
2. How did workers strategize to improve work conditions? How did collective behavior on the part of workers turn into a social movement?
3. What improvements can you make as a consumer in your food choices? What are some ways that you can ensure that the food you consume is from companies with fair and equitable labor practices?

Shut 'Em Down

Social Movements Confront Mass Homelessness and Mass Incarceration in Los Angeles

Jordan T. Camp

Jordan T. Camp, Selections from "Shut 'Em Down: Social Movements Confront Mass Homelessness and Mass Incarceration in Los Angeles," *Incarcerating the Crisis: Freedom Struggles and the Rise of the Neoliberal State*, pp. 134–138, 141–145, 206–208, 210–212, 217–253. Copyright © 2016 by University of California Press. Reprinted with permission.

> This day of action will promote the human right to housing and reinforce the hip hop community's responsibility to social justice causes.
> —Chuck D, Operation Skid Row music festival, Los Angeles, January 2012

On a cordoned-off block stretching between Fifth and Sixth Streets and Gladys in downtown Los Angeles, which on most days houses a soup kitchen, a vacant lot, and a single-room-occupancy hotel, Chuck D and Public Enemy performed for free at the Operation Skid Row music festival. The festival, which took place on January 15, 2012, the weekend of Dr. Martin Luther King Jr.'s birthday, was co-organized by Chuck D and the Los Angeles Community Action Network (LA CAN), a housing and human rights organization. More than fifteen hundred people crammed the street to listen to Public Enemy as well as the music of famed LA hip-hop performers such as Freestyle Fellowship, Medusa, Kid Frost, Yo-Yo, and Egyptian Lover, and artists from the neighborhood such as the Skid Row Playas. In the face of threats from the Los Angeles Police Department to shut the festival down, Public Enemy opened with one of their signature songs of defiance, "Shut 'Em Down."[1] They did so before an audience of Skid Row residents and community organizers; members of social movement organizations such as the Bus Riders Union, Critical Resistance, Food Not Bombs, and INCITE! Women of Color Against Violence; and fans from across the city. This effort to connect hip-hop with the struggle for human rights was significant for its timing and location. During the fifth year of the worst economic crisis since the Great Depression, this festival highlighted the material conditions in Skid Row—an area in downtown Los Angeles where Black people constitute 75 percent of the population, and where there is the highest concentration of poverty, policing, and homelessness in the United States. More than just a day of entertainment, the Operation Skid Row musical festival helped circulate a critique of the crisis through expressive culture.[2]

FIGURE 25.1   Chuck D and Public Enemy performing at the Operation Skid Row music festival, Los Angeles, January 15, 2012.

Image by Ernest R. Savage III, www.asavagecity.com.

Artists and activists connected to social movements in Los Angeles have taken up a dramatic fight over the meaning of the crisis by calling for the human right to housing in Los Angeles, the "First World capital of homelessness." The Operation Skid Row festival was one manifestation of this effort.[3] It illuminated the material conditions experienced by the racialized poor, and how they have resisted them. Indeed, Operation Skid Row confronted the truth of the crisis, as Stuart Hall observed, "The social formation can no longer be reproduced on the basis of the preexisting system of social relations." This effort to

1. Steve Diaz, "Operation Freedom and Freedom Now!," *Community Connection,* January–February 2012, http://cangress.wordpress.com/tag/community-connection/; Ernest Hardy, "Public Enemy Puts Spotlight on Skid Row," *Los Angeles Times,* January 17, 2012.
2. Gary Blasi and the UCLA School of Law Fact Investigation Clinic, *Policing Our Way Out of Homelessness? The First Year of the Safer Cities Initiative on Skid Row* (Los Angeles: UCLA and USC Center for Sustainable Cities, September 24, 2007); Christina Heatherton, ed., *Downtown Blues: A Skid Row Reader* (Los Angeles: Los Angeles Community Action Network, 2011); Jordan T. Camp and Christina Heatherton, *Freedom Now! Struggles for the Human Right to Housing in L.A. and Beyond* (Los Angeles: Freedom Now Books, 2012); Nicholas Dahmann with the Los Angeles Community Action Network, "Los Angeles: I Do Mind Dying, Recent Reflections on Urban Revolution in Skid Row," *Los Angeles Public Interest Law Journal* 2 (2009–10): 210–19.
3. Mike Davis, *A Planet of Slums* (New York: Verso, 2006), 36; Neil Smith, "New Globalism, New Urbanism: Gentrification as Global Urban Strategy," *Antipode* 34, no. 3 (2002): 427–50; Craig Willse, "Neo-Liberal Biopolitics and the Invention of Chronic Homelessness," *Economy and Society* 39, no. 2 (2010): 155–56.

highlight material conditions in downtown Los Angeles during the present crisis of global capitalism shows how expressive culture has provided distinct counter-narratives of the crisis.[4]

Public Enemy's performance of songs such as "Shut 'Em Down" at Operation Skid Row did not simply reflect the crisis, but called attention to it and, in doing so, attempted to confront it.[5] The performance enabled grassroots social movements working on homelessness and poverty to circulate their critique at a different geographical scale. The politics of scale are crucial for the poor, evicted, and homeless residents of Skid Row. There are more homeless people in Los Angeles than in any other city in the country, affecting between sixty and one hundred thousand people. The state's response to the crisis has been to contain poor and homeless people within particular geographical boundaries. Revanchist policing strategies trap Black, Brown, and poor people in space in order to protect the interests of capital and the state. Such traps on Skid Row include the mass arrest (under the guise of public safety) of residents for activities such as loitering, jaywalking, public urination, and public drunkenness, and the mass eviction of residents from single-room-occupancy hotels in the name of reclaiming downtown through condo and loft conversions for high-end real estate development. This strategy of "accumulation by dispossession" has been sustained and justified by racial narratives. Such narratives purport that poor people of color are individually responsible for their own loss of wealth, a consequence of their attitudes, behaviors, and cultures of ineptitude.[6]

Under such logic poor people suffering from homelessness were not to be assisted through public services and employment; rather, city officials have promoted revanchist strategies of crisis management.[7] Since 2006 Los Angeles city officials have pursued a "broken windows" strategy of policing they called the Safer Cities Initiative (SCI). Developed by the Manhattan Institute and implemented at the local scale by then Mayor Antonio Villaraigosa and Chief William Bratton, SCI represented an update on the revanchist policies that Bratton helped usher in with then–New York Mayor Rudolph Giuliani in the 1990s. Bratton assumed control of the LAPD in 2002. By 2003 he implemented broken windows policing in Skid Row. With the ideological and political support of the Manhattan Institute and the criminologist George Kelling of Rutgers (who was paid at least $500,000 in consulting fees), the LAPD unleashed an unprecedented deployment of police power in less than one square mile of the Central City area, which

4. Clyde Woods, " 'Sitting on Top of the World': The Challenges of Blues and Hip Hop Geography," in *Black Geographies and the Politics of Place,* ed. Katherine McKittrick and Clyde Woods (Cambridge, MA: South End, 2007), 49; Clyde Woods, "Traps, Skid Row, and Katrina," in *Downtown Blues,* 51; Clyde Woods, "The Challenges of Blues and Hip Hop Historiography," *Kalfou* 1, no. 1 (2010): 33–34; Stuart Hall, *The Hard Road to Renewal: Thatcherism and the Crisis of the Left* (New York: Verso, 1988), 96; Robin D. G. Kelley, *Race Rebels: Culture, Politics, and the Black Working Class* (New York: The New Press, 1994), 207.

5. Clyde Woods, "Do You Know What It Means to Miss New Orleans? Katrina, Trap Economics, and the Rebirth of the Blues," *American Quarterly* 57, no. 4 (2005): 1005; George Lipsitz, "The Struggle for Hegemony," *Journal of American History* 75, no. 1 (1988): 146–50.

6. George Lipsitz, *Footsteps in the Dark: The Hidden Histories of Popular Music* (Minneapolis: University of Minnesota Press, 2007), 108; Mike Davis, *A Planet of Slums,* 36; Clyde Woods, "Les Misérables of New Orleans: Trap Economics and the Asset Stripping Blues, Part 1," *American Quarterly* 61, no. 3 (2009): 769–96; Christina Heatherton, ed., *Downtown Blues,* 4–6; David Harvey, *The New Imperialism* (New York: Oxford University Press, 2003), 137–82; Robin D. G. Kelley, *Yo' Mama's Disfunktional! Fighting the Culture Wars in Urban America* (Boston: Beacon Press, 1997), 8; Stuart Hall, "Gramsci's Relevance for the Study of Race and Ethnicity," *Journal of Communications Inquiry* 10, no. 5 (1986): 24.

7. Neil Smith, "Giuliani Time: The Revanchist 1990s," *Social Text* 57 (Winter 1998): 1–20.

became a laboratory for applying new policing and security technologies. This political project has required ideological legitimation. The broken windows metaphor is revealing, since, as Fred Moten observes, broken windows are not repaired—they are replaced—much as Black, Brown, and poor people are literally removed from space. The metaphor also highlights the fact that this policing strategy has a revenge-driven logic. It represents the homeless, poor, and housing-rights activists as enemies of the neoliberal state. In doing so, it has been part of an ideological and political campaign to legitimate Los Angeles's own version of incarcerating the crisis.[8]

This [reading] asks and answers the following questions about these dynamics: What was the relationship between structures and processes of racialization, gentrification, and the policing of urban space in the aftermath of the global financial crisis of 2008? How have the dominant representations of the crisis provoked resistance and criticism at the grassroots? How have grassroots activists and artists confronted the parallel crises of mass homelessness and mass incarceration? What kinds of alternatives to criminalization are made possible when conceived from the perspective of the social movement for the human right to housing? Drawing inspiration from the struggle for the human right to housing, I make four principal arguments. First, the racial and spatial dynamics of the global financial crisis in 2008 underscore the need to theorize its historical and geographical origins in cities such as Los Angeles. I illustrate how contemporary housing policies have been deployed in response to shifts in the political economy in the wake of the twentieth-century Black freedom struggle.[9] I suggest how they have ensured a racially and spatially differentiated organization of the landscape in U.S. cities.[10]

Second, while there are different methodological approaches to tracing the roots of this crisis, I argue that it is crucial to analyze it as a conjuncture. Conjunctural analysis helps to grasp its relationship to the neoliberal turn in U.S. and global capitalism. It will help us periodize the shifting relationships between capital, the state, and social movements. Through a concrete analysis of the struggle for housing rights, we can better understand alternatives to the neoliberal settlement, which has justified the privatization of public housing, education, and health care and the rise of mass incarceration in globalizing California. It suggests that consent to this settlement has been secured through purportedly colorblind narratives.[11]

8. Ruth Wilson Gilmore and Christina Heatherton, "Fixing Broken Windows Without Batons," in *Freedom Now!*, 1. See Gari Blasi and Forrest Stuart, "Has the Safer Cities Initiative in Skid Row Reduced Serious Crime?" (Los Angeles: UCLA Law School, September 15, 2008), http://wraphome.org/downloads/safer_cities.pdf; Fred Moten, "The Meaning of 'Broken Windows,' " talk presented at Eso Won Books, Los Angeles, June 23, 2005; Manhattan Institute, "Why Cities Matter," YouTube.com, March 21, 2014; Gary Blasi and the UCLA School of Law Fact Investigation Clinic, *Policing Our Way Out of Homelessness?*, 23; Alex S. Vitale, "The Safer Cities Initiative and the Removal of the Homeless: Reducing Crime or Promoting Gentrification on Los Angeles's Skid Row?" *American Society of Criminology* 9, no. 4 (2010): 867–73.

9. Edward W. Soja, *Seeking Spatial Justice* (Minneapolis: University of Minnesota Press, 2010), 131–132;

10. Robert D. Bullard and Charles Lee, "Introduction: Racism and American Apartheid," in *Residential Apartheid: The American Legacy,* ed. Robert D. Bullard et al. (Los Angeles: Center for Afro-American Studies Publications, UCLA, 1994), 7.

11. Stuart Hall and Doreen Massey, "Interpreting the Crisis," *Soundings: A Journal of Politics and Culture* 44 (Spring 2010): 57–71; Stuart Hall, "The Neoliberal Revolution," *Soundings: A Journal of Politics and Culture* 48 (Summer 2011): 10; Cindi Katz, "Vagabond Capitalism and the Necessity of Social Reproduction," *Antipode* 33, no. 4 (2001): 724; Vijay Prashad, "Second-Hand Dreams," *Social Analysis* 49, no. 2 (2005): 191–98.

Next, I show how these narratives have been deployed to naturalize this transformation of the political economy as inevitable. This line of argument enables us to understand how the crisis came to be represented in terms of security. It can also help us assess how racist ideologies have reinforced the logic of the current political settlement.[12] They have endorsed the withdrawal of the social wage at precisely the moment when the military, prisons, and policing have become central to the political economy of the U.S. empire.[13]

Finally, remaining attentive to the structural underpinnings of the current conjuncture, this [reading] examines the perspective of events articulated in the expressive culture of social movements in Los Angeles.[14] It argues that contemporary struggles represent a continuity of campaigns waged by the long civil rights movement to contest racial capitalism's organization of space. These grassroots activists and artists show that the resolution of crisis by racialization, mass criminalization, and neoliberalization is not inevitable. The [reading] proceeds in three parts: it looks at dominant depictions of the current crisis, then turns to the historical confrontation in Los Angeles between housing struggles and emergent securitization, and concludes with a consideration of what we might learn from Los Angeles about the prospects for alternative futures.[15] [...]

The Epicenter of the Crisis

> We dared to rise up, dared to struggle, and dared to put this country on notice about the inequality.
>
> —Bilal Ali, Black Panther and LA CAN housing organizer in
> *Freedom Now! Struggles for the Human Right to Housing in Los Angeles and Beyond*, 2012

12. Cindi Katz, "Childhood as Spectacle: Relays of Anxiety and the Reconfiguration of the Child," *Cultural Geographies* 15 (2008): 15–17; Stuart Hall and Doreen Massey, "Interpreting the Crisis," 58.

13. Nikhil Pal Singh, "The Afterlife of Fascism," *South Atlantic Quarterly* 105, no. 1 (Winter 2006): 71–93; Avery F. Gordon, "The U.S. Military Prison: The Normalcy of Exceptional Brutality," in *The Violence of Incarceration,* ed. Phil Scraton and Jude McCulloch (New York: Routledge, 2009), 174; Stephen Graham, *Cities Under Siege: The New Military Urbanism* (New York: Verso, 2010), 94; Daniel Martinez HoSang, *Racial Propositions: Ballot Initiatives and the Making of Postwar California* (Berkeley: University of California Press, 2010), 20–23.

14. See Daniel Widener, *Black Arts West: Culture and Struggle in Postwar Los Angeles* (Durham, NC: Duke University Press, 2010), 11; Gaye Theresa Johnson, "A Sifting of Centuries: Afro-Chicano Interaction and Popular Musical Culture in California, 1960–2000," in *Decolonial Voices: Chicana and Chicano Cultural Studies in the 21st Century,* ed. Arturo J. Aldama and Naomi H. Quiñonez (Bloomington: Indiana University Press, 2002), 320–23.

15. Cedric J. Robinson, *Black Marxism: The Making of the Black Radical Tradition* (1983; reprint, Chapel Hill: University of North Carolina Press, 2000); Neil Brenner, Jamie Peck, and Nik Theodore, "After Neoliberalization?" *Globalizations* 7, no. 3 (2010): 327–45; George Lipsitz, "Learning from Los Angeles: Another One Rides the Bus," *American Quarterly* 56, no. 3 (2004): 511–29.

In the aftermath of Ronald Reagan's election as president, there was a pervasive and persistent assault on federal funding for affordable housing. Activists and policy analysts have shown that contemporary mass homelessness emerged as a result. At the same time, city officials passed laws criminalizing homelessness and poverty. In turn, Skid Row in downtown Los Angeles became an "open-air prison" for people deemed disposable. As Laura Pulido's research demonstrates, the production of this securitized space has been shaped by the "geography of past racial regimes."[16]

Since the late 1970s and early 1980s the Los Angeles City Council has promoted the "containment" of homelessness on Skid Row as a way to trap Black and poor people in space.[17] Deindustrialized Black workers from South Central L.A. were forced to migrate to Skid Row as part of a survival strategy to gain food, shelter, and other basic necessities because there was a concentration of social services in this section of the city. According to the legal scholar Gary Blasi, Skid Row went from being 67 percent white and 21 percent Black in the 1970s to majority Black by the end of the 1980s. During the 1990s California ranked forty-ninth out of fifty states in terms of providing public housing. Currently Skid Row has the highest concentration of homeless people in the city and the most concentrated poverty in the United States. By analyzing the mass criminalization of the poor and disproportionately Black low-income residents and homeless people in the capital of homelessness, we can gain clarity on the dynamics of racialization, gentrification, incarceration, and capital accumulation during the continuation of a "cold war on the streets of Downtown."[18]

The gentrification of downtown Los Angeles has been accompanied by mass criminalization. These political, economic, ideological, and geographical processes need to be theorized in their totality. In an alliance with finance capital, the neoliberal state has provided police presence downtown to facilitate the production of new condos and lofts. Aggressive policing and surveillance has been deployed to criminalize resistance to these uneven developments. Real estate speculators and developers transformed single-room-occupancy hotels that were rented for about $500 a month into condos and lofts that rent for between $2,000 and $5,000 a month. As housing and land prices rose, state officials, local real estate developers, and journalists appealed to moral panics about race, crime, and law and order to justify the restructuring of the space in the interest of capital and the state. In transforming the landscape by constructing art museums, coffee shops, restaurants, dog grooming services, and other amenities for gentrifiers and owners, the city has made gentrification a centerpiece of its efforts to compete with other cities in attracting capital. Policing has been central to this urban strategy of capitalist development. Homeless residents and civil rights activists downtown are persistently subject to arrest as a result. The

16. Michael Anderson et al., eds., *Without Housing: Decades of Federal Housing Cutbacks, Massive Homelessness, and Policy Failures* (San Francisco: Western Regional Advocacy Project, 2010); Jordan T. Camp and Christina Heatherton, "Housing Question," in *Freedom Now!,* 83; Laura Pulido, "Rethinking Environmental Racism," 561.

17. Gilda Haas and Allan David Heskin, *Community Struggles in Los Angeles* (Los Angeles: UCLA School of Architecture and Urban Planning, 1981), 13–19; Mike Davis, *City of Quartz: Excavating the Future in Los Angeles* (1990; reprint, New York: Verso, 2006), 232.

18. Christina Heatherton and Yusef Omowale, "Skid Row in Transition: An Interview with Gary Blasi," in *Downtown Blues,* 36; The Labor/Community Strategy Center, *Reconstructing Los Angeles from the Bottom Up* (Los Angeles: Labor/ Community Strategy Center, 1993), 31–32; Gary Blasi and the UCLA School of Law Fact Investigation Clinic, *Policing Our Way Out of Homelessness?,* 1–9; Richard Walker, "Golden State Adrift," 5; Mike Davis, *City of Quartz,* 234.

LAPD and the Manhattan Institute have engaged in an ideological campaign to justify neoliberal forms of aggressive policing rather than social spending as a strategy of managing the crises of mass homelessness and poverty.[19]

Consider for example an article that appeared in the Manhattan Institute's *City Journal*. Penned by LAPD Chief Charlie Beck along with Bratton and the coauthor of the broken windows theory, Kelling, the article argues that the Safer Cities Initiative represents a significant effort "to reduce crime, lawlessness, and disorder." In turn, Beck, Bratton, and Kelling assert that the problem they seek to solve has been "lawlessness" rather than "homelessness."[20] Yet such "lawlessness" can be read in an inverse and negative procedure as the dissent of homeless and housing activists challenging systematic human rights abuses in the revanchist city. This policing strategy combines vengeful security politics with the elite desire for reclaiming space from aggrieved communities. Revanchism provides the ideological underpinning for the strategy. Skid Row residents—the homeless, low-income renters, the evicted, the unemployed; in short, the surplus population—have endured increasing authoritarianism because of these revenge-driven policing and security policies. This intensified securitization has included the installation of security cameras on Skid Row, which as Richard Winton of the *Los Angeles Times* observes, makes "the downtown area the most heavily monitored part of the city." In promoting an image of L.A. as safe for gentrifiers, the local state has enacted a strategy of regulating public space through extensive policing and surveillance. Read in this context, the mayor's office depicts the police as protecting the homeless when poor and homeless residents actually need protection from the police. Indeed, as Alex Vitale has suggested, we need to ask whether or not the goal of the policy was to "reduce crime and homelessness or instead to remove a large concentration of poor people forcibly from Skid Row in hopes of encouraging the subsequent gentrification of the area." This is particularly important in a context where "a major effort to gentrify the Skid Row area has been underway for several years." At the very moment that developers have sought to invest in the area the city's policy has been to cycle poor and homeless people "through the criminal justice system" or force them to move "into other poor areas with already inadequate social services."[21]

19. David Wagner and Pete White, "Why the Silence?," 45; Neil Smith, "New Globalism, New Urbanism," 442; David Harvey, "The Right to the City," *New Left Review* 53 (2008): 34–35; Daniel Martinez HoSang, "The Economics of the New Brutality," *Colorlines,* December 10, 1999, http://www .colorlines.com/articles/economics-new-brutality; Ellen Reese, Geoffrey Deverteuil, and Leanne Thach, " 'Weak-Center' Gentrification and the Contradictions of Containment," *International Journal of Urban and Regional Research* 34, no. 2 (2010): 311. For an elaboration of the transitions on Skid Row, see the interview with Gary Blasi by Christina Heatherton and Yusef Omowale, "Skid Row in Transition," 38–40.

20. Charlie Beck, William J. Bratton, and George L. Kelling, "Who Will Police the Criminologists? The Dangers of Politicized Social Science," *City Journal* 21, no. 2 (Spring 2011). On the failures of the broken-windows policing approach on both empirical and theoretical grounds, see the systematic analyses by Bernard E. Harcourt, *Illusion of Order: The False Promise of Broken Windows Policing* (Cambridge, MA: Harvard University Press, 2001); Don Mitchell, *The Right to the City,* 195–222.

21. Neil Smith, *The New Urban Frontier,* 220, 222; Neil Smith, "Giuliani Time," 10; Richard Winton, "LAPD Adds 10 Cameras to Curb Skid Row Crime," *Los Angeles Times,* September 15, 2006, http://articles.latimes.com/2006/sep/15/local/me-cameras15; George Lipsitz, "Learning from Los Angeles: Producing Anarchy in the Name of Order," in *Freedom Now!,* 33–40; Daniel Martinez HoSang, "The Economics of the New Brutality"; Alex S. Vitale, "The Safer Cities Initiative and the Removal of the Homeless," 870–71.

In 2010, Deborah Burton, a Skid Row resident and organizer with LA CAN, traveled to Geneva to deliver a statement to the United Nations Universal Periodic Review about the human rights abuses represented by mass homelessness in Los Angeles. She explained that "Instead of providing the solution to homelessness—which is housing—Los Angeles and other cities choose to use the police to harass, move, and incarcerate homeless people. ... Black people by far are the most impacted by homelessness." "My organization," Burton declared, "LA CAN, works in partnership with dozens of other organizations built and led by impacted residents. We are building power. We will make progress. We can win. But the task is huge and we will need the international communities to join us in pressuring the U.S. government." Burton's intervention underscores the importance of the ideological and political struggle over the meaning of the policing of the crisis. As the historian Rhonda Williams argues, focusing on the critiques of neoliberal governance articulated by African American working-class women activists helps us to understand "a key element of poor women's political movement ideology." Much as the long civil rights movement worked to overcome geographical boundaries by making their appeals in terms of human rights, so too have public housing residents, low-income renters, single-room-occupancy tenants, and members of the disproportionately Black homeless and marginally housed population claimed the human right to housing to circulate their struggles in different cities around the country and the planet. The demand for the human right to housing and access to the social wage represents a confrontation with the racial regime of U.S. capitalism.[22]

As the cofounder and codirector of LA CAN Pete White explains, "We believe that one thing that encourages safety is housing. Housing for all. We believe that safe spaces, green spaces, parks, educational opportunities, [and] occupational opportunities ... define what safety would feel like to us." He adds, "There's $100 million, $87 million of which went to policing, that could have gone to solutions that encourage safety in a whole different way." LA CAN has exposed racism as a central contradiction in the state form. By organizing based on a democratic platform of civil and human rights, the organization has articulated a social vision that shows how antiracism is in the interest of the urban multiracial working class as a whole. Implementing their program would require the abolition of homelessness, the production of public housing, full employment, and an end to the Safer Cities Initiative. This would mean access to and redirection of a surplus budget of more than $87 million spent annually on policing. This would require

22. Deborah Burton, statement at the United Nations Universal Periodic Review, in *Freedom Now!*; Doudou Diène, *Report of the Special Rapporteur on Contemporary Forms of Racism, Racial Discrimination, Xenophobia and Related Intolerance* (Geneva: Human Rights Council, April 2009), 20; *Universal Declaration of Human Rights* (Geneva: United Nations Department of Public Information, 1948); Rhonda Y. Williams, " 'We Refuse': Privatization, Housing, and Human Rights," in *Freedom Now!*, 15. On the politics of scale, see Neil Smith, "Contours of a Spatialized Politics: Homeless Vehicles and the Production of Geographical Scale," *Social Text* 33 (1992): 54–81; Bobby Wilson, "Scale Politics of the Civil Rights Movement," paper presented at the Association of American Geographers, New York, February 2012. On the stakes in feminist struggles for the social wage, see Cindi Katz, "Vagabond Capitalism and the Necessity of Social Reproduction," 709–28. For a critique of the human rights paradigm, see Randall Williams, *The Divided World: Human Rights and Its Violence* (Minneapolis: University of Minnesota Press, 2010).

a shift in the urban political economy away from militarism and toward a social wage that would entail radical social transformations.[23]

Through their political campaigns, direct-action protests, and community meetings as well as their newspaper *Community Connection* and innovative use of new media such as blogs, documentary filmmaking, and Facebook, LA CAN documents and challenges the pervasive and persistent criminalization experienced by homeless and poor residents. As part of a regional alliance, the Western Regional Advocacy Project (WRAP), LA CAN codirector Becky Dennison explains they have "really expanded the bandwidth of the opposition to the criminalization of homelessness. In four or five different states, we had four substantive homeless Bills of Rights moving." By organizing directly with the poor at multiple scales—local, regional, national, and international—in a struggle for survival, they have generated antisystemic protest. This organizing demonstrates in practice that the demand for the human right to housing is part of a broader struggle for a better social wage. LA CAN and their allies in organizations around the city and state, including the Community Rights Campaign, Californians United for a Responsible Budget, the Youth Justice Coalition, the Stop LAPD Spying Coalition, the Labor Community Strategy Center, and Critical Resistance Los Angeles, are engaged in a dynamic struggle against criminalization and for racial and economic justice in the neoliberal city.[24]

Drawing on the social vision of the long civil rights movement, LA CAN has organized Black, Brown, poor, and homeless people downtown to contest criminalization and press for economic human rights, a social wage, and the right to the city. For example, in 2009 the United Nations Special Rapporteur on Adequate Housing, Raquel Rolnik, visited Los Angeles (cohosted locally by LA CAN) and other U.S. cities to assess the housing crisis. She found that the "subprime mortgage crisis has widened an already large gap between the supply of and demand for affordable housing. The economic crisis which followed has led to increased unemployment and an even greater need for affordable housing."[25] She concluded that gentrification and the foreclosure crisis have been the leading causes of the spike in homelessness. Accordingly, renters and homeowners alike have been affected. Poor people who lost their housing are

23. Daniel Fischlin, Ajay Heble, and George Lipsitz, *The Fierce Urgency of Now: Improvisation, Rights, and the Ethics of Cocreation* (Durham, NC: Duke University Press, 2013), 42; Clyde Woods, "Life After Death," *Professional Geographer* 54, no. 1 (2002): 64; Mike Davis, *Prisoners of the American Dream* (New York: Verso, 1986), 310; Robin D. G. Kelley, *Yo' Mama's Disfunktional!,* 155; Clyde Woods, *Development Drowned and Reborn: The Blues and Bourbon Restorations in Post-Katrina New Orleans,* ed. Laura Pulido and Jordan T. Camp (Athens: University of Georgia Press, forthcoming); Jordan T. Camp and Christina Heatherton, "Asset Stripping and Broken Windows Policing on L.A.'s Skid Row: An Interview with Becky Dennison and Pete White," in *Policing the Planet: Why the Policing Crisis Led to Black Lives Matter,* eds. Jordan T. Camp and Christina Heatherton (New York: Verso, 2016).

24. *Community Connection,* September–October 2011, https://cangress.files.wordpress.com/2011/10/cc42-final-small-for-web.pdf; Don Mitchell, *The Right to the City,* 21; Robin D. G. Kelley, "Ground Zero," in *Downtown Blues,* 13, 15; Jordan T. Camp and Christina Heatherton, "Asset Stripping and Broken Windows Policing on L.A.'s Skid Row," in *Policing the Planet.*

25. Raquel Rolnik, *Report of the Special Rapporteur on Adequate Housing as a Component of the Right to an Adequate Standard of Living, and on the Right to Non-Discrimination in This Context* (Geneva: Human Rights Council, February 12, 2010), 8.

increasingly forced into homelessness. The neoliberal state has responded to this increase by "producing anarchy in the name of order." Perhaps this is nowhere more evident than downtown L.A.[26]

Social movement organizations, including LA CAN and WRAP, have underscored the importance of confronting this crisis politically. According to WRAP Organizing Director Paul Boden, "Local 'anti-homeless' police enforcement campaigns, separate court systems, property confiscations and the closing of public spaces—these are in the forefront of today's civil rights battles." This intervention compels us to reckon with the unfinished business of the long civil rights movement in confronting mass homelessness and mass incarceration. To do so, we need to listen to activists who are demanding "house keys, not hand cuffs." They suggest that another city is not only possible but a burning necessity.[27]

Bibliography

Ali, Mazher, et al. *State of the Dream 2011: Austerity for Whom?* Boston: United for a Fair Economy, 2011.

Anderson, Michael, et al., eds. *Without Housing: Decades of Federal Housing Cutbacks, Massive Homelessness, and Policy Failures.* San Francisco: Western Regional Advocacy Project, 2010.

Blasi, Gary, and the UCLA School of Law Fact Investigation Clinic. *Policing Our Way Out of Homelessness? The First Year of the Safer Cities Initiative on Skid Row.* Los Angeles: UCLA and USC Center for Sustainable Cities, September 24, 2007.

Blasi, Gari, and Forrest Stuart. *Has the Safer Cities Initiative in Skid Row Reduced Serious Crime?* Los Angeles: UCLA Law School, September 15, 2008.

Brenner, Neil, Jamie Peck, and Nik Theodore. "After Neoliberalization?" *Globalizations* 7, no. 3 (2010): 327–45.

Bullard, Robert D., and Charles Lee. "Introduction: Racism and American Apartheid." In *Residential Apartheid: The American Legacy.* Edited by Robert D. Bullard et al. Los Angeles: Center for Afro-American Studies Publications, 1994.

Camp, Jordan T., and Christina Heatherton. *Freedom Now! Struggles for the Human Right to Housing in Los Angeles and Beyond.* Los Angeles: Freedom Now Books, 2012.

———. *Policing the Planet: Why the Policing Crisis Led to Black Lives Matter.* New York: Verso, 2016.

Dahmann, Nicholas, with the Los Angeles Community Action Network. "Los Angeles: I Do Mind Dying, Recent Reflections on Urban Revolution in Skid Row." *Los Angeles Public Interest Law Journal* 2 (2009–10): 210–19.

Davis, Mike. *City of Quartz: Excavating the Future in Los Angeles.* New York: Verso, 2006.

———. *A Planet of Slums.* New York: Verso, 2006.

———. *Prisoners of the American Dream.* New York: Verso, 1986.

Diène, Doudou. *Report Submitted by the Special Rapporteur on Contemporary Forms of Racism, Racial Discrimination, Xenophobia And Related Intolerance.* Geneva: Human Rights Council, April 2009.

Fischlin, Daniel, Ajay Heble, and George Lipsitz. *The Fierce Urgency of Now: Improvisation, Rights, and the Ethics of Cocreation.* Durham, NC: Duke University Press, 2013.

Gordon, Avery F. "The U.S. Military Prison: The Normalcy of Exceptional Brutality." In *The Violence of Incarceration*, 166–86. Edited by Phil Scraton and Jude McCulloch. New York: Routledge, 2009.

Graham, Stephen. *Cities Under Siege: The New Military Urbanism.* New York: Verso, 2010.

Haas, Gilda, and Allan David Heskin. *Community Struggles in Los Angeles.* Los Angeles: UCLA School of Architecture and Urban Planning, 1981.

Hall, Jacquelyn Dowd. "The Long Civil Rights Movement and the Political Uses of the Past." *Journal of American History* 91, no. 4 (March 2005): 1233–63.

26. Don Mitchell, "Homelessness, American Style," in *Downtown Blues*, 42; Mazher Ali et al., *State of the Dream 2011: Austerity for Whom?* (Boston: United for a Fair Economy, 2011); Michael Anderson et al., eds., *Without Housing*, 6, 42; George Lipsitz, "Policing Place and Taxing Time on Skid Row," in *Policing the Planet.*

27. Paul Boden, "Didn't Work Then, Won't Work Now," HuffingtonPost.com, January 31, 2013; Clyde Woods, "Traps, Skid Row, and Katrina"; Christina Heatherton, ed., *Downtown Blues*, 55; Jack O'Dell, *Climbin' Jacob's Ladder*, 113–16, 263–93; George Lipsitz, "Learning from Los Angeles: Another One Rides the Bus," 511–29; Daniel Widener, "Another City Is Possible: Interethnic Organizing in Contemporary Los Angeles," *Race/Ethnicity: Multidisciplinary Global Perspectives* 1, no. 2 (2008): 189–219; Jacquelyn Dowd Hall, "The Long Civil Rights Movement and the Political Uses of the Past," *Journal of American History* 91, no. 4 (2005): 1261.

Hall, Stuart. "Gramsci's Relevance for the Study of Race and Ethnicity." *Journal of Communications Inquiry* 10 (1986): 5–27.

———. "The Neoliberal Revolution." *Soundings: A Journal of Politics and Culture* 48 (Summer 2011): 9–27.

Hall, Stuart, and Doreen Massey. "Interpreting the Crisis." *Soundings: A Journal of Politics and Culture* 44 (Spring 2010): 57–71.

Harcourt, Bernard E. *Illusion of Order: The False Promise of Broken Windows Policing.* Cambridge, MA: Harvard University Press, 2001.

Harvey, David. *The New Imperialism.* New York: Oxford University Press, 2003.

———. "The Right to the City." *New Left Review* 53 (2008): 23–40.

Heatherton, Christina, ed. *Downtown Blues: A Skid Row Reader.* Los Angeles: Los Angeles Community Action Network, 2011.

HoSang, Daniel Martinez. *Racial Propositions: Ballot Initiatives and the Making of Postwar California.* Berkeley: University of California Press, 2010.

Johnson, Gaye Theresa. "A Sifting of Centuries: Afro-Chicano Interaction and Popular Musical Culture in California, 1960–2000." In *Decolonial Voices: Chicana and Chicano Cultural Studies in the 21st Century*, 316–29. Edited by Arturo J. Aldama and Naomi H. Quiñonez. Bloomington: Indiana University Press, 2002.

Katz, Cindi. "Childhood as Spectacle: Relays of Anxiety and the Reconfiguration of the Child." *Cultural Geographies* 15 (2008): 5–17.

———. "Vagabond Capitalism and the Necessity of Social Reproduction." *Antipode* 33, no. 4 (2001): 709–28.

Kelley, Robin D. G. *Race Rebels: Culture, Politics, and the Black Working Class.* New York: New Press, 1994.

———. *Yo' Mama's Disfunktional! Fighting the Culture Wars in Urban America.* Boston: Beacon Press, 1997.

Lipsitz, George. *Footsteps in the Dark: The Hidden Histories of Popular Music.* Minneapolis: University of Minnesota Press, 2007.

———. "Learning from Los Angeles: Another One Rides the Bus." *American Quarterly* 56, no. 3 (2004): 511–29.

———. "Policing Place and Taxing Time on Skid Row." In *Policing the Planet: Why the Policing Crisis Led to Black Lives Matter.* Edited by Jordan T. Camp and Christina Heatherton. New York: Verso, 2016.

———. "The Struggle for Hegemony." *Journal of American History* 75, no. 1 (June 1988): 146–50.

Mitchell, Don. "Homelessness, American Style." In *Downtown Blues: A Skid Row Reader*, 42–49. Edited by Christina Heatherton. Los Angeles: Los Angeles Community Action Network, 2011.

———. *The Right to the City: Social Justice and the Fight for Public Space.* New York: Guilford, 2003.

Moten, Fred. "The Meaning of 'Broken Windows.' " Talk presented at Eso Won Books, Los Angeles, June 23, 2005.

O'Dell, Jack. *Climbin' Jacob's Ladder: The Black Freedom Movement Writings of Jack O'Dell.* Edited by Nikhil Pal Singh. Berkeley: University of California Press, 2010.

Prashad, Vijay. "Second-Hand Dreams." *Social Analysis* 49, no. 2 (2005): 191–98.

Pulido, Laura. "Rethinking Environmental Racism: White Privilege and Urban Development in Southern California." *Annals of the Association of American Geographers* 90, no. 1 (2000): 12–40.

Reese, Ellen, Geoffrey Deverteuil, and Leanne Thach. " 'Weak-Center' Gentrification and the Contradictions of Containment: Deconcentrating Poverty in Downtown Los Angeles." *International Journal of Urban and Regional Research* 34, no. 2 (2010): 310–27.

Robinson, Cedric J. *Black Marxism: The Making of the Black Radical Tradition.* Chapel Hill: University of North Carolina Press, 2000.

Rolnik, Raquel. *Report of the Special Rapporteur on Adequate Housing as a Component of the Right to an Adequate Standard of Living, and on the Right to Non-Discrimination in This Context.* Geneva: Human Rights Council, February 12, 2010.

Singh, Nikhil Pal. "The Afterlife of Fascism." *South Atlantic Quarterly* 105, no. 1 (Winter 2006): 71–93.

Smith, Neil. "Contours of a Spatialized Politics: Homeless Vehicles and the Production of Geographical Scale." *Social Text* 33 (1992): 54–81.

———. "Giuliani Time: The Revanchist 1990s." *Social Text* 16, no. 4 (Winter 1998): 1–20.

———. "New Globalism, New Urbanism: Gentrification as Global Urban Strategy." *Antipode* 34, no. 3 (2002): 427–50.

———. *The New Urban Frontier: Gentrification and the Revanchist City.* New York: Routledge, 1996.

Soja, Edward W. *Seeking Spatial Justice.* Minneapolis: University of Minnesota Press, 2010.

United Nations. *Universal Declaration of Human Rights.* Geneva: United Nations Department of Public Information, 1948.

Vitale, Alex S. "The Safer Cities Initiative and the Removal of the Homeless: Reducing Crime or Promoting Gentrification on Los Angeles's Skid Row?" *American Society of Criminology* 9, no. 4 (2010): 867–73.

Wagner, David, and Pete White. "Why the Silence? Homelessness and Race." In *Freedom Now! Struggles for the Human Right to Housing in Los Angeles and Beyond*, 42–48. Edited by Jordan T. Camp and Christina Heatherton. Los Angeles: Freedom Now Books, 2012.

Walker, Richard. "Golden State Adrift." *New Left Review*, no. 66 (2010): 5–30.

Widener, Daniel. "Another City Is Possible: Interethnic Organizing in Contemporary Los Angeles." *Race/Ethnicity: Multidisciplinary Global Perspectives* 1, no. 2 (2008): 189–219.

———. *Black Arts West: Culture and Struggle in Postwar Los Angeles.* Durham, NC: Duke University Press, 2010.

Williams, Randall. *The Divided World: Human Rights and Its Violence.* Minneapolis: University of Minnesota Press, 2010.

Williams, Rhonda Y. " 'We Refuse': Privatization, Housing, and Human Rights." In *Freedom Now! Struggles for the Human Right to Housing in Los Angeles and Beyond.* Edited by Jordan T. Camp and Christina Heatherton. Los Angeles: Freedom Now Books, 2012.

Willse, Craig. "Neo-Liberal Biopolitics and the Invention of Chronic Homelessness." *Economy and Society* 39, no. 2 (2010): 155–84.

Woods, Clyde. "The Challenges of Blues and Hip Hop Historiography." *Kalfou* 1, no. 1 (2010): 33–54.

———. *Development Drowned and Reborn: The Blues and Bourbon Restorations in Post-Katrina New Orleans.* Edited by Laura Pulido and Jordan T. Camp. Athens: University of Georgia Press, forthcoming.

———. "Do You Know What It Means to Miss New Orleans? Katrina, Trap Economics, and the Rebirth of the Blues." *American Quarterly* 57, no. 4 (2005): 1005–18.

———. "Les Misérables of New Orleans: Trap Economics and the Asset Stripping Blues, Part 1." *American Quarterly* 61, no. 3 (2009): 769–96.

– – –. "Life After Death." *Professional Geographer* 54, no. 1 (2002): 62–66.

– – –. "'Sittin' on Top of the World': The Challenges of Blues and Hip Hop Geography." In *Black Geographies and the Politics of Place*, 46–81. Edited by Katherine McKittrick and Clyde Woods. Cambridge, MA: South End Press, 2007.

– – –. "Traps, Skid Row, and Katrina." In *Downtown Blues: A Skid Row Reader*, 50–55. Edited by Christina Heatherton. Los Angeles: Los Angeles Community Action Network, 2011.

Wilson, Bobby. "Scale Politics of the Civil Rights Movement." Paper presented at the Association of American Geographers, New York, February 2012.

Post-Reading Questions

1. According to the excerpt, how do poverty, homelessness, gentrification, and policing efforts intersect with one another to create situations of social injustice?
2. To address the crisis of homelessness, what must be done? What are some viable interventions and solutions we can implement?
3. How are organizations such as the LA Community Action Network (CAN), the Western Regional Advocacy Project (WRAP), and other groups addressing the crisis of homelessness?

CONCLUSION

The readings in this anthology are designed to enhance your sociological knowledge and inspire public service. Hopefully, after reading this collection, you are compelled to make positive changes in society. By adopting the framework of public sociology, you can gain a deeper understanding of social injustices and learn how to address them effectively. Then, you can carry the sociological knowledge you have gained in the classroom into the outside world to inspire positive social change.

Many of the excerpts in this anthology focus on the injustices that marginalized groups face in society. Perhaps you have faced similar injustices in your own life. You can address these struggles through a variety of social actions. I encourage you to contemplate how you can use the knowledge you have gained in this book to transform your own community. By embracing public sociology, you can go beyond just learning about social problems to create social interventions and enact solutions.

You can start the process by having a dialogue about public sociology with people in your community. For example, you can share what it means to adopt a sociological imagination and inspire people to look at their personal circumstances in a new light. This may prompt the recognition that the individual troubles we face often reflect widespread community concerns. By realizing that we are all united by our environment, we can find common ground in our shared struggles, which can inspire collective engagement to make our communities stronger. This is public sociology in action.

Conversations about public sociology will likely continue for many years, both in academic circles and the civic sphere. Some scholars question the viability of public sociology in scholarship and practice. Yet, many people, both within and outside of academia, find the approach to be inspirational and full of promise. Internal debates will continue in the field, leading to various interpretations of the philosophy, but for many, the core mission of public sociology remains the same.

Regardless of our social positions, as people inspired by sociology, we can unite around this powerful tool. We can bring sociological knowledge from the classroom into our communities. We can fight together against injustices and unite to work to reduce and eliminate inequities. I sincerely hope that you feel inspired to create positive social change after reading this anthology. By embracing public sociology together, we can make the world a better place.

Printed in the USA
CPSIA information can be obtained
at www.ICGtesting.com
LVHW020927090823
754690LV00011B/30